Praise for *The Leader Within*

"To see yourself as others see you is an invaluable gift that comes from thoughtful reflection of one's behavior and its effectiveness. To expand one's ability to be more versatile in adapting different styles of behavior as needed to enhance one's effectiveness is a hallmark of great leadership. *The Leader Within: Learning Enough About Yourself to Lead Others* provides the blueprint for both reflection and learning that can help any manager to be a better leader. It is an essential resource for any manager's development and growth!"

Bob Nelson, Ph.D., President, Nelson Motivation, Inc., and author of *1001 Ways to Reward Employees* and *The 1001 Rewards & Recognition Fieldbook*

"Having an understanding of how beliefs, feelings, and values motivate behavior has made a significant impact on the process of change at the WD-40 Company. A different culture has evolved. The learnings in this book helped that process add value to the 'new' WD-40 Company culture."

Gary Ridge, President and CEO, WD-40 Company

"The authors have written an absolute must-read book for present and future leaders who are focused on serving their organizations and staff. It challenges your thoughts and views about yourself and the method in which you lead. If you truly want to succeed at the highest level, you owe it to yourself and those around you to read this incredible insight on leadership."

Nicolas de Segonzac, CEO, Debtco, Inc.

"Finally someone has written a definitive work on the inner psychic aspects of leadership. Read this book and your leadership approach will be positively changed forever!"

Dick Lyles, author of *Winning Ways* and *Winning Ways*

"In our training, coaching, and development work with leaders, we have found that many lack sufficient understanding of both themselves and others to effectively influence people and situations. We have found this unique book an invaluable resource, like no other, for providing vital insights to help leaders become more effective."

Bret Skousen, Director—Training and Development, Black & Decker

"I've personally benefitted immensely and make daily use of the practical wisdom about understanding and managing people—including ourselves—and situations that are essential to successful leadership of organizations. The valuable 'know-how' contained in this book continues to be a key resource for our ongoing business success. I strongly recommend it as a 'MUST READ AND TAKE ACTION ON' to anyone charged with responsibility for managing people and organizations."

**Jeffrey Mitchell , Executive Vice-President and General Manager,
H.O. Penn Machinery Company, Inc.**

"I found this book not only an excellent, comprehensive guide on leadership, but it was also very thought provoking. Our world needs a breakthrough in the improvement of our leadership—the kind of leadership this book teaches and inspires. In the meantime, you can learn from this book and make your world better for yourself and those around you."

Tom Cleveland, President, H.O. Penn Machinery Company, Inc.

"This book helps us have a more positive impact for all our stakeholders. It's a powerful resource on our lifelong journey as learning, growing leader/managers. It's full of insights gleaned from decades of research and practical experience by Michael O'Connor and the other contributing authors—insights that can help the reader deliver more leadership and management results at both the strategic and tactical levels, help all our stakeholders achieve more success, and yield a much greater personal sense of accomplishment for all of us in our organizations and business ventures. If you are going to read one book and take action on it starting *now*, this is the one I'd recommend."

Nick Betzold, Chairperson, President & CEO, The Betzold Companies

"As a manager, business owner, board member, and advisor to executives/managers throughout my career I've made great practical use of the knowledge about our human "wiring" that is a tremendous resource for effectively managing ourselves and leading others and organizations to greater success. If you're serious and committed to your ongoing career success and growth, this is an essential resource for achieving great results and personal fulfillment along the way."

Pete Refakis, Prinicipal & General Manager, Holt-Refakis Equipment Company

The Leader Within
Learning Enough About Yourself to Lead Others

The Leader Within
Learning Enough About Yourself to Lead Others

Drea Zigarmi
Ken Blanchard
Michael O'Connor
Carl Edeburn

PRENTICE HALL
An Imprint of PEARSON EDUCATION
Upper Saddle River, NJ • New York • London • San Francisco • Toronto • Sydney
Tokyo • Singapore • Hong Kong • Cape Town • Madrid
Paris • Milan • Munich • Amsterdam

www.ft-ph.com

Library of Congress Cataloging-in-Publication Data

A CIP catalogue record for this book can be obtained from the Library of Congress.

Production Editor and Compositor: *Vanessa Moore*
VP, Executive Editor: *Tim Moore*
Development Editor: *Russ Hall*
Full-Service Production Manager: *Anne R. Garcia*
Marketing Manager: *Martin Litkowski*
Manufacturing Buyer: *Maura Zaldivar*
Manufacturing Manager: *Alexis Heydt-Long*
Cover Design Director: *Jerry Votta*
Cover Design: *Chuti Prasertsith*
Interior Design: *Gail Cocker-Bogusz*

© 2005 Drea Zigarmi, Ken Blanchard, Michael O'Connor, Carl Edeburn
Published by Pearson Education, Inc.
Publishing as Prentice Hall
Upper Saddle River, NJ 07458

Prentice Hall offers excellent discounts on this book when ordered in quantity for bulk purchases or special sales. For more information, please contact: U.S. Corporate and Government Sales, 1-800-382-3419, corpsales@pearsontechgroup.com.
For sales outside of the U.S., please contact: International Sales, 1-317-581-3793, international@pearsontechgroup.com.

Company and product names mentioned herein are the trademarks or registered trademarks of their respective owners. The authors wish to thank the following companies for allowing the inclusion of their proprietary models within the text and acknowledge that appearance of these models herein has no impact on their exclusive ownership: the KEN BLANCHARD COMPANIES for their SITUATION LEADERSHIP® II model; LIFE ASSOCIATES for their DISC model; and LIFE ASSOCIATES and OUT OF THE BOX LEARNING, INC. for their TICS model.

All rights reserved. No part of this book may be reproduced, in any form or by any means, without permission in writing from the publisher.

Printed in the United States of America
1st Printing

ISBN 0-13-147025-6

Pearson Education Ltd.
Pearson Education Australia Pty., Limited
Pearson Education South Asia Pte. Ltd.
Pearson Education Asia Ltd.
Pearson Education Canada, Ltd.
Pearson Educación de Mexico, S.A. de C.V.
Pearson Education—Japan
Pearson Malaysia S.D.N. B.H.D.

*To Susan, who has helped me to understand
these ideas and concepts with my heart.
— Drea Zigarmi*

*To Margie, my best friend and partner,
who has been with me every step of the way.
— Ken Blanchard*

*To my wife Mary Ann, my family, friends, co-authors,
and leaders, whose unique talents have enabled me to
contribute to this much-needed book.
— Michael O'Connor*

*To Cleo Ann, who has inspired and
supported me for thirty-five years.
— Carl Edeburn*

Contents

PREFACE   xvii
ACKNOWLEDGMENTS   xxi

Chapter One: Leaders and Change   1

LEADERS   1
    The Importance of Leadership   1
    The Conundrum   2
    Two Examples   2
    Questions to Ponder   2
    Bob's Self-Perceptions   3
    Others' Perceptions of Bob   4
    Antonio's Self-Perceptions   5
    Others' Perceptions of Antonio   6
    The Four Tragedies   7
    The Abetting System   9
    Kissing Off the Organization   9
    The Leadership Vacuum   10
    The Covenant   13
ONIONS   15
    The Layered Self   15

    The Leadership Onion   15
    Peeling the Onion   17
    The Challenge of Discomfort   17
    Flavoring the Stew   18
    The Michelangelo View   20
CHANGE   20
    Changing Ourselves   21
    Creating Reality   21
    Beliefs as the Basis of Reality   22
    Language and Reality   22
    Clinging to Accepted Realities   23
    Confining Yourself   23
    Fear and the Shadow Self   24
    Me and My Shadow   25
    Masculine/Feminine Shadows   26
    Fear—Your Emotional Brakes   27
    It's All Part of the Game   28
    Alternative Realities and Behaviors   30
    Working on the "Self"   31
    Personal "Why" of Leadership   32
    Change and Failure   33
SUMMARY   34
    Endnotes   34

Chapter Two: Personality and Context   37

PERSONALITY   37
    In a Nutshell   37
    A Model for Experience   38
    Positive and Negative Response Modes   39
    Behavior Is the Medium   41
    Definition of Personality   42
    Personality Is Dynamic   43
    Personality Is Influenced by Life History   44
    Diversity Within Pattern   45
    Subdivision of Personality: Disposition, Values, and Persona   46
    The Disposition-Values-Persona Connection   49
    The Leadership Onion and Personality   50
CONTEXT   52
    Definition of Context   52
    Definition of Role Behavior   53
    Organizational Philosophy and Values Are a Basis for Role   53
    Role Behavior as the Basis for Leadership   54

CONTENTS

    Importance of the Role Concept   55
    The Leader Behavior Subset   57
    Context Versus Situation   57
    One-to-One Context   58
    Group Context   59
    Organizational Context   59
    Need to Know Yourself   62
SUMMARY   63
    Endnotes   63

Chapter Three: Preference and Disposition   65

PREFERENCE   65
    Unconscious Preference   65
    Roots of the Idea   66
    Definition of Preference   66
    Definition of Disposition   67
    "Wired" and "Acquired" Disposition   67
    Neither Good Nor Bad Disposition   68
    DISC Pattern   69
    Familiar Ways of Responding   69
    Modes of Responding   70
    Flight Versus Fight   71
    Accept Versus Control   71
    Extroversion Versus Introversion   72
    Direct Versus Indirect   74
    Perceive Versus Judge   75
    Risk-Taking Versus Risk-Assessing   76
    Optimistic Versus Pessimistic   77
    Change-Oriented Versus Continuity-Oriented   78
    Summary of Basic Response Modes   79
COUPLES   80
    The "D" Direct Controller   81
    The "I" Direct Accepter   84
    The "S" Indirect Accepter   87
    The "C" Indirect Controller   91
FUNDAMENTAL PRINCIPLES   95
    DISC Principle #1   95
    DISC Principle #2   97
    DISC Principle #3   100
    DISC Principle #4   103
    DISC Principle #5   104
    DISC Principle #6   107

The Platinum Rule   108
SUMMARY   110
Endnotes   111

Chapter Four: Beliefs and Points of View   113
BELIEFS   113
Beliefs as Building Blocks   113
Importance of Beliefs   114
The Power of Beliefs   114
Mechanism of Self-Change   114
The Concept of Belief   115
BELIEFS AND VALUES   116
What Is a Value?   116
Values Criteria   117
Values Process   120
Types of Values   120
Value Systems   121
The Value of Values   122
POINTS OF VIEW   125
Self/Other Focus   126
Rights/Responsibility Focus   127
THE TRADITIONALIST POINT OF VIEW   130
Key End Values—Social Ends   130
Key Means Values—Social Means   130
Self-Esteem Conflict   131
General Perspective   132
Specific Issues   132
Work Style   133
Growth Actions   133
Summary of the Traditionalist   134
THE CHALLENGER POINT OF VIEW   135
Key End Values—Personal Ends   135
Key Means Values—Personal Means   135
Self-Esteem Conflict   136
General Perspective   137
Specific Issues   137
Work Style   138
Growth Actions   138
Summary of the Challenger   138
THE INBETWEENER POINT OF VIEW   139
Key End Values—Personal Ends   139

Key Means Values—Social Means   140
Self-Esteem Conflict   141
General Perspectives   141
Specific Issues   141
Work Style   142
Growth Activities   142
Summary of the Inbetweener   143
THE SYNTHESIZER POINT OF VIEW   143
Key End Values—Social Ends   144
Key Means Values—Personal Means   144
Self-Esteem Conflict   145
General Perspectives   145
Specific Issues   146
Work Style   146
Growth Activities   147
Summary of the Synthesizer   147
Caveats to Points of View   148
Endnotes   150

Chapter Five: Perceptions and Persona   151

PERCEPTIONS   151
Psychological Bifocals   151
An Example of Lateness   152
An Example of Support   152
Connections to Self   153
General Research Findings   153
ICEBERGS   154
Self Versus Others' Perceptions   154
Self-Perception   155
Others' Perception of the Disposition-Values Connection   156
The So Whats   157
The Merger   157
The Misunderstood Challenger   158
Relaters as Inbetweeners   159
Introverts as Traditionalists   159
Controllers as Synthesizers   160
PERSONA   161
Self-Esteem   161
Negative and Positive Modes Revisited   162
The Esteem, Disposition, and Values Connection   163
The Definition of Persona   164
Implications of Persona   165

Role-Dependent Persona   166
Self-Indulgent Persona   167
The "So What" of Persona   168
SUMMARY   169
Endnotes   170

Chapter Six: Behaviors and Situations   171
BEHAVIORS   171
Managers Versus Leaders   172
Viva la Difference   173
A Prescription   173
Leadership Defined   174
Leadership Style Defined   175
Two Basic Elements of Influence Behavior   175
Directing, Structuring, Focusing Behavior   176
Supporting, Collaborating, Inspiring Behavior   176
An Example Across Context   177
A Three-Context Responsibility   178
Seven Is Not Magic   178
Situational Leadership® II   180
No "Single Best" Leadership Style   180
The One-to-One Context   181
Situational Leadership in a One-to-One Context   182
Development Level   182
Subdivisions of Competence   183
Subdivisions of Commitment   184
Development Levels Are Somewhat Sequential   184
Regressive Cycle   186
Development Level Is Task or Goal Specific   186
STYLES   187
A General Concept of Style 1—Directing   189
A General Concept of Style 3—Supporting   192
A General Concept of Style 2—Coaching   195
A General Concept of Style 4—Delegating   196
SITUATIONS   198
When to Use Style 1 in a One-to-One Context   198
When to Use Style 2 in a One-to-One Context   201
When to Use Style 3 in a One-to-One Context   203
When to Use Style 4 in a One-to-One Context   205
Does Situational Leadership Work?   205
Development and Regressive Cycles   206

CONTENTS

Development Cycle 206
Regressive Cycle 206
Using Situational Leadership Theory 208
SUMMARY 209
Endnotes 209

Chapter Seven: Vision and Learning 211
VISION 211
Dimensions of Vision 211
Purpose 212
Values 214
Image 215
Gravity 216
Starfish 217
LEARNINGS 220
The "So What" of Personality on Leadership Behavior 220
Disposition and Leadership Behaviors 221
"D-ness" and Leadership Behavior in a One-to-One Context 222
"I-ness" and Leadership Behavior in a One-to-One Context 224
"S-ness" and Leadership Behavior in a One-to-One Context 227
"C-ness" and Leadership Behavior in a One-to-One Context 229
Values and Leadership Behaviors 232
Leader Values and Follower Perceptions of Leader Behaviors 232
Persona and Values Point of View 234
Traditionalists and the Organization 236
Morale and Leader Values 237
Challenger Point of View and Follower Morale 237
Inbetweener Point of View and Follower Morale 238
Synthesizer Point of View and Follower Morale 240
The End of the Beginning 240
EPILOGUE 241
The Expression of Character 241
Definition of Character 241
Character on a Personal Level 243
Endnotes 244

Bibliography 245

Index 257

Preface

THE BOOK'S ORIGIN

The Leader Within is the result of our many years of experience training, consulting, coaching, and researching American business managers and leaders. At the heart of this book is a seven-year, in-depth, statistical study of the influence behaviors used by American corporate executives. Although the report's statistics are not included (to reduce reading time and save space), the conclusions presented in this book are sound and substantiated.

THE BOOK'S PURPOSE

This book is a self-development resource; its purpose is to help you learn more about yourself so that you can change, grow, and become a better leader. Its primary objective is to present some well-developed models that help you re-create or reinvent your leadership approach so that you can bring about better organizational results and greater human satisfaction.

Knowing yourself is key to being an effective leader. The models explained in this book can help you examine the inner self that you bring to your organizational life's frequent "moments of influence." Examining how you presently behave as a leader, and then contrasting and comparing those behaviors with possible alternatives, can provide you with invaluable insights for becoming a more effective leader.

THE BOOK'S INTENDED AUDIENCE

We wrote this book for managers and leaders—people who earn a living by influencing others within organizational settings. However, other audiences will also find it informative and helpful. Consultants can utilize the information within this book to better understand the executives they coach. Human resource professionals can use this book as a tool for broadening and refining their executive development programs. College and university faculty can use this book as a challenging and stimulating text for their own leadership teaching or research, and the research formulated by the students they advise.

THE AUTHORS' FRAME OF REFERENCE

The working definition of leadership used in this book is, of course, values based, as is any definition of worth. We define a leader as anyone who acts to arouse, engage, and satisfy the motives of the follower—within an environment of conflict, competition, or change—that results in the follower taking action toward a mutually shared outcome or vision.

As you will see, that vision must be growthful for the follower, ultimately societal, and also contribute to the well-being of all involved. The values inherent in this definition involve the follower's growth and development; they imply the follower's eventual independence and autonomy of action when serving the (organizational) outcome or vision.

The term *servant leader* might come to mind. The leader who is a servant judges his or her success not only in the accomplishment of the outcome, but also by the effects the accomplishment has on those who do the accomplishing. Are those who are led healthier, happier, committed, and more apt to become leaders themselves? The true intent of the servant leader is to serve both the vision *and* all those who seek to achieve that vision. The servant leader's inner intent is not self-oriented, but other-oriented. Such a leader ensures that other people's high-priority needs are being served.[1]

THE BOOK'S ORGANIZATION

The book is organized into seven chapters, which move from a discussion of an individual's inner makeup or personality dimensions, to the role of a leader, to the implications inner personality has on an individual's potential to carry out the leader role. Each chapter is divided into two sections that help organize the seven key chapters.

- Chapter 1 discusses the leadership challenge of self-change.
- Chapter 2 defines the parameters of personality and leadership.
- Chapters 3, 4, and 5 present in-depth discussions and models for understanding the three key aspects of personality: disposition, values, and persona.
- Chapter 6 discusses leader behaviors in a one-to-one context.
- Chapter 7 makes the important connection among disposition, values, and leadership behaviors. This chapter examines the relationship between personality and leadership behaviors that may help you become a more effective leader.

THE AUTHORS' HOPES

We wrote this book with the hope that increased self-awareness would result in better leadership and fewer negative personalities in organizations. We hope for less ego, politics, personal hurt, and psychological turn off on the part of all people in organizations; and we hope for more organizational *go*, action, personal joy, and liberation of personal energy and motivation for organizational purpose. Our dream of healthier organizations will happen more readily if leaders become more self-aware and elicit more self-awareness from their followers.

Discovering who you are and what you can be is a lifelong challenge. Connecting to the "lost" or as yet undiscovered facets of your humanness will make you a better leader and will go far to rekindle the spirit of the people you lead.

D.Z., K.B., M.O., C.E.
March 2004

Endnotes

1. Greenleaf 1991.

Acknowledgments

No good work, especially one of this scope and magnitude, can be done alone. We wish to thank the colleagues and friends who, in the early days of this project, gave their time, expertise, and love. They are Renata Zenner, Patrice DeVeau Simpson, Tara Wallace, Margie Blanchard, Eunice Parisi-Carew, Don Carew, Laurence Hawkins, Pat Zigarmi, and Warren Bennis.

We owe special thanks to the team at Prentice Hall, particularly Russ Hall Tim Moore, and Vanessa Moore, who helped make this book a reality. We also want to warmly thank Judd Sills, Jenner Marcucci, and Karen Manz, who read this book and offered much-needed criticism and encouragement.

Finally, we are deeply grateful to Maril Blanchard, who coordinated, edited, and nurtured the manuscript through the days of discouragement as well as the final days of optimism and accomplishment.

CHAPTER 1

Leaders and Change

"One's self is at the base of everything. Every action is a manifestation of the self. A person who doesn't know himself can do nothing for others."

— EIJI YOSHIKAWA[1]

LEADERS

The Importance of Leadership

We all know the importance of effective leadership. Leaders not only make a difference in the results of their organizations, they also make a difference in the satisfaction levels of the people working within the organizations.[2] The relationship between follower satisfaction and lower absenteeism, lower turnover, and higher productivity has been clearly substantiated.[3]

Getting along with the boss is the number one factor affecting job happiness, according to a recent national survey.[4] All we need to do is think about our *own* experiences with people who managed us to understand how important the leader-follower relationship is to our organizational well-being, and therefore, how crucial a good leader is to follower satisfaction.

The Conundrum

If it is so important, why don't more people lead others more effectively? There are several reasons. Lack of know-how and lack of commitment to use that know-how are the two primary reasons for lack of effective leadership. However, we do not believe that leaders get up in the morning and go to work with the intent to mismanage or mislead those with whom they are charged to work. Instead, we are optimistic that the intent to effectively lead others is behind most leaders' behavior. Therefore, let's look at two examples to better understand the problem.

Two Examples

Consider Bob and Antonio, the two male executives described in the pages that follow. These men are *incredibly typical* of the leaders we encounter within the many organizations in which we work. It is not that there are villainous people in leadership positions, but, sadly, there seem to be few heroes to follow. Instead, the visionless, myopic, self-oriented Bobs and Antonios who do not inspire others toward meaningful work *are the norm*. The tragic part is that these negative leader descriptions come to us through the words of those being led.

Questions to Ponder

As you read the descriptions of these far too typical leaders, ask yourself the following questions:

- Are the leaders in my organization like those described here?
- What effect do they have on the motivation of their followers?
- What is the intent, never mind the effect, of such leaders?
- Is there something of them in me?
- What prevents leaders such as these from growing, learning, and changing?

CHAPTER 1 ■ LEADERS AND CHANGE

- What is the long-term effect of this type of leadership on the output and well-being of the organization?
- How can the organization afford to have these leaders continue to lead others?

In short, we believe that those who are being led deserve better. Organizations will not prosper, change, and grow if better leadership is not forthcoming. However reluctant you may be to admit it, if you see something of yourself in these examples, then you must commit yourself to change and growth. If people such as Bob and Antonio lead others in your organization, then you must find ways to help them change before your organization can become truly functional.

If your leadership is not perceived the way you had intended or expected, then it is in your best interest to change. If the people you seek to lead are either not productive or seem skeptical of your leader behaviors, then you need to explore other ways of leading and becoming more effective.

Bob's Self-Perceptions

Bob is a 42-year-old chief financial officer for a $30-million, privately owned company. He manages the accounting department, which includes numerous direct and indirect reports. Bob relishes the processes and procedures of accounting, and believes that similar rational lines of thinking can and should be applied to all parts of the company. As CFO, Bob is called into several high-level meetings with other VPs of service, product development, sales, and marketing.

Although an introvert by nature, Bob would say that he is flexible enough to present a social exterior of *distant* informality. His main strength, as he sees it, lies in helping others apply rational thinking to daily events and problems. This process will take time. He believes that "haste makes waste," and urgency must take its place in line behind thoroughness. For Bob, making a decision without due consideration of all the risks signifies poor judgment.

Good team meetings, in Bob's opinion, are ones in which a leader guides the process so that everyone can speak, agendas are followed, and risks are noted. He believes that "passionate conflict" between team members should be kept to a minimum. When unresolved issues do arise, they should be dealt with offline. The conflicting parties should observe proper decorum, stick to the issues, and be tactful. If Bob has differences with either his boss or peers, he mentions these differences in team meetings as issues to be considered. If his perspective is not heeded, then he feels underappreciated and disrespects those who disagree with his warnings and wisdom.

Bob sees himself as a serious, hard-working company man who performs all tasks, even charity work, with a certain efficiency and industry. In team meetings with those who report directly to him, he wants the meeting to move along quickly. He displays little tolerance for what he considers "petty interpersonal" issues between his people. He sees "channels of communication," procedures, and policies as extremely important to solving problems.

Others' Perceptions of Bob

Bob's people see him as coming to meetings with his mind made up and emphasizing process to minimize resistance. The employees on "his team" view him as reaching decisions by using the group to examine possible risks to his own ideas, downplaying alternatives, and moving to closure around his position. Then, the decision is represented upward as a team decision.

Bob is seen as evading both open-ended discussions that entail conflict and free-flowing dialogue in which other ideas may gather momentum. Others' ideas are regarded as combative. Both direct reports and peers view him as becoming tense at the possibility of values or interpersonal issues overtaking the business at hand. Direct reports feel Bob would be uneasy if the group met without him.

Most of his direct reports say that Bob is unreceptive, tactful, critical, and political. In tense situations, Bob gets angry, attacks, and shuts down what little alternative thinking he may do in favor of avoiding risk. He is seen as following process to minimize even healthy differences of opinion, lessen possible conflicts, make the outcomes more efficient, and improve the bottom line.

Bob is perceived as someone who is not having much fun. His people think he has extremely poor "people skills." He garners little loyalty from his people, partially because they do not know him as a *person*. They see him as someone who tries to fulfill a role without engaging either his heart or theirs. They see his work pace as slow, methodical, thoughtful, and controlling. He delegates very little and tells his people that he wants to see "final" products or reports "for an information check" before they go out. He is seen as task focused, not people focused. People matters seem to be somewhat of an energy drain to him. He tends to be seen as pessimistic about life events.

Bob is perceived as an uncommunicative soul who "suffers in silence" to all but a few. He tends to avoid most conflict until he can't take it anymore, then he explodes with his own brand of attacking diplomacy. Using tactful accusations, he will try to gain some control over others through procedure and process. He is seen as choosing to block or avoid the expression of his own passion and humanness in favor of a self-alienating compliance to procedure and rational process.

Bob's effect on direct reports produces a stultifying, boring, initiative-draining environment where emotionless, bureaucratic procedures replace the passion and enjoyment possible in a work setting. As a result, in spite of stable departmental performance and growth, many of his employees leave for greener pastures.

Antonio's Self-Perceptions

Antonio is a 36-year-old vice president of research and development for a large, $700-million health-care company. He heads a group of people responsible for researching and documenting the relationship between health-care costs, effective medical treatments, and customer perceptions of health care. He serves as the HMO's spokesman to legislative groups, customer organizations, and physician groups. Antonio has published extensively, gained industry-wide recognition, and "caught the eye" of those who run the corporate holding company that owns the HMO.

Antonio sees himself as someone who can give a good presentation and make a favorable impression. He is well dressed and plays golf in the low 80s. He views himself as the head of a proud Hispanic family and is proud of his eight- and ten-year-old sons, who attend private schools. He travels incessantly, enjoys his work, appreciates the power and status of his role, and has adjusted well to the changing face of the health-care industry.

In extended conversations with Antonio, we heard him rationalize that those who left his unit were incompetent workers whose previous leader had not addressed their performance issues. The interesting thing about Antonio is that this bright, articulate man mostly agreed with much that his direct reports and peers said about him, after first giving some face-saving rationale. Antonio's reaction to hearing these perceptions was to offer extensive support of his own perceptions, followed by avoidance of further dialogue and promises to do what he could in the future.

Others' Perceptions of Antonio

Antonio's peers, direct reports, and boss describe him as incredibly bright and energetic. He is seen as a competent researcher who is ambitious and articulate, with an excellent grasp of health-care industry issues.

Although his direct reports appreciate his brightness, almost all of them describe him as arrogant, disrespectful, and demeaning. They say he communicates a know-it-all attitude and conveys an air that everyone else has inferior skills and knowledge. Employees describe Antonio as someone who says he wants directness and honesty, yet becomes irate when they suggest alternatives to his ideas or even ask for the rationale behind his decisions.

Most of Antonio's peers see him as self-centered. They say that he does only what he wants to do. He keeps his image intact by silence, diplomacy, avoidance, and, when all else fails, attacks and public beratings. Antonio is perceived as an intimidating, smooth, political, dishonest, unethical, results-oriented man who creates a stressful work environment for both direct reports and peers. They believe Antonio keeps only the promises and appointments that serve his personal agenda, and operates on a plan unknown to those who are responsible for supporting it.

In the seven months that Antonio has led the research and development unit, seven of his thirteen direct reports left. In doing background interviews with his direct reports (some who had left as well as those still working for him) prior to our discussions with Antonio, we found that some would not talk to us for fear of reprisal. Antonio's boss sought our help because it was time to either help Antonio improve or let him go. His boss understood that Antonio could not stand alone, but must succeed within the context of others. Antonio's peers were beginning to work around him, thus stretching already overextended organizational resources.

Antonio's effect on others was easily seen in the disdain, disrespect, and anger expressed by his direct reports and peers. In his short seven months as VP of research and development, Antonio hit some home runs by publicizing the organization's output and "catching the eye" of the holding company's top brass. But, because of his effect on others around him, it is just a matter of time before this interpersonal "time bomb" goes off and Antonio self-destructs.

The Four Tragedies

The situations with Bob and Antonio are variations on a theme. Each man, as described by direct reports, is ineffective. Antonio views himself as others do and knows that people consider him ineffective. In fact, the questionnaires given to both Antonio and his people revealed the same profile. Bob, on the other hand, views himself as an effective leader and was surprised to receive feedback contrary to his own view. Bob's and Antonio's ineffectiveness results in at least four tragedies.

The first tragedy lies in the fact that Bob is not aware of the effect he is having on his direct reports. What creates his *myopia*? What causes him to misunderstand the effect he is having on people? Does he know what to do to change his behavior?

The second, even more apparent tragedy, lies in Antonio's knowing how he is viewed by his people, yet choosing not to change. Antonio certainly lacks the *will* to change, regardless of whether he has the knowledge and skill to change.

Both Bob and Antonio, like the executives they typify, lack knowledge. They lack an understanding of the true meaning of leadership. They lack the self-knowledge necessary to clearly see why they act the way they do. They have little understanding of their impact on others, and they have few ideas about possible alternatives that could be used. However, even if they considered the possible alternatives, they do not show the courage or self-discipline to use them.

The third tragedy is found in the impact these men have on those they are supposed to lead. Their leadership does not help others be more productive and energized. Instead, they create anger, fear, resentment, frustration, and flight. Their direct reports hate coming to work each day. In some instances, their direct reports refused to describe their perceptions to us and blamed the organization for letting this happen.

The fourth tragedy lies in the loss these typical leaders create for the organization they are supposed to serve. The organization's resources are not well spent supporting this type of leadership. Additionally, the organization loses employee creativity, energy, efficiency, commitment, and productivity. In some cases, this type of leader garners employee resentment and ill will to the point of employee sabotage.

These tragedies are typical, but not exhaustive, of the leadership problems existing in today's organizations. In most cases, individuals in leadership positions are well meaning. However, because of a general lack of individual and organizational awareness concerning what effective leadership behaviors could and should be used, these problems persist.

The Abetting System

Such "leaders" work and act within organizations that permit or even foster this kind of ineffective behavior. Organizations, through the individuals that head them, too often promote the Bobs and Antonios into positions of power and control. Thus, poor leadership begets more poor leadership because poor leaders often select managers who possess the same traits they themselves demonstrate. Because human issues are not valued as much as the bottom line, effective corporate leadership continues to be evaluated solely on how it appears to affect shareholder value. Human issues take longer to "fix," and thus the Bobs and Antonios of corporate America continue to be in charge of others.

From our vantage point as corporate consultants, there is more competition than collaboration among executives. Too often, short-term issues displace long-term future considerations. Too often, focus on profits supersedes the relationship with employees and customers, efficiency is substituted for genuine quality, and rationality drives out joy in the workplace. This lack of leadership is exacting a dreadful toll.

Kissing Off the Organization

The fallout created by a pyramid of ineffective executives, as typified by Bob and Antonio, is devastating and pervasive. Our observations lead us to believe that people in organizations *feel* sad and dissociated from their organizations. Too many employees have long since moved from skepticism to cynicism with regard to their leaders and their organizations. The incidence of truly loyal employees (employees committed to the organization and planning to stay at least two years) remains at just 24 percent nationally, the same as in 1999. Thirty-four percent of U.S. employees are at risk (employees neither committed to the organization nor planning to stay), as compared to 33 percent in 1999.[5]

Too many of those who work in organizations do so merely to make a living, not to make a meaningful, fulfilling contribution to their organizations. Instead, they are merely spending time on the job to make enough money to do what they really want to do off the job. In short, many employees don't *nurture their organization*; they merely meet the job requirements.

People go to their place of employment, but aren't fully engaged with either their minds or hearts. Too many employees seem to lead stressful organizational lives because they choose or are forced to abandon their personal beliefs, values, and hopes "at the organization's doorstep." They go to work simply to lay bricks, rather than envisioning the creation of a cathedral.

A recent *Fortune* article[6] documented how the "best and brightest" don't want to be part of corporations due to the organization's lack of creativity, autonomy, and vision. Instead, the more talented among the younger generation are looking for alternatives to corporate life. If they do become part of a corporation, then it is only to learn and earn enough to get out, be on their own, and create their own vision, independence, and freedom. Younger workers have little interest in building their organization's future and show little interest in their organization's health or well-being. Today's workers feel owned instead of having a sense of psychological ownership in their organization's purpose. They feel weak, not strong; they are cynical, not hopeful; they feel despair, not commitment. Instead of viewing themselves as a partner, they feel apart, separated from their organization's purpose, the possibility of meaningful work, and the joy of mutual effort. They have no commitment to something greater than their own self-interest or reward for their own individual efforts.

The Leadership Vacuum

A great deal of fault lies at the feet of the leaders. Poor leadership results not from conscious malice, but from inadequate leadership knowledge, values, and behaviors. Many leaders we encounter do not fully realize that the biggest competitive edge they have lies more in the people they lead and less in technology, capitalization, or market share.

People in leadership positions do not know themselves well enough to escape the "disease of me."[7] This lack of leader self-knowledge results in organizational systems, policies, practices, and stories that do not create energizing environments of true hope and worth for those who work in them. Just over one-half (54 percent) of the employees surveyed believe their organizations treat employees fairly. Additionally, an atmosphere of genuine care and concern for employees was only experienced by 44 percent of the surveyed population.[8]

Those in positions of authority are the products of the very systems that need to be changed. Too often, those who are technically proficient, politically astute, or have a strong desire for power or wealth are in charge. The succession processes of many corporations seem to sift out those who are not politically aware and driven toward power and bottom-line results. The process of natural selection reinforces a culture of "self"-oriented individuals. A 1999 National Business Ethics Study reported that only 47 percent of the employees surveyed thought their leaders were highly ethical. Additionally, 56 percent of the population surveyed felt that expectations of ethical behavior had been well communicated within the organization. Yet, only a third of the employees surveyed felt comfortable reporting ethical misconduct.[9]

Those who usually rise to the top of the many organizations with which we are acquainted sacrificed much of their joy and compassion to get there. They have neither the sense nor desire to produce an energizing work environment that includes both a social vision and values for others they may lead. Instead, these individuals are caught up in their own personal quest to climb the corporate ladder. There seems to be a profound lack of purposefulness, except to make it to the top.

More often than not, we see leaders who do not have a vision that manifests a clear set of beliefs for leading their organizations into the future. Instead, many in management or leadership positions find themselves shaped by corporate culture, rather than shaping or changing the culture to emotionally ignite the minds *and* hearts of those who carry out the organization's purpose. Thus, it is understandable that leaders have little or no vision. They are followers who are promoted to leadership positions with no precedents for what leadership could be.

Not knowing what to do to move their organizations toward an energizing work environment with social vision and values is understandable. What is disturbing is that many of those in leadership positions do not have the energy, tolerance, or perspective to *want* to lead their organizations into the future.

Corporate leaders often lack the self-knowledge necessary to act effectively for themselves, their followers, or the long-term, overall positive welfare of their organizations. Those in authority lack an appreciation of the nature of leadership. They often dwell on concepts that divide and separate people, rather than on concepts that reflect the interconnectedness and commonality of people. They become forgetful of purpose and values that explain *why* and *what for*. They have very little awareness of the context of their office or the external environment that frames whatever it is they are responsible for. They seldom see themselves as learners who are creating new realities for themselves and others.

Corporate leaders are often physically out of shape and emotionally blocked. In the worst cases, they are spiritually starved executives who live terribly imbalanced lives chained to corporate titles, responsibility, and, of course, large financial payoffs. These executives are workaholics. They are the "respectable addicts" of an imbalanced system and, more often than not, they create or allow environments that produce dysfunctional employees.

Executives are often driven by personal aims. From executive boardrooms to the small entrepreneurial offices of most organizations, there can be found a group of ego-driven, personally myopic, provincially interested people competing for power and energy with almost everyone else. In most instances, that drive results in pain, dissatisfaction, broken marriages, dissolved partnerships, and disintegrated personal relationships. For many, the "road to the top" is a relentless grind in which an individual must choose to make the supreme sacrifice of personal fulfillment on an altar of organizational power and influence.

We could provide extensive economic, sociological, and medical data to verify the need for better leadership in organizations. Instead, we ask you to ponder these questions:

- Does the leadership of your organization promote the healthy, integrated growth of *all* key stakeholders (employees, owners, and customers)?
- Are the organization's members becoming physically, emotionally, and spiritually healthier?
- If you were the leader, how would organizational members honestly answer these questions about you and your organization?

Leaders are not independent beings merely attaining personal financial goals and greater career opportunities. They must, as Socrates advocates, "See their office as a social responsibility, a trust, a duty, and not as a symbol of their personal identity, prestige and lofty status."[10]

It's as if leaders forget that what is done to others, is done to self. They overlook the interconnectedness of humanity. The leaders' aim should be to build energy among those who share the same business purpose and values, because business purpose and values represent the key to individual commitment. Without clarity and agreement around these elements, everyone's energy is limited. The leaders' aim should also be to create integrity in the treatment of the customer, as well as integrity in the treatment of organizational members who serve the customer. It is vital for leaders to understand that *how* employees are treated by the organization is *how* the employee is likely to treat the customer.[11] Without this understanding, individual and organizational wholeness is unfeasible or improbable.

The Covenant

Leaders must understand that a covenant is established between each employee and the organization—a covenant in which the employee decides whether to give more or take more. Some research indicates that approximately 26 percent of a company's workforce is engaged (loyal and productive), 55 percent is not engaged (putting in time), and 19 percent is actively disengaged (unhappy and spreading discontent).[12] What kind of a covenant is established within your organization?

What kind of covenant do you establish if the company continually communicates messages that workers are expendable, interchangeable, dispensable, or second-class? What kind of covenant do you establish if the organization has no vision or values, or the stated vision and values are not actually in use? The data is clear and obvious. Because of the perceived low ethical standards of executives, employees feel justified in responding in a like manner. They retaliate through absenteeism, sabotage, theft, indifference, or poor productivity.[13]

By now you might think we have little faith in humanity. We do not think people are inherently self-serving, uncaring, or socially irresponsible. In fact, we believe just the opposite is possible. With the right leadership, most people are capable of a great deal of human connectedness, organizational productivity, and self-integration. However, the naturally striving and growing individual is vulnerable to being controlled and made to feel ineffective in corporate settings. The organizational context can either be nurturing or antagonistic toward the individual's integrated sense of self, and therefore the covenant formed between the individual and the organization is influenced positively or negatively.

This covenant is profoundly shaped by the leaders who represent and embody the "organization" in the mind of the employees. Leaders who do not possess self-awareness, integrity, and character, or do not recognize the value in social purpose and connectedness, negatively influence employees to become takers. Such employees learn to act in compliance or defiance with the organization's policies and procedures. They take as much as possible and give as little as possible.

It is up to leaders to embody sharing, connectedness, and self-integration so they can help others develop the same qualities. Good leadership starts from the inside of an individual leader, and then is demonstrated outwardly. Good leadership is founded in a state of being, not just doing. Good leadership is about *your* outlook, *your* orientation, *your* character, and *your* inner thoughts and emotions.

Good leadership results in creating new realities for others to follow, or for others to be allowed to create. However, if you are to do that for others, then you must do it for yourself first! You cannot expect your organization, team, or direct reports to change if you are not willing to change. The ideas in this book can help you in your lifelong quest to become a better leader and produce an environment that fosters the well-being of others.

ONIONS

What do onions have to do with leadership? It is a metaphor that can help you understand yourself, the leader you are, and the leader you wish to become. Think of the qualities and characteristics of an onion. The main characteristics of the onion are its layers, strong and undeniable aroma, and striking taste that enhances the flavor of other foods. In most cases, the onion is commonly used to spice up the main course.

The Layered Self

Like an onion, there are "layers" of the self. The layers, in the form of your disposition, values, and resultant leadership "skin," give shape and substance to you as a leader. Each layer can and must be clearly understood before you can "transform" your leadership character.

A journey of self-understanding begins at the inner layers, and then moves outward to the layer of observable leader behaviors. Your leader behaviors rest on the often less visible and less examined inner layers of self, which are formed through the self's evolutionary interaction with your life's events. The development and expansion of your leadership character will come from understanding each important layer.

The Leadership Onion

The self consists of multiple layers, from complex inner layers to more simple outer layers. The layers of importance are: (1) the core unconscious self, (2) the dispositional layer, (3) the values layer, (4) the persona, and (5) the leadership skin. Figure 1.1 depicts the multilayered self within the metaphor of the leadership onion.

The dispositional layer is divided into *wired* and *acquired* preferences. The values layer is made up of various *programmed* and *developed* values. The values and dispositional layers combine to form a values/dispositional layer, a persona, which also shapes your leadership behavior over time. The persona is the self you want to present to others, while the leadership skin is the outward behavior others can observe. More definition and specificity about these layers will be added in subsequent pages. At this point, however, familiarize yourself with the names and sequence of the layers, and then read on.

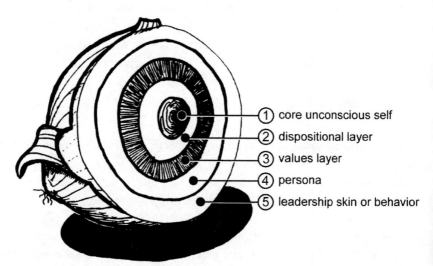

FIGURE 1.1 *The leadership onion.*

For example, your value base—what you believe, what you perceive as valuable, what business you are in as a human being—is central to your approach to leadership. The vision you hold for yourself and others stems from the important *values* layer you bring to the "moments of management." The values layer is your unique essence, which gives form to your "leader" self. This layer is not only form giving, but because it is between other layers, it also gives strength and substance to the layers above and below it. Your values layer is independently linked to your *dispositional* layer—another dimension of the leadership onion.

Peeling the Onion

Besides its multiple layers, a second characteristic of an onion is the unique aroma it releases when its core is exposed. Anyone who cuts into an onion knows the discomfort to eyes and nose. There can be a similar discomfort when peeling back the layers of self.

Kierkegaard, the Scandinavian philosopher, wrote that life must be lived forwards, but can only be understood backwards.[14] The process of peeling the onion requires you to constantly grow through introspection and reflection. Peeling the onion requires a *loving tolerance* for who you are and who you are not. It requires a humble acceptance of your strengths and, more important for growth, a patient acknowledgment of your weaknesses.

A loving tolerance of self implies a creative tension in life. It is a condition of pleasurable tension in which you are moving toward something better, while also cherishing the past. Peeling the onion fosters the duality of being and becoming. It requires a change in thought and action, while building on what is.

Peeling the onion implies that you are accountable for your own development. You must assume responsibility for your own experiences and must possess the courage to recognize both your glorious functionality *and* the adaptive potential of your dysfunction. Peeling the onion requires you to have the courage to intentionally move away from your existing comfort zones, confront your not-so-successful self, and, in reflective tolerance, face the harsh realities of self-change.

The Challenge of Discomfort

Often, discomfort comes from loss of control or predictability. When you use unfamiliar behaviors, you dislike the feeling of *incapacity*, never mind the less-than-perfect results. As an experiment, write your full name on a piece of paper. Now, using your other hand, write your full name again. How did you feel during this experience? What was your reaction? Did you like the results of your efforts with the alternate hand? Did you feel as powerful the second time you wrote your name as the first time? Most people report that they would not want to do this too often. People typically respond by saying they feel like a child in school, waiting for the teacher to correct their efforts. Some say they don't like their efforts with the opposite hand and need more time to practice.

We asked you to try this exercise because it effectively demonstrates the mental work that must be done to change an outward behavior. It allows you to touch the mental aspects you and others may bring to a behavioral change. Change is not only based in practicality and logic, but in personal emotion, security, and self-concept. Peeling the onion requires that you become more comfortable in creating the *self* that you want to become.

Attaining comfort and effectiveness with infrequently used behaviors is an anticipated outcome of this book. You must understand why you depend on certain patterns of behavior *and* why you avoid others that you could use to become a more effective leader. This journey will require courage and persistence. It will take courage to make mistakes, and to *feel* and *be* vulnerable as you lead others. It will take persistence to reinvent yourself in the presence of others' judgments.

Flavoring the Stew

Unless you are in the habit of making a meal out of a platter of onion rings, you most likely use onions to spice up or add flavor to other foods. Usually, you use moderate-to-small amounts of onions in your meals. So it is with leadership. Leadership in organizations is not the main course. The main course of organizational life is the organization's purpose and those who accomplish that purpose. Leadership ultimately provides a service, much as the onion does to the stew. Leadership "allows" the way for the main body of people to accomplish the purpose.

Most of us find that eating onions by themselves is difficult. A serious problem with most books on the topic of leadership is the separation of the analysis of leader behaviors from the analysis of followership. *Those books are all onions and no stew!* There can be no leadership without "followership," and that is why, in this book, you will always find a discussion of leader behaviors in light of follower needs. You will also find an in-depth discussion regarding followers' perceptions of leaders with specific points of view or dispositions. The chapters in this book are focused more on the examination of leadership than they are on followership. *But do not, for one instant, think that leadership is the whole stew.*

A noteworthy, telltale sign of the off-kilter, monarch-like emphasis on today's corporate leadership is found in an examination of executive salaries. New York Federal Reserve Bank President William McDonough cites a recent study showing that during the past 20 years, the average CEO's compensation has grown from 42 times that of the average production worker to more than 400 times as much. That translates to an average CEO salary of $10 million a year versus $25,467 for the average worker.[15] In fact, you may be chagrined to note that executives get millions just to retire.[16] Someone must think the leader is the whole stew.

Too many individuals believe that to lead means to take charge, provide the energy, motivate, be responsible for, and control, rather than to attribute meaning to an already energetic, motives-driven workforce that seeks satisfaction through their work and enriched responsibility. Not enough potential or existing leaders see themselves in the service of those who follow. The mind-set of a servant-leader means others' needs must come before yours. It means *serving* their hopes and dreams.

It is as if many business leaders see only themselves and act as if the organization is an extension of *their* own self-purpose. Events and people become the instruments of their desires, reality, and being, instead of promoting *common* purpose and *common* values that *lead* to a meaningful reality for them and others.

The Michelangelo View

Many executives lack a highly developed perspective of leadership. Their egocentricity puts them, alone, in the center and they are compelled to show the way. When Michelangelo talked about the creation of the "David" and many other sculptures, he was fond of saying that the figure was already there. All he did was uncover it by knowing what to chip away. This is what we mean by a highly developed leadership perspective. You are uncovering, visioning, and verbalizing what is already present in others.

You can only do this by using yourself as a source of learning. Understanding what is in your heart allows you to understand what is in the hearts and minds of others. It is the perspective of wholeness—which starts with self-knowledge—that allows a leader to *envision* beyond self and uncover what is in others.

Most people can behave in ways that will make them much more effective as leaders. They are capable of growing by using a wider range of behaviors than they are currently using. Growth is about doing the "self" work necessary to become a better leader. You can benefit by discovering and applying certain less used aspects of yourself to become more effective. To grow is to change your realities and, therefore, yourself. To grow, you must connect to those *lost* parts of yourself that extend your range of humanness to help and serve yourself and others. You must examine how you *now* behave as a leader and understand what future behaviors might be possible within you.

CHANGE

Accept the idea that people are multilayered beings who sometimes experience discomfort with self-examination. View leadership as service to both organizational purpose and those who carry out organizational purpose. Remember that inherent in the process of leadership is the requirement that other people change and grow. With such attitudes, you can go about the business of validating, improving, or re-creating yourself and your approach to leadership. But, to reinvent or re-create yourself will require your constant desire to change and grow. How can you ask others to grow and develop without your being open to change and growth? To illustrate the problems of change and growth, consider the following joke from Woody Allen's movie *Annie Hall*.

Changing Ourselves

A man walks into his psychiatrist's office and promptly says that the doctor needs to help him with his brother. He says to the psychiatrist: "Doc, it's my brother . . . he thinks he's a chicken." The doctor asks, "Why don't you just tell him he's *not* a chicken?" The man replies, "I can't, I need the eggs!"

There is much wisdom in this old joke. This anecdote illustrates the following: (1) people *create* their own reality, (2) people seem to *cling* to their realities because of fear of losing what they have, and (3) people *confine* themselves to their present realities because they do not usually envision other alluring and functional realities.

Creating Reality

When two people observe the same event, they are likely to see different things and have different interpretations. This variability stems from differing views of reality, which are constructed from a combination of each person's distinctive personal experience and interpretation of life's events. No two people are exactly alike, and while there are broad patterns that are similar, everyone is unique enough to be somewhat unpredictable.

People sometimes change from one set of behaviors to another because of life-threatening circumstances. Yet, the moment the threat is past, most people return to their earlier realities. Profound, persistent behavioral change that is fully integrated into total being occurs only through the reexamination and reconstruction of reality. A reconstructed or "new" reality allows new behaviors to continue in the presence of shifting environmental forces.

Your reality is "created" or formed through interaction with the events and people of your experience. You form beliefs around these events and experiences. A common language and experiences with others help firm up these beliefs and "your" reality is formed.

Beliefs as the Basis of Reality

Everyone forms beliefs about the world, themselves, and their interactions in the world. These beliefs create an intricate web called a "point of view" or "belief window." This self-constructed point of view is a window through which you see events and people.

In other words, you experience the world—people, places, and things—and over time, form beliefs that allow you to function in the present and anticipate the future. The advantage of forming beliefs lies in being purposeful and reducing the time-consuming effort of understanding how and why each experience is connected to others. Your belief window can serve to reduce the uncertainty of life and particular circumstances.

Language and Reality

Your reality is both distinctively original *and* socially shaped by shared experiences with other people. Language is one shared experience that shapes your reality. A simple example can be found in the differences between the English and Eskimo languages. English-speaking people use one word for snow, while there are numerous different words for snow in the Eskimo language. The latter allows for the distinction between different types of snow and conditions, while the English language does not. The non-Eskimo language does not stimulate an individual to experience the different snow types. Even if the non-Eskimo could actually see, taste, or feel the difference in those snow types, he or she would not be able to express it.

An intricate web of common beliefs and common experience is confirmed through a common language; thus, your reality is connected to those with whom you live and love, work and play, nurture and protect. Just as beliefs and language are the keys to reality formation, they are also a basis for self-change. In the subsequent chapters, we offer some ideas and concepts to change your beliefs about leadership. These ideas and concepts also offer you the chance to create a new language about leadership so that you can create your new leadership behavior.

Clinging to Accepted Realities

Not only do you create your own reality, but you also cling to it because other people experience similar realities. Lily Tomlin's fitting quote, "Reality is just something on which there is consensus," helps to explain how you function in the social milieu. You reach intersubjective agreement about a person, place, or thing. Your reality is connected to others through language, and your needs are met with and through others by clinging to realities that other people support. You cling to old realities not only because others support that reality, but also because you are fearful of what others might think if you were to act outside those realities or "norms."

Confining Yourself

Family, social, and cultural norms create certain realities that define what is and is not; what is good and bad; and what the self can and cannot be. It is easier to function when operating by what others accept, because adherence to certain realities allows you to see yourself as acceptable and good. Yet, there is a hidden cost to following the crowd: Accepted societal "goods and bads" and other dichotomous cultural concepts often misrepresent, misshape, or deprive existence of a wider range of possibilities, as the example of Eskimo "snows" would imply. In other words, conforming to accepted realities can be confining.

Confinement emerges when you formulate beliefs that preshape your response. It occurs when your beliefs are not supported by your experiences, yet you act as if those beliefs are supported. "Assumed constraints" result when you fail to examine an experience *because* of the beliefs you hold. Moreover, confinement results when cultural or social acceptance runs counter to your experiential understanding, yet you choose behaviors that gain acceptance rather than new, more experientially appropriate behaviors. Although accepted realities may be confining, it is difficult to form new realities. Too often, fear arises when you act outside accepted norms or reality.

Fear and the Shadow Self

Like the onion seed, you start less developed but, at least, relatively whole. Your experience is seamless and whole—whole in the sense that your experience of existence is not limited by concepts or notions that are segmented, parted by time, divided into good, bad, future, present, past, self, or others. You are whole, in the sense that you contain a myriad of untapped response possibilities that allow you to express your humanness. Whole also means that you are capable of responding with flexibility to environmental requirements, using a wide range of behaviors.

As you develop, the world changes: Objects, experiences, and people become separate. You begin to judge and divide everything you experience into good and bad. You select what is acceptable to your significant others, group, or society. You learn what thoughts, emotions, and behaviors must be *suppressed* or *put away*. You begin to create your shadow self. Of course, some of this sorting is necessary for societal functioning, but that which is "put away" *does not go away*. The nonacceptable (according to others or society) parts of yourself take on a life of their own—your shadow self. Your shadow self is the unfulfilled, illegitimate, and almost despised parts of yourself.

Through language, experience, and association with others, you form beliefs concerning what is true and not true, what is acceptable and unacceptable, and what is possible and impossible. You learn what not to do in order to be loved; you learn what to do in order to not be rejected. To be unloved or constantly rejected is painful. Pain produces fear of future pain. Gradually, you associate fear with certain behaviors and *learn* to fear certain socially unacceptable parts of yourself. Often, you become what you least fear becoming. Often, what can and does happen, through a *trained incapacity*, is that you develop a less flexible self, a less understood self, and a less self-accepted person.

For example, there are many executives whose shadow selves are afraid to lose. They fear growing old and being weak, soft, and caring. They are afraid to relinquish control, slow down and reflect, or face the conflict that is the natural by-product of human interaction in organizations. There are many other executives who are afraid to take charge, be strong, or generate conflict.

At first, it is not the fears that limit; rather, it's the failure to *explore* the fears that limit. To use our chicken analogy, people are "chicken" to face their fears. It is the "care and feeding" of an unexamined "shadow" that you must seek to change.

Me and My Shadow

In Jungian or Freudian language, the shadow self is mostly unconscious. That which is unacceptable from a cultural, organizational, or family point of view becomes what people do not devote much conscious energy or time to. You block your self-acceptance and development through conscious avoidance and nonexploration. You eventually deny certain possibilities in your self. Thus, the shadow self is not explored. It is seldom identified, discussed, or managed in the habits of life. Unlike other cultures of the past or present, in today's society there are almost no rituals or healing ceremonies to accept or integrate your shadow self.

However, this shadow side or aspect of self does not go away. You still have the capacity to be and want to be these unaccepted aspects, but it will take energy *not* to use or act on these capacities of self. It is quite possible that the shadow side of yourself can, at times, manifest itself behaviorally in place of more rational self-control.

Societies throughout history denied and controlled the shadow side by "projecting" or assigning that which is not socially or culturally acceptable to other groups or races. This technique of projection resulted in the annihilation of six million Jews, the genocide of Native Americans, and the enslavement of blacks, to mention a few real and frightening examples.

The implications of the shadow can be easily seen at an organizational level. There is a shadow side to every organization.[17] Ask yourself, "How important and reliable is the rumor mill in your organization? What is not openly addressed in meetings? Who are perceived as the 'second-class citizens' of the organization? What are people saying in whispers? Who gets blamed for system errors?" The avoidance and nonconfrontation of issues feeds the organization's shadow. Certain unacceptable human/organizational issues are forced into the shadows and require perpetual energy to keep them there.

As previously discussed, the socialization process serves a purpose. Socialization prevents anarchy or self-oriented, indiscriminate, socially harmful behaviors that pander to the possible destructive side of every person. However, it is the authors' opinion that certain antisocial *behaviors,* such as murder, rape, theft, lying, and so on, should be labeled as undesirable, unacceptable, or unhealthy, and therefore should be prevented. Still, it is unfortunate that when certain behaviors are labeled as unacceptable, they have major negative consequences for the wholeness of self if not integrated and accepted by the individual. Integrating these less acceptable social capacities does not always mean acting on them. However, it does mean acknowledging them and understanding the implications for a wise choice.[18]

Masculine/Feminine Shadows

An excellent example of the formation of the shadow self can be found in the cultural meaning and expression of masculine and/or feminine psychic aspects. Many people have written about the different socialization processes that males and females experience. Many authors have reported the stereotypical behavior required of men and women in this culture.[19]

The cultural meaning and expression of these masculine and feminine dimensions has also been explored extensively in a leadership context.[20]

The socialization of males or females results in a set of widely known, acceptable behaviors for males and another set of acceptable behaviors for females. Both cross-cultural studies[21] and U.S. studies[22] confirm that males are more commonly socialized to assume individual, independent, aggressive, task leadership orientations, while females are shaped to assume nurturing, collectivist, compromising, caring, relational leadership orientations. The point is that each individual, regardless of gender, possesses the capacity to learn these two sets of behaviors and therefore can have the ability to respond to events and opportunities using either set of behaviors.

Normally, genders are not expected to show behaviors outside these orientations. For example, recall the impact that crying had on Edmund Muskie's presidential campaign or the implications given to Hillary Clinton's assertive, aggressive, controlling role when lobbying for health-care reform. The fact that each individual is capable of both orientations, yet socialized toward one, results in the development of latent aspects of self that need to be explored and perhaps capitalized on when appropriate.

People possess the capacity to understand and *express* both orientations, even though socialized toward one. The socialization process results in both self and others valuing some behaviors while devaluing others, whether intentional or not. A second confounding element arises when the devalued behavior may be natural to the individual *and* perhaps even more functional in specific role situations. It may be fitting that a woman manifests an independent, assertive, task leader approach if the situation warrants it. It also may be more effective for a man to use nurturing, caring, compromising, relational leader practices. The free and frequent use of the undeveloped and less socially accepted shadow-self behaviors takes courage and persistence. It takes courage and conviction to act in the face of disapproval, rejection, and, in some cases, even social punishment.

Fear—Your Emotional Brakes

Fear is an emotional brake on possible alternative actions. It is normal and, of course, healthy in some circumstances. Fear of falling from a precarious perch or publicly making a speech in front of a hundred people may "feel" the same. Sweaty palms, the flow of adrenaline, and body chemistry may reflect a heightened state of readiness. But the potential negative consequences are different. In most situations, it is life preserving to have a fear of falling from a precarious perch, but this is not necessarily so with making a public speech. Fear in life-threatening situations may be life preserving, but fear in learning situations may be "life" threatening or, at least, limiting. A better understanding of self requires the exploration of thought and feelings, which may stimulate old and new fears.

It's All Part of the Game

Do you think that people can and do change? Do you believe that you can change? These questions are important because to grow means that you must believe people can and do change. Because your reality is in some ways self-constructed, it follows that you can alter it. If you change your thoughts (realities), then you will eventually change your behaviors. Individual change means the shift from one set of patterns or behaviors (realities) to another over time, but an absolute prerequisite to change is the belief that you have the potential to change.

The belief that you can change is essential to your future. If you believe that you (or other people) cannot change, then you become trapped in your present limitations and strengths. On this issue, the experts tend to disagree and the battle rages.[23] Consider this: What are the implications for you if you were to live as if you cannot change your patterns of behavior?

This book is based on our findings that most people *can* change. People can and do change major patterns of behavior—with effort and education. Read no further if you believe that you cannot change. However, if you want to change, the ideas within the following pages will help.

To be more illustrative, let's examine a real management example. One of us was advising a baseball coach for the Major League Chicago Cubs. The discussion centered on reprimanding a player for not adhering to a bunt sign. The coach had previously reprimanded the player in front of the other players.

CHAPTER 1 ■ LEADERS AND CHANGE

When the coach was asked to share his rationale for the public reprimand, he said he did it to teach this player and, more important, the other players, what *not* to do in the future. Further inquiry led to the coach actually disclosing that he didn't want the others to think he was soft. He was indeed *the boss* and was to be respected through compliance to his directives. Let's grant that the player should have adhered to the bunt sign. However, what alternatives to the public reprimand would produce better results for the coach, the player, and the team?

There are very few circumstances where public reprimands are advantageous. In this case, negative consequences are appropriate, but not a public reprimand because it creates a defensive, resistant, fearful individual who *feels* violated (even if he is wrong). The player's natural reaction to a public reprimand may be to make excuses, blame the coach, or defensively shut off any constructive feedback that may accompany the public reprimand. The onlookers are not thinking, "Oh, I guess I'll be careful in the future." Typically, they are thinking, "That poor teammate, I'm glad I'm not him . . . that coach is not being fair . . . he makes mistakes as we all do . . . if he ever does that to me . . ."

Instead of producing a learning experience for others about the need to adhere to bunt signs, the coach reduced his own credibility, introduced fear into a learning situation, and produced sympathy for a teammate—probably the last thing that he wanted to do. Indeed, what the coach succeeded in doing was transferring his fear to those around him—disguised in the name of teaching and authority. What makes matters worse is that the shadow side of the coach was not acknowledged or explored. His shadow side was revealed by his fear of being soft or losing control through softness. Those fears blocked his capacity to explore other behaviors.

One common solution known to work in this type of situation is to pull the individual aside (out of earshot of others, but not necessarily out of eyesight) and, after exploring the individual's point of view, to deliver the reprimand if it is still warranted. Using this approach, the player's dignity is still intact, and he also hears the message without the tension of a public reprimand. The other players see that consequences result from missed directives, and they also feel that they will be treated with discretion in similar circumstances.

When the coach heard this alternate solution, he said, "Maybe so, but now the players know who is boss." The coach said *being the boss* was *what was important*, and he probably would not use the alternative. It seemed that, in the reality he had created, he needed the eggs!

Stop for a moment. Given that you may not know all the facts behind the example, do you find yourself agreeing with the coach? Do you believe that public reprimands are effective and appropriate? If your answers are yes, what would it take to change your point of view? What *emotion* is connected with such a change? What is preventing you from using the suggested alternative? You must acknowledge your fear of change and loss of what you presently do as an individual and as a leader. Then, in the spirit of learning, you must courageously go where you have not gone before.

If you confine yourself to unquestioned, "created," familiar realities, then you act in that confinement. You can peel back the layers by understanding that you act in the presence of other alternatives, and consciously acknowledging your fears. As you receive feedback from those you seek to lead, you must face your possible weaknesses. You should cherish your weaknesses, not hide them from yourself. Your weaknesses can be a pathway to new and more growthful possibilities. You can recognize and use your fears to change to better alternative realities.

Alternative Realities and Behaviors

It is said that true insanity is repeating the same ineffective behaviors over and over yet expecting different results. The fear factor is one reason people do not change behavior, however a second and more debilitating reason is the lack of alternatives. Some people possess almost no sense of different alternatives. As you read further, you will gain a clearer understanding of potential alternatives. Try them, use them, and make them your own as you become more versatile.

CHAPTER 1 ■ LEADERS AND CHANGE

Collecting information and having the willingness to look at the effect of your behavior is a beginning. You must seek to understand and acknowledge the patterns that you presently use. Understanding presently used behaviors is the first step, but the "true" work begins in "bypassing" the fears of the shadow self, and then using other, more functional possibilities. Repeating the same ineffective behavior over again, yet expecting different results, will not enable you to grow or develop. To grow requires that you become more versatile. Thus, the second step is finding and using suitable alternative behaviors that will achieve better results for you. To use other possibilities requires the reconstruction of your reality in light of real and ideal results.

Working on the "Self"

If the baseball coach wants adherence to the bunt sign *and* respect as a leader, if he wants performance *and* motivated ballplayers, then a change in his reality is necessary. His reality must be re-created to allow for other attitudes and behaviors that could produce the desired results. This advice holds true for you. First, note your patterns of frequent behaviors. At the same time, note those patterns you *do not* use frequently. Those infrequently used behaviors are the key to your fears and growth.

The redefinition of your reality—who you are—may be accomplished if new possibilities can be found in your shadow side. Those different alternatives can be found in behaviors you fear to use. In the case of the coach, his shadow side had within it the belief that it is unacceptable to be seen as weak and not in control. Those beliefs, those fears of the shadow side, prevented him from acknowledging and using alternative possibilities.

The work comes in *realizing* those other possibilities when necessary. In the coaching example, the coach must understand that his values and disposition at that leadership moment evolved into a need for others to see who has the "power." This need took precedent over the coach's need to have the player understand the conditions that led to the bunt sign, the impact that not bunting had on the status of game, and the impact that noncompliance had on the team.

Assuming the bunt sign was the best strategy at that moment in the game, it is desirable for the player to see the same conditions that the coach saw, which prompted the bunt sign in the first place. Will the leader's actions produce "that reality" for this player?

This example may seem a bit extended, but there is a tendency for all people, at various times, to act on familiar realities instead of looking for a wider range of more effective alternatives. This is especially true in times of stress or pressure.

Personal "Why" of Leadership

As we consult with managers, we often ask if they like managing people. More than half of the managers say no. The results may cause you to wonder why people end up in positions of leadership. What psychic rewards do you receive from being in a leadership position? Is it to be of service? Is it because it is the only way to earn more money or achieve more status? What motives keep you going? As you read the subsequent pages of this book, they will provide you with insight as to what drives you to seek positions of leadership.

Underlying your leadership growth and your purpose as a leader is the issue of your organization's social purpose and your ability to provide leadership in light of its social purpose. Is the first organizational purpose to provide "value" that adds to the lives of others through your organization's product or service, or simply to make money? Can you envision the advancement of social purpose while business goals are being reached, and not the converse? The furthering of social purpose mandates caring about followers inside the organization, as well as the customers outside.

Too many business leaders see their goals only in terms of organizational profits. Profits are necessary and desirable, but remember that profit is a by-product of a greater, broad-ranging vision. Profit is an indirect result of the organization's interaction with a public or a society that wants or needs the organization's service or product. To improve organizations, you must deal with people (both internal and external to the organization), and their individual and collective actions that relate to achieving the organization's social purpose. Of course, capital and fiscal resources are important inputs, but labor and people are still the most potentially defining resources in organizational output.

Being a profitable organization (or fiscally responsible in the case of a noprofit organization) is not at issue. Those who try to argue for either profit over people or people over profit are limiting their capacity to lead. Profit is absolutely essential to maintain growth, provide jobs, and meet the demands of the marketplace. *How* people are treated and grow while the organization is profiting is the issue. In the long run, making a profit and treating people humanely are not mutually exclusive.

Change and Failure

It is essential for leaders to understand the multilayered self as it is brought to the moments of influence and within the context of furthering the organization's social purpose. Your personality as "it" seeks to meet the requirements of the situation (as you see it) will result in the demonstration of your character. Each moment of leadership can be either well met or poorly executed. All great leaders fail at times, so why not allow yourself that possibility? An examination of the lives of great leaders, such as Gandhi, Henry Ford, Winston Churchill, Golda Meir, and others, confirms the early failures of those we know changed history.[24]

Your challenge is to know yourself well enough to change yourself. You must learn to "read" the situation and sometimes use behaviors with which you may not be comfortable, if you want to meet the requirements needed to be more effective. For example, the baseball coach needed to be more flexible in his private self-reality so that he could be more behaviorally effective. However, most leaders want others to change behaviors for certain organizational results; they much less often meet the challenge of changing their own behavior with the same gusto they expect from others.

SUMMARY

To recap: People are multilayered, can and do experience discomfort when involved in self-examination, and may not view leadership as service to others. People create and live in their own realities. They cling to these realities because they fear their shadow selves and tend not to look for alternatives. But change is possible, with self-understanding and growth.

You can use the ideas and models in this book to make the challenges of self-understanding and growth easier and more effective. We found that being an effective leader is, more than anything else, a learned set of behaviors. For the benefit of present and future generations, let's proceed with that learning now.

Endnotes

1. Yoshikawa 1981.
2. Kim 2002.
3. Eby et al. 1999; Rainey 1997; Petty, McGee, and Lavendar 1984; Tett and Meyer 1993 (to mention just a few).
4. Doehrman 2000.
5. Walker Information 2001.
6. Labich 1995.
7. Riley 1993.
8. Walker Information 2001.
9. Hudson Institute and Walker Information 1999.
10. Nair 1994.
11. Schmit and Allscheid 1995; Johnson 1996.
12. Buckingham 2001.
13. Patterson and Kim 1991.
14. Vitullo-Martin and Moskin 1994.
15. *USA Today* 2002.
16. Husted 1995.

17. Egan 1994.
18. Johnson 1991; Abrams and Zweig 1991; Bly 1988.
19. Rokeach 1979, 1986; Feather 1970, 1984; Bem 1979; Bem and Lenney 1976; Fletcher 1994.
20. Sargent 1983; Kanter 1977; Korabik and Ayman 1989; Powell and Butterfield 1994; Murphy et al. 1995; Blanchard and Sargent 1984 (to mention a few).
21. Fromm 1965; Kohlberg 1964, 1973; Weber 1990; Schein and Mueller 1992; Adler and Izreli 1989.
22. Hofstede 1980; Powell 1990; Jensen, White, and Singh 1990.
23. Goldsmith 1983; Keller et al. 1992; Nicholson 1998; Ornstein 1993; Prochaska et al. 1992; Tellegen et al. 1988.
24. Fagan, Bromley, and Welch 1994.

CHAPTER 2

Personality and Context

"Watch your thoughts; they become words. Watch your words; they become actions. Watch your actions; they become habits. Watch your habits; they become character. Watch your character; it becomes your destiny."

— Frank Outlaw[1]

PERSONALITY

In a Nutshell

Our message throughout this book is quite simple: *Who you are (inside) governs, to a large extent, how you act and react (outside).* In other words, your external leader or managerial behaviors[2] are based largely on your internal preferences and values. Although the context in which you act affects both the words you express and actions you exhibit, the context is less influential than your personal inner values and dispositions. In fact, your personal values and disposition even shape how you view the context or situation.

That's our message in a nutshell. Although simple, several corollaries and qualifiers first need to be explained and understood before you can integrate that message into your leadership behaviors. Let's begin by exploring a model for experience that can help you understand how you "shape" and are "shaped" by the environment within which you function.

A Model for Experience

Although living and working in an organizational setting is more complex than Figure 2.1 implies, it does provide a basic reference point for understanding our model for experience.

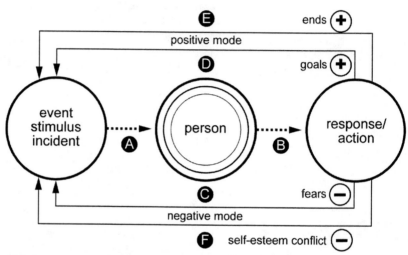

FIGURE 2.1 *A model for experience.*

In this model, we state that experience both triggers and tempers your inner life. For example, an event (circle: event/stimulus/incident) occurs within your organizational environment. In a work setting, that event could be a memo, meeting, customer or vendor call, and so on. You (circle: person) perceive that event as one requiring a response (line A), which you provide (line B). Your response (circle: response/action) *reveals* the essence of who you are, what you think, and what you value. In other words, *you* are the response at that moment in time, and people know you through what you say and do—your behaviors.

Additionally, your response may *initiate* a behavior that creates an event for others. Your initiated behaviors also reveal who you are at a specific instance in time.

Although your behavior reveals who you are, there is a distinction between you the person (circle) and you the behavior (line B). This distinction represents the difference between the inner world you experience (thoughts, values, and preferences that no one else can experience) and the outward demonstration of that experience (behavior that others can see). Using the analogy developed in Chapter 1, your behavior is akin to the outer skin of the onion, while your "person" really involves many inner layers. In other words, you first mediate or *filter* events through your disposition, values, and other inner layers, and then you produce an outer layer response.

Positive and Negative Response Modes

As shown in Figure 2.1, your response can be classified as either positive and proactive (lines D and E) or negative and reactive (lines C and F). The notion of positive and negative modes refers to the *origin* and *focus* of the energy from which the response arises; it does *not* describe how well you function in relation to the demands of the situation. For example, if you respond from energy that is confident, proactive, and relaxed, then the resultant behavior is considered positive. Your proactive, goal-oriented, and initiating response results in behavior that attempts to achieve, accomplish, or bring about some desired end state. However, if you respond from energy that is fearful, anxious, or tense, then the resultant behavior is considered negative. Your reactive, reflexive, and fearful response results in behavior that attempts to fend off, protect, or cope with some immediate problem or threat.

The concept of negative and positive modes is related to the heightened states of pleasurable excitement or anxiety. In Figure 2.1, the positive mode is further divided into *ends* (line E) and *goals* (line D), while the negative mode is divided into *fears* (line C), and *self-esteem conflicts* (line F). This twofold division within modes relates to the disposition and values layers discussed in Chapter 1—a response can be disposition and/or values driven.

While ends and goals are both future-oriented, there are differences. An *end* response is a ***values-based, premeditative, rational, belief-oriented,*** and *desired* state of existence; for example, the desire for world peace epitomizes an end response. A *goal* response is a *disposition-based, intuitive,* and *instinctive* outcome; for example, wanting to be liked or accepted typifies a goal response.

A *fear* response is also disposition-based, instinctive, and reflexive; for example, a reluctance to speak up in meetings may illustrate a fear response. A *self-esteem conflict* response, which takes into account your rational beliefs, is *values-based, meditative,* and *analytic*; for example, a dilemma arising from wanting to be either honest or right demonstrates a self-esteem conflict response. (The concept of self-esteem is primarily belief/value based, and will be more fully explained in Chapter 4.)

Positive Response Mode

If you are in positive response mode, then your behavior often displays high levels of activity that serves some meaningful purpose in the future you hope to create. In addition, a high sense of personal worth and security, enhanced openness toward alternative perspectives and possibilities, and positive expectations about your own goals and those of others often characterize your behavior.

Negative Response Mode

If you are in negative response mode, then your behavior often displays fear-driven, reactive undertakings that are short-term oriented, centered around predetermined views, or non-negotiable. In addition, you may feel negative about possible outcomes and/or less confident about your ability to influence inevitable results. Unlike people who respond from a positive mode, you are less receptive to other perspectives, possibilities, or alternative response modes. In keeping with the onion analogy (Figure 1.1) presented in Chapter 1, the concept of a multilayered self, with ends, goals, fears, and self-esteem conflicts, can be represented in the manner shown in Figure 2.2.

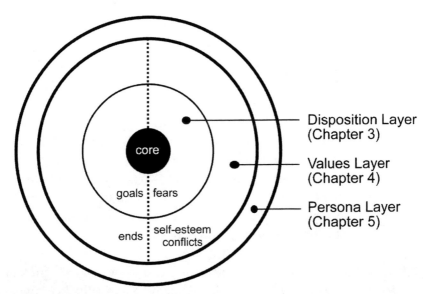

FIGURE 2.2 *A model of the multilayered self.*

As you will see in the following pages, the patterns around positive and negative response modes vary. However, in times of stress, knowing your own end, goal, fear, and self-esteem conflict patterns can be helpful, especially because your self-esteem is definitely related to consistent positive- and negative-response behaviors.

Behavior Is the Medium

As you can surmise, those you seek to influence can only see your outer skin—your behavior. Thus, it is your behavior—what you say and do—that is the medium by which you express and others interpret your intent. Red Auerbach, the famous general manager and coach of the Boston Celtics, is quoted as saying: "I'm not so concerned with what I say to my players as much as I am concerned with what they heard me say." Clearly, he understood that *the essence of any leadership attempt lies in others' reaction to your behaviors.* Therefore, you must examine your inner layers, understand your intent, *be* the message, and become aware of other perspectives. You must stay keenly aware of what you say from the viewpoint of those you seek to influence. You must be aware of your responses, actions, or behaviors from the point of view of those who receive it.

Definition of Personality

Someone once said, "What's a diamond but a little coal, pressure, and time?" Your personality also develops much like a diamond. Experience, in the form of both threats and opportunities, exerts "pressure" on your basic embryonic core—your genetic makeup—to form the facets and "flaws" in your personality and, ultimately, character. It is this personality—the sum total of your genetic and experiential makeup, the forming and formed diamond—that is brought to the "moment of management."

To bring perspective to the disposition and value layers of the onion, consider the following definition of personality and qualifiers of personality.

We use the term *personality* to broadly refer to your personal preferences and beliefs, plus your history with those preferences and beliefs. Your personality includes every *factor that describes your values, sensitivities, fears, goals, habits, and inclinations for coping with stressful situations*.[3] As noted in Chapter 1, the self—the sum total of your personality—consists of a multilayered set of dimensions that include disposition and values.

You can best understand personality as your inner thoughts and emotions, held over time. Of course, these inner thoughts and emotions are expressed outwardly within the context of living and leading, but personality itself is defined as the inner thoughts and emotions that you bring to the *moment of living . . . and leading*.

Your personality is constantly being formed and reformed through interaction with ideas, people, experience, and feedback. You are in a state of constant flux between being and becoming. There are parts of your personality that are clear to you, while other aspects are not. You may understand many of your own patterns of thought and emotions quite well, or you may not. Your personality can be modified and changed to some extent, at any point in time. However, your personality, or the tendency to think or emote in certain ways, is patterned over time. This predictable pattern of personality is what is brought to each moment of interaction and the influencing process.

Personality can be viewed through a threefold qualifying framework: (1) personality is dynamic, (2) personality is influenced by life history, and (3) personality shows diversity within a pattern.

Personality Is Dynamic

Environmental forces can influence personality, which means that personality is dynamic and changeable. Many leaders have changed their personality as they sensed the environmental demands necessary to gain results. For example, the young, introverted, and shy Gandhi struggled to make the necessary changes to become a strong public speaker.

A growing body of research on reared-apart twins addresses the question of how much of one's personality is associated with heredity and environment. Researchers[4] established that approximately 40 percent of the personality variance is related to genetic factors, whereas about 60 percent of the variance is associated with environmental factors and test error.

Given this research, it can be argued that your personality is not cast in stone. You are continually weighing your behavior in light of prevailing (external) social norms and role expectations. You are constantly comparing your behavior to others. Yet, most of the time, you evaluate your behavior in terms of its usefulness in serving your internal needs and fears, which may or may not result in the desired impact on others. Most of the time, when behavior does not serve your conscious or preconscious needs and fears, you will modify the behavior accordingly. If your behavior *does* meet your internal needs through interactions with the environment, then you are more likely to repeat the behavior; you are "reinforced" to use the behavior again. That is why you may create, cling, and confine yourself to a certain, sometimes limited, range of behaviors.

Personality Is Influenced by Life History

Personality is cumulative. Reoccurring life experiences provide you with a chance to learn. Threats or opportunities give you a chance to either repeat behaviors or develop other behaviors when responding to external or internal needs. As your life unfolds, your internal fears and goals will shift as you overcome certain challenges from which you learn. Thus, what may be a fear or goal at one point in your life may not be a fear or goal at another point.

There is evidence to suggest that certain life experiences remain in your psyche as symbols[5] showing the way you should or should not act. These symbolic word pictures, or "vignettes," serve as a shortcut for your analysis of the current situation. These vignettes provide you with the "learned" response to all "like" situations.[6] It is in this way that your past life experiences influence current action.

Many biographers study their subjects from birth to death, trying to analyze how early life experiences or critical events create and shape certain actions and reactions over time. These writers are interested in discovering how life events shape the inner psychological makeup of their subjects. For example, it is fascinating to see how Churchill's early experiences with his parents affected his resiliency in later life.[7] Likewise, it is intriguing to see the influence Gandhi's early sexual experiences had on some of his doctrines concerning abstinence.[8] There is even evidence to suggest that if certain early life experiences are not understood and dealt with, then the lack of resolution may contribute to the failure of some executives as they move up the corporate ladder and more responsibilities are incurred, yet less control is imposed.[9]

To narrow this book's focus, a discussion of how past life events shape personality will not be given. Instead, this book is primarily concerned with the description of *personality dimensions*, no matter how they are formed. Instead of discussing events, and thus personality development over time, you will be asked to "pose for a snapshot in time." This snapshot highlights personality, without discussing why, formulation, stage analysis, or cultural perspective. To further keep the snapshot as simple as possible, a layer of historical analysis will not be added.

Diversity Within Pattern

Several writers describe how individuals, despite an abundance of variability and idiosyncrasy, seem to fall into certain patterns of development and growth. The classic works of Levinson[10] and Sheehy[11] postulate that most individuals within the same cultural context are faced with the same life issues at approximately the same ages in their lives. These authors support the idea that certain stages or patterns show both a continuity of personality and the change that is possible over time. Specifically, Levinson describes various life stages, and then explains how people may respond differently or similarly to the same life issues. For example, he depicts five-year cycles in which the central issue of man's life changes from "breaking away from the nest," to "what am I going to be," to "getting into the real world," and so on.

Howe and Strauss's book,[12] *Generations,* is a comprehensive discussion of value patterns that occur in specific age groups. The authors maintain that these patterns repeat themselves over approximately 80-year cycles. Because values are a key part of personality, it is important to examine *both* disposition and values.

Everyone is unique. Because of the uniqueness, it is impossible to totally predict your own or other people's behaviors. You must expect that, accept that in yourself and others, and yet seek to understand yourself as fully as possible. At the same time, there are logical, consistent patterns amid human variation. In other words, behavior is thematic. There is observable behavior around a theme.

For example, human-growth cycles seem to show that almost all people experience a midlife crisis or dilemma associated with the realization that more than one-half of his or her life is over. While different people handle this realization differently, the behaviors are still focused around the identifiable theme of a midlife crisis or dilemma.

Subdivision of Personality: Disposition, Values, and Persona

The concept of personality is divided into five layers or subconcepts: (1) the subconscious core, (2) the disposition layer, (3) the values layer, (4) the persona, and (5) the leadership skin. The behavior you use to influence others is based on both your more *instinctive* needs, thoughts, or emotions (dispositions), and your *premeditated, cognitive standards* of thought and emotion (values). Research shows that managers use both their sense of right or wrong, *and* their understanding of personal goals and fears when they are influencing others.[13] Interestingly enough, some managers are more "values driven," and others are more "needs driven."

Let's start by differentiating between the fundamental values and disposition layers.

Definition of Disposition

Disposition is defined as the tendency, over time, to prefer one response or behavior to another. It is instinctive, somewhat genetic, chemical, somatic, and, much of the time, preconscious. An example would be the disposition to either stay and *fight* or to take *flight*. The *preference* to fight (or flight) at one instance in time is called a *disposition* when consistently exhibited over several instances in time. (A full explanation of these concepts and the resultant typology is the topic of Chapter 3.)

Disposition is both triggered and tempered by context. For example, your fight or flight tendency is generated or "revealed" by the situation, yet the situation shapes your outward demonstration of the tendency. *How* you fight or flight may depend on how instrumental or functional the behavior may appear in light of your understanding of the situation. How and around what issues you fight or flight may also be affected by your system of values and what you consider to be right or wrong, good or bad.

CHAPTER 2 ■ PERSONALITY AND CONTEXT

The Importance of Energy

Your expression of preference or disposition is not as important as your awareness of the energy required to use that preference. In simple terms, you may choose to engage or move away, but one of these two behavioral tendencies will always be harder for you to do. One behavior or choice may require more thought, focus, and effort than the other. For example, it may be easier for an introverted manager to stay in his or her office to complete necessary paperwork than it is to interact and become acquainted with employees. Your true disposition is always revealed by the energy requirements made on you over time. *Disposition, when naturally acted upon, energizes you.* Likewise, not acting on your natural dispositions requires more energy than normal, and may result in your feeling discomfort, fatigue, and stress.

Many people will take the path of least resistance[14] and act in those patterns that take less energy; however, all people possess the capacity to adapt and, therefore, act differently. Most people can act outside their *comfort zones*, if they choose to.

Your comfort zones are habitual ways of acting that allow you to respond to personal, environmental, or role-related demands. These habituated or patterned actions let you more readily sustain your energy. These patterns of preference, developed through experience, can help you reduce stress, simplify problematic situations, learn from the past, and/or prepare for the future. However, when you use influence behaviors that are new to you, unfamiliar to your *normal* influence patterns, you will use more energy.

At first, your self's energy is focused outward toward coping, learning, and solving physical, economic, social problems, and so on. Then, your self-energy is focused inward toward assimilating what you learn, growing as you expand, changing, and evolving.

Being aware of your energy requirements means understanding and coping with the compatibility or incompatibility between the functional *requirements* of a situation and your *natural* disposition to meet those requirements. There are adverse consequences to the expenditure of life energy when not replenished. There should be at least a moderate fit between role and disposition if stress and tension are to be handled effectively.

For example, suppose you were looking for someone to fill a salesperson position. Among other things, this job requires the jobholder to constantly meet new people, establish a network of contacts through other people, and be seen as approachable, likeable, and personable. In short, the sales role requires the outward demonstration of persuasiveness, openness, affability, friendliness, and interest in others. Someone with an extroverted disposition would find it easier to fulfill these requirements than someone with an introverted disposition, regardless of his or her value-based tendency to be interested in people.

However, if the person who filled the position displays a strong introverted disposition, then he or she must be aware of the energy needed to continually exhibit extroverted behaviors in the course of acting in the salesperson role. This does not mean that an introverted person should not be in a sales role. Rather, he or she is advised to find ways to accept and become comfortable with the role's energy requirements, and also to find ways to rejuvenate his or her energy.

Definition of Values

Values are the guiding "shoulds" of your life. While dispositions are instinctive, preconscious, "would-do" behaviors, values are thoughtful, meditative, "should-do" behaviors. *A value is an enduring belief that a particular end or mean is more socially or individually preferable than another end or mean.*[15] In other words, people believe that certain ends or means are better principles on which to make choices for themselves and/or others.

To act in a way that is consistent with your values initially requires *thoughtful reflection*. In essence, this is a cognitive process. It is necessary to weigh what is better, right, or more right against what may be worse, wrong, or more wrong, based on your driving inner beliefs and related assumptions. (Chapter 4 provides a full explanation of the values concept, plus a model for understanding your own value pattern.)

Criteria for a Value

Thoughts and ideas not acted on over time should not be considered values. Those thoughts and ideas that, over time, are neither personally cherished nor premeditatedly acted on are not enduring beliefs. They are instinctive preferences or *programmed* values. For example, people acting on a set of standards for right and wrong may affectively or emotionally adopt these standards from family members, peer group associates, or societal organizations—without examining the alternatives. These adopted social modes of behavior are then unquestionably adhered to over time, resulting in conditioned responses to environmental demands.

Only beliefs that are genuinely self-owned, "cherished," and consistently *acted* on can be considered values. For behavior to be values driven, the value must be freely chosen from among alternatives, with the choice's implications or consequences somewhat understood. For example, in most cases, to eat is not a value, but what is eaten could be values driven. Values meeting these criteria are called *developed values*.

The Persona

The persona will be more fully explained in Chapter 5. For now, think of the persona as a historical self, which emerges because of the innate human capacity to reflect on experience. In other words, your persona is the result of your life experiences with your disposition and values. Over time, you reflect on those experiences and begin to form ideas about (1) the self you wish to be, (2) the self others expect you to be, and (3) the internal and external realities that may limit the achievement of the self you want to be.

The persona is concerned with the presentation of self to the "outside world." It is constantly evaluating your historical life experiences, in relation to your disposition and values, to shape your future behavior.

The Disposition–Values–Persona Connection

Sometimes, disposition and values act in concert. Other times, they do not. Consider the following example: Suppose someone speaks to you in a mildly threatening manner. On a dispositional level, you may tend to engage or withdraw. If your disposition and values are in concert, then your choice is simple. Your natural energy and thoughtful meditative values are aligned, making behavior less problematic. If, on the other hand, your disposition is to fight but your values say fighting is wrong, then you must become either disposition-driven or values-driven before you can act.

There is a connection between values and disposition. In certain instances, your values could limit or support the expression of your natural preferences over time. In other instances, your disposition may override your values and you could end up being rationally discontented, yet emotionally excited, with your behavior. An example may further your understanding of this idea. Imagine you are a manager who holds the value that to publicly reprimand an employee is unfair and, in the long run, ineffective. Yet, due to a bad day and a series of costly errors, you blast one of your employees in the presence of several others.

It is possible that the natural disposition to be direct, assessing, and a fighter outweighed your rational, logical value structure about fairness, and thus you ended up behaving in a more instinctive way that was incongruent with your values. In this example, the persona is being "formed" as you reflect on this experience. If you are displeased with your instinctive dispositional behavior *and* the ideal self-image you want to present to the outside world is not to publicly embarrass others, then this experience may provide the opportunity to learn. When you find yourself in a similar situation, in the future, you may choose an alternative to a public reprimand. (A more in-depth treatment of the interactive effect among disposition, values, and persona is provided in Chapter 5.)

The Leadership Onion and Personality

Let's recall the onion figure (Figure 1.1) from Chapter 1. However, let's add some additional concepts.

The circle's broken lines in Figure 2.3 intentionally suggest the dynamics of forming and reforming both your values and disposition. The circle's broken lines symbolize the lack of formation and clarity that you may feel about your own value patterns and disposition. The solid lines represent the predictable, known, and formed patterns of your thoughts and emotions. Note that there is a disposition/values connection, or persona, by which disposition or values may *influence* each other to shape both present and future behavior.

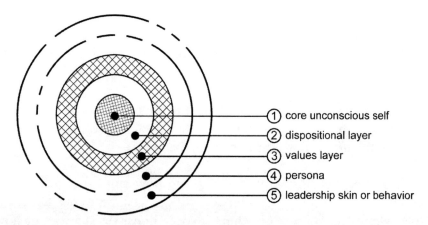

FIGURE 2.3 *Concept of personality.*

The sum total of your disposition and values, as represented in Figure 2.3, is your *personality*. It is the internal psychic activity that is eventually reflected externally or interpersonally. Your internal psychic activity derives from an experience that you remember and from which you learn. You extract "learnings" from that experience, which you use to both pre-shape and shape your future experiences.

Personality results from *repetitive thoughts* or vignettes[16] that you "play back" to yourself. It broadly refers to your personal preferences and beliefs, plus the historical life experiences that impact such preferences and beliefs. It also includes the limitations you may impose on yourself by defining yourself through behavior that you do not prefer or value. Personality is the combination of dispositions, values, and developed strengths that you bring to the influence context.

CONTEXT

Mr. Jones, wanting to impress his out-of-town cousin, asked Elmer, the town dullard, over and introduced him to his cousin. Whispering, Jones said to his cousin, "Watch this." Jones held out a dime and a nickel to Elmer and said, "You can have one of these, Elmer. Which one do you want?" Elmer said, "I'll take the big one, please."

Jones put away the dime and whispered to his cousin, "Can you believe how dumb he is?" The cousin's sympathies were aroused and the next day he happened to meet Elmer on the street. He said to Elmer, "Don't you know that the small coin is worth twice as much as the big coin?" Elmer said, "Sure, I know that." "Then why do you let him make a fool of you?" asked the cousin. With a slight smile, Elmer said, "Because the first time I pick up the dime, he will stop playing the game."

What makes this story both amusing and powerful is not just Elmer, but also the context in which Elmer acts. To get what he wants, Elmer plays a role within the context of others' expectations. He is aware of how his personality is played out in the role.

To become an outstanding leader, you also must understand *self-action in the context of a role*. The Elmer story can help you understand both the concept of role and, more generally, personality in context. People often don't think of the context; rather, they listen only to the "reality in their head." But an effective, functional personality in context is akin to fish in water. There is a separateness, but it is ultimately an integratedness that maintains the existence of both. Therefore, an effective leadership personality requires an aptitude for engaging in "situational" activities: to observe, analyze, stop, think, and then choose the most appropriate behavior for the desired outcomes.

Definition of Context

Context is a broad term that refers to many levels of expectations. Levels of expectations range from general to particular, starting from cultural expectations to social, to organizational, to specific job- or role-related expectations. For example, you could live in a Jewish culture, reside in Israel in a kibbutz, and work as the director of nursing. Or, you might be an American, live in Chicago, and work for IBM as a salesman.

A *role* is a more narrow set of expectations than the context may dictate; however, the context involves not only *expectations* at a cultural, societal, and organizational level, but also includes the focus of issues, problems, and expectations. In the salesman example, there might be product knowledge issues, customer demand problems, and sales volume expectations. Thus, a role is always fulfilled within a larger context.

Definition of Role Behavior

Role behavior is a set of actions associated with an organizational function, office, or position.[17] For example, your work position requires you to perform certain actions that accomplish specified organizational tasks. In turn, your position's required activities—its *role requirements*—define or limit potential behaviors that you, as a manager/leader, are expected to demonstrate.

Your position's role requirements result from a set of expectations defined by its role set. Your *role set* consists of all the people—boss, direct reports, associates, internal and external customers, vendors, and others—who interact with *your position* to accomplish their work.

Organizational Philosophy and Values Are a Basis for Role

Many role behaviors are embedded in a context of implicit or explicit visions, values, norms, or customs; these are often known as *organizational cultures* (or subcultures). Organizational culture may be clear and consistent, because the values or norms are publicly announced and reinforced through its people and practices. However, in other instances, the values *in use* are not the same as the organization's espoused values, thus resulting in conflicting role behaviors. Lack of role clarity can stem from ambiguous, ill-conceived vision and/or values, as well as confusing job descriptions and action plans.

Various factors temper the expectations of people within a role set; for example, factors impacting expectations include technology, profession or industry, positional level within the organization, laws, and various values/philosophies of the organization's culture. Expectations and resultant behaviors centered on serving the organization's purpose are called *work*. But, those people who find pleasure in engaging in such required activities might not always see it as "work."

Role Behavior as the Basis for Leadership

Within groups and organizations, there exists a necessity for collective action toward a common purpose. However, because of specialization of interests and function, individuals within the group or organization may hold differing points of view as to which collective actions should be taken. The leadership role blends and integrates these different viewpoints toward a shared vision or end state.

Leadership, in its best form, is granted by those being led. How many people would continually and willingly follow a leader who repeatedly demonstrated incompetence? The prerogative to lead, within the framework of an organization, comes about partly because of your expertise, skills, and commitment to organizational outcomes. Others *give* you the right to lead them because they believe you have the expertise to help achieve the organization's outcomes.

Additionally, others grant you the right to lead based on the legitimate power that comes with the organizational office you hold. People *expect* a company president to lead, and the president, as the office holder, wants and expects that prerogative. In hierarchal organizational structures, the decision-making prerogative is passed up and down the organization according to position, job description, and reporting relationships. In positions *under* a leader, people *give over* the right to make certain decisions—the employees grant the leader the right to lead. Sometimes, however, employees may not give the leader the right to lead. At that point, either the employee or leader leaves, or the employee stays and passively resists the leader.

In all cases, leadership does not exist apart from the organizational context that spawned it. There can be no leadership without followers. There can be no leadership role without followers' roles.

Importance of the Role Concept

The concept of role is emphasized for several reasons. First, it is important to understand that leadership is the result of your interactions with the contextual requirements. There are no *great* men or women. There are only extraordinary circumstances in which you may act extraordinarily. Thus, you must learn to appreciate the context. According to Warren Bennis, you must learn to read the "social architecture."[18] You are not the whole stew!

Second, the concept of role is emphasized because the absence or presence of extraordinary behavior is typically a product of disposition and values *in a role*. Extraordinary behavior results from your values and disposition acting to fit the role requirements. The presence or lack of leadership behaviors results from many years of history with your own disposition and values brought to the role. In other words, leadership behavior will be absent if your inner self is at odds with the role requirements. In the vast sweep of historical events, people such as Nixon, Carter, Clinton, or Patton, to mention a few, were not prepared to meet some of the contextual role requirements of their leadership position. Their dispositions and values did not prepare them to either *see* what was required or to act in ways that would more than meet those requirements.

The lack of effective leadership behavior is not just lack of preparation. Failure is not only an "inward deficit." *Effective leadership results from an inner state of readiness (or nonreadiness) in light of external role requirements.* The leadership role *serves* the organization's purpose. The "would-be" leader must understand the organizational context and clearly see the issues, expectations, situation, and role in light of the organizational purpose. The leader must then choose with which part of the inner self to respond to the role requirements. The leader should never forget that a role is just that—a role.

Third, the concept of role is emphasized because you can be taught to act in ways that meet the role requirement's context, *if* you realize how your values and disposition affect your perceptions of the role and actions required to fit that role context. Leaders are both born *and* made. Leaders are born, because dispositions are shaped and expanded from the initial genetic material. But leaders are also made, because dispositions and values are historically formulated. Thus, you must seek to understand your inner self to become more adaptable. Your *inner* work is as important as your understanding of the role. In the best of times, your personality and role requirements are compatible, even synergistic. The real challenge lies in those times when the context *requires* more than you are prepared to *give*.

In other words, when influencing others in an organizational position, you fulfill a role. People in the organization have expectations for your behavior. Your boss, your boss's boss, your peers, your direct reports, your internal and external customers, and your organization's owners, investors, and suppliers all have expectations for your behavior. Each of these people maintains personal and organizational requirements for your behavior, based on both their personalities and organizational roles.

Yet, at the same time, influencing others is shaped as much by the organizational context as it is by the role set. Reading the organizational context requires that you ask questions such as: "Toward what goal am I leading people?" "Who are my followers?" "What are the criteria for success?" "What resources do I have?" "Why is this important work?" "What expectations are held for my behavior?" Your answers, which are shaped by the organizational context within which you asked the questions, set the stage for the leadership act.

CHAPTER 2 ■ PERSONALITY AND CONTEXT

The Leader Behavior Subset

Leader behaviors are a specific subset of role behaviors. Typically, you are expected to do other things besides lead. For example, you might be expected to produce reports, generate budgets, solve customer problems, and respond to your bosses' needs, to name just a few tasks. These additional role requirements—which can involve budgets, technical knowledge, time management, business plan development, and unit representation to outside groups—are examples of role behaviors that are not *direct* leader behaviors.

These nondirect leader behaviors can and do influence the way you are seen by others you lead. These behaviors can indirectly shape the way others perceive your influence style. Telling your employees that you want to empower them but choosing not to consult them when developing next year's budget sends a confusing message. Therefore, you must seek to use these "indirect influence" actions, such as developing a budget, in concert with your overall set of influence behaviors, *if* you want to convey a total and consistent message as to the way you are viewed.

Effective leadership is *the act(s) of arousing, engaging, and satisfying followers' motives—within an environment of conflict, competition, or change—that results in followers taking action toward a mutually shared vision*. In an organizational setting, leadership can result in the accomplishment of organizational goals. In the broader sense, leadership is also an act of allowing, facilitating, or reframing experiences for others so that organizational effort serves a societal purpose. A great deal more will be said about this in Chapter 6. Before doing so, however, let's examine the various contexts in which you are asked to lead.

Context Versus Situation

Leadership occurs within different *contexts* or settings, and there are variations within a given context. These contextual variations create different leadership *situations*. In other words, each context requires specific leader behaviors, while some situations within the same context require a variation of those specific leader behaviors.

The terms *context* and *situation* are intentionally used to denote two different concepts. *Context* designates three basic *settings* in which you may be required to influence others: (1) a one-to-one context, (2) a group context, and (3) an organizational context. While context designates the setting in which influence is required, *situation* designates the *variation* in a particular setting that sets it apart from other situations. For example, the situation may vary within a one-to-one context, depending on an employee's competency and commitment to a task. Or, the situation may vary in an organizational context, depending on whether you are at the planning or implementation stage of a change effort.

These three contexts—one-to-one, group, and organizational—may be a challenge for you to understand, because they each have organizational, technical, physical, psychological, and emotional dimensions that create different situations. The Situational Leadership® II model presented in Chapter 6 will help you understand the appropriate use of leader behaviors, within a given situation. However, let's first look at the three contexts and some of the situations that you may encounter.

One-to-One Context

The first context in which you may need to influence others is within a one-to-one setting. For example, you and one of your direct reports may be in a meeting to set goals, develop budgets, troubleshoot a problem, or engage in a performance-review session. In this one-to-one context, your focus is simply concerned with *the individual*.

However, each one-to-one context can be quite different, if the individual, the task, or both are different. Your influence attempt must be concerned with an understanding of the *situational* variables, such as the task or issue being discussed and/or the individual's competence and commitment to achieve the necessary outcomes. For example, the influence behaviors required for a new employee would be quite different from those required for one of your top-performing veterans.

Group Context

The second context in which you may need to influence others may occur in small groups or teams of three to twelve people. The group to which you belong could be a group of associates or it could be a team of direct reports over which you have hierarchical position power. In either case, you may be concerned with the *group's* effectiveness and morale, rather than that of any one member. In this setting, you are interested in facilitating group processes, interactions, and outcomes.

The group situation could vary considerably, depending on the stages of group morale and productivity. Variation within groups depends on the past history of group interaction, presence or lack of effective group norms, group members' ability to work in groups, and task interdependence. These and other issues create variation in the group context, which results in a different *situation*. Compared to a one-to-one setting, the complexity of a group setting is more vast, certainty of outcomes is lesser, and development time needed for the team to be self-sufficient may be greater.

Organizational Context

The third context in which you may need to influence others is organizational. You might be a CEO or CFO. You may be the head of a large subunit within an organization, such as finance, sales, or marketing. While you have a group of direct reports with whom you may team, your direct reports also have employees who report to them. In this context, you are influencing more than one level below you in the organizational structure.

The variation that occurs at the organizational context involves two or more of four key factors that dynamically interact to shape the performance of the organization. These factors are: (1) the organization's culture (formal and informal), (2) strategic direction and strategies, (3) processes and systems (including its managerial, operational, financial, and human resource processes), and (4) people—especially those who exert the most impact. The strengths and weaknesses of these four factors will account for the variance in performance at the organizational context level, similar to what occurs at the group or individual level.

The scope of the influence attempt could involve a change in organizational vision and value positions, or corporate policy, structure, and long-range plans. For example, you may want to implement a program on quality throughout the organization. Or you may want to improve the bottom line, incorporate a new product line, or put in a new code of ethics for the company. Implementing any of these examples involves the promulgation of ideas throughout the organization or subunits you seek to influence. These changes will affect many or all of the organization's systems and processes, such as budgeting, staffing, accountability, data, and rewards, to mention a few.

In an organizational context, your focus is on both the process and *systems* that shape individual and group performance and motivation; it is not on specific individuals or groups per se. For example, if you want to institute a new product line, to make it a success, your influence behaviors would be more concerned with information systems, data systems for tracking outcomes, and support systems that increase sales and affect customer usage. Additionally, your influence behaviors may be concerned with the informal and formal organizational rituals and ceremonies that reward new product sales.

The variation that occurs in this context centers on the organization's readiness, as reflected through its accountability, data, feedback, training, and reward systems, to support the proposed organizational change. The systems' readiness may account for situational variance, just as individual competence and commitment explain one-to-one context variance or productivity and morale account for group context variance.

Organizational context produces the greatest amount of complexity. The certainty of the outcomes is greatly reduced, and the time needed for implementation of change is the longest of the three contexts. These contexts might be viewed as depicted in Figure 2.4.

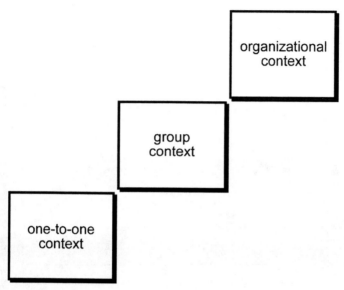

FIGURE 2.4 *Hierarchy of contexts.*

These contexts shape or define the role that you fulfill, as well as the behaviors you need to use. To clarify what has been explained thus far, our initial model for experience (Figure 2.1) can now be seen more specifically as shown in Figure 2.5 on the following page.

In this more comprehensive picture of experience (Figure 2.5), the stimulus (line A) now originates from various contexts or settings and requires a response (line B) appropriate to all the different contexts or settings. You are able to see the complexity of the *stimulus* more accurately. Your organizational context may be *in force* as you sit down with an employee in a one-to-one context. In fact, an organizational perspective, in the form of expectations, purpose, and values, should be *in force* when you meet with an employee in a one-to-one context.

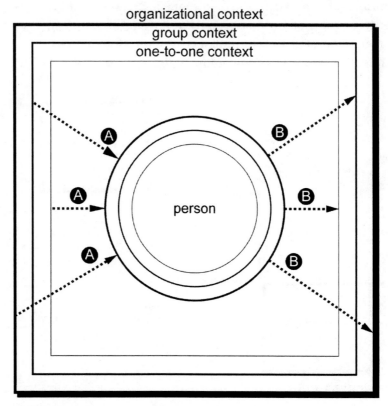

FIGURE 2.5 *Expanded model for experience.*

Need to Know Yourself

Your *response* may be made in a one-to-one context, a group context, or an organizational context, but expectations for your behavior stem simultaneously from the several levels of contexts. It becomes vitally important to know yourself, given the levels of expectations you will experience as a leader. The *diamond* self is being formed and flawed within the pressure of organizational life. Your personality, in the basic forms of disposition and values, results in responses that meet the situation *well* or, perhaps, *not as well* as you might like. To meet the situation well, you must come to know yourself. If you don't know yourself, you are not likely to be as effective as those who do.[19]

SUMMARY

So here you are, being and becoming, revealing and manifesting yourself in each leadership attempt, in each "moment of truth" with those you lead. You show continuity and change in your behavior. You operate from your own values and dispositional base, as well as from your past history of successes and failures in influencing others. Knowing yourself requires both action and reflection. Action without reflection can result in uninformed future action. Reflection without action can result in sterile, ungrounded thinking. As already said, you must "peel the onion." *You must practice learning about yourself.* Your self-understanding can be limited by the paradigms you use to guide your actions and reflections.

The models in this book are intended to serve as your guide. If you do not reflect on your experiences, if you do not try to understand *yourself* (not just why some behavior was effective or not), you may be doomed to repeat failures, and you may continue to be less effective than you could be otherwise. But if, through reflection and action, you can let go of your ego, habits of preference, or personal needs, then you can become more adaptive, more tolerant. You are able to access your *other* inner aspects, which can help you become a more versatile, effective, and humane leader. This tolerance requires a special class of courage, the courage to live not only with your strengths but also with your vulnerabilities.

The beauty of self-understanding is that it can help you recognize the expectations inherent in the context in which you lead. It can help you understand that the self is a microcosm of others and a mechanism for seeing similar and dissimilar patterns within others. The concepts contained in the following pages can increase your self-understanding.

Endnotes

1. Outlaw, *www.quotemeonit.com*.
2. The terms *manager* and *leader* are not synonymous. Leaders and managers think and act differently. A discussion of the differences can be

found in Chapter 6 (pages 172-173). We use both terms initially to be inclusive of all influencing behaviors demonstrated by both.

3. Kahn et al. 1964.
4. Keller et al. 1992; Goldsmith 1983; Tellegen et al. 1988.
5. Lombardo 1986.
6. Lombardo 1986.
7. Manchester 1983.
8. Erickson 1969.
9. Ket de Vries 1989.
10. Levinson et al. 1978.
11. Sheehy 1974, 1995.
12. Strauss and Howe 1991.
13. Deci 1995; England 1967.
14. Fritz 1984.
15. Rokeach 1973.
16. Lombardo 1986.
17. Kahn et al. 1964.
18. Bennis 1989.
19. Atwater and Yammarino 1992.

CHAPTER 3

Preference and Disposition

"Chains of habit are too light to be felt until they are too heavy to be broken."

— WARREN BUFFET[1]

PREFERENCE

Unconscious Preference

As previously discussed, personality is divided into several layers. The two basic layers are *disposition* and *values*. Your behavioral responses are based on the dynamics of both disposition and values. In some instances, your response is more values driven than disposition driven. In other instances, the opposite is true. In still other instances, these layers combine to shape your response.

For the sake of simplicity, let's examine the disposition layer before describing its relationship with your valuing processes. In actuality, your disposition and preferences may not be free to shape your behavior, independent of your values or valuing process. However, let's take the subelements of personality one layer at a time, as an initial step in learning the concepts.

Roots of the Idea

The idea of behavior patterns or dispositions is not new. Much of what is described in this chapter is rooted in the writings of many people, most notably the works of Carl Jung.[2] Jung hypothesized that there are deep-rooted psychological types, or patterns, in the human psyche that are consistently demonstrated over time. These patterns may even be passed on genetically, existing in the "collective unconscious" of each individual. Jung cites evidence of these patterns in dreams, art, literature, and myth.[3]

Several behavioral models derive from Jung's concept of psychological types. For example, Marston[4] applied Jung's ideas to more common, non-psychotherapy circumstances, while the DISC model draws from the combined ideas of both Jung and Marston.

We use the DISC model to establish and explain the concept of disposition and preference. We chose the DISC model for its user-friendliness and history in management and business applications. Additionally, we selected DISC because its model and instrumentation are easy to use in research. There are other models used to examine disposition and preference, such as the Myers-Briggs Type Indicator (MBTI).[5] However, regardless of which model is used, the main point is that these concepts are credible, here to stay, and an excellent tool for self-learning.

Definition of Preference

Preference is defined as a *preconscious* tendency to act or react, in a certain way, to an event experienced in the environment. In other words, preference describes how you might act in a single instance in time. Preference is "would-do" behavior. It is instinctive, emotional, unanalyzed, and unplanned. A preference is not, in and of itself, bad or good, functional or dysfunctional. Instead, it is a behavioral manifestation of "who you are."

An example might be helpful. One bright, sunny afternoon, a man took a walk in the hills behind his home. His seven-year-old daughter and one of her playmates accompanied him. The threesome walked for about an hour; unexpectedly, one of the children noticed a medium-sized snake

CHAPTER 3 ■ PREFERENCE AND DISPOSITION

crossing the path ahead of them. One child showed her fear by retreating and yelling loudly, "Stop, stop, go back!" The other child could not conceal her fascination and demonstrated her interest by quietly inching closer to the rapidly moving reptile.

To debate the wisdom of either child's' response is not the issue. Each child displayed a different response to the same incident. In their simplest forms, one response was to move away or withdraw (*flight*), while the other was to move toward or engage (*fight*). The encounter *revealed* an instinctive preference, relatively unencumbered by past history, which allowed each child to react differently. (Both children said that, before this incident, they had never seen a snake outside of a cage.)

Definition of Disposition

Disposition is defined as a *repeated*, demonstrated preference for a certain behavior, *over time*. In the case of the two children, if they encountered other snakes on other walks and responded in the same manner, we could say they are *disposed* to flight or fight in this context. If, in the face of other unrelated events, such as meeting with a schoolyard bully or participating in a public recital, the two children displayed similar response preferences, we could say they show an even stronger pattern or disposition to flight or fight.

To use an adult example, suppose you manage two people. You just announced a decision that you know is unpopular with both of them. One of these people might naturally tend to openly contest the decision, while the other might naturally submit to the decision. Their responses are indicative of their preference for certain behavior.

"Wired" and "Acquired" Disposition

Wired disposition springs from your unique variation of the standard genetic codes for all human beings. For example, tolerance for pain, frustration, and ambiguity; and degree of visual, auditory, olfactory, and visual-spatial acuity are all genetically determined. These physiological differences lie at the base of your *wired* disposition.[6]

Because you are also a "product of your environment," a secondary disposition base usually develops if the environment "requires" some adaptation. You adapt by acquiring *learned* responses for coping with environmental variables. For example, you may learn certain extroverted responses in the presence of a gregarious set of parents, even though you retain a strong wired tendency to be contained and self-controlled. Or, you may exhibit deliberate, premeditative, logical responses, even though your wired tendency is to be uninhibited and spontaneous. The *acquired* disposition feels somewhat uncomfortable, requires more energy, and is secondary to the core wired disposition. It is, however, present in patterned form and secondarily used in selected situations.

You may not be sensitive to the difference in energy requirements. However, if your *acquired* disposition is radically different from your *wired* disposition, then you could experience confusion, depression, and energy loss. In most people, the difference between wired and acquired disposition is complementary, not antagonistic, and therefore not too divisive. The relationship between acquired and wired disposition will be more evident later in this chapter.

Neither Good Nor Bad Disposition

When reading the preceding examples, you may tend to judge the disposition of both the children and employees as good or bad, appropriate or inappropriate, depending on your own set of dispositions or values. Regarding the example of the children encountering the snake, you might argue that you want your children to stay away from all snakes because a few could be dangerous and life-threatening. Or, you might say that cautious curiosity at a distance is the better approach, because an intelligent understanding of nature is better accomplished without too much fear.

From a managerial point of view, you could argue that it is better to let employees voice their objections so that the manager can more clearly understand their objections. From an opposite point of view, you might argue that the decision is already made and the sooner employees get on with it, the better.

CHAPTER 3 ■ PREFERENCE AND DISPOSITION

Dispositional patterns are more or less functional, depending on environmental or role-related demands. They are neither good nor bad. The choice of flight or fight is functional or dysfunctional, depending on the context of the behavior and impact on the individual. Therefore, please suspend your judgment, which may emanate from either your disposition or values, while we build a composite picture of dispositional patterns.

DISC Pattern

The letters D, I, S, and C are used to identify the dispositional patterns of responding. Each letter represents a *distinctive* dispositional pattern, while each pattern denotes an individual who prefers certain response modes. Although we will fully explain the DISC patterns, for now, please understand that a "D" dispositional type is different from an "I," "S," or "C" disposition. As you will see when we discuss response modes, the order of these preferences will not always be DISC. Instead, the preference order could be ISDC in one response mode, SCDI in another.

At first, only these four letters will be used, to aid you in suspending judgment until the explanation is complete. Remember, each dispositional pattern includes its own strengths and weaknesses, which are intertwined. In other words, what you are disposed to do may be a *strength*, if the situation requires that behavior. On the other hand, what you are disposed *not* to do could be a *weakness*, if the situation demands that behavior.

Familiar Ways of Responding

Each person embraces various ways of responding to the circumstances he or she experiences. Consider the following story. A young Italian immigrant, who could speak no English, found it hard to cope in his new American environment. Even getting a meal at a restaurant was difficult. Undaunted, he entered a diner, sat down, and observed a truck driver order apple pie and a cup of coffee. Rehearsing the order a few times, he proudly said in an unfamiliar language, "Apple-a-pie and a-cup-a-coffee." To his delight, he received what he ordered.

After several days of a steady diet of apple pie and coffee, he decided to learn some new words, for the sake of variety. He heard another patron order a ham and cheese sandwich and lemonade. Again, he rehearsed his order and said, "Ham-a-an-a-cheese-samwich and lemonada." The brusque waitress fired back, "You want that on wheat or rye?" The confused immigrant quickly said, "Apple-a-pie and a-cup-a-coffee."

There are several points illustrated by this story. The first important point is that each individual, when under stress, reverts back to his or her most familiar pattern of behavior. Uncertainty may cause the individual to close off new behaviors or modes of responding. Boring comfort feels better than risky ambiguity and social ridicule.

The second important point is that there are a wide variety of options to choose from on the menu of behaviors. However, an individual raised or accustomed to using one mode of coping may not use other behaviors. The individual's common modes of responding are so familiar, through language and experience, that he or she may not consider other possible behaviors.

Modes of Responding

The third point is that while there are different solutions to life's problems and opportunities, these solutions are often composed of several *modes of responding*. For example, recall the children and the snake. Their preference to either engage or withdraw is one instinctive mode of responding. A second mode of responding is shown by the children's preference for either outward excitement or inward quietness.

Thus, one child exhibited *extroverted flight* behavior, while the other displayed *introverted fight* behavior. In the apple pie story, the immigrant showed *introverted flight* behavior; he did not engage the waitress.

Let's examine some of the very basic response possibilities you may use. Then you can learn how they might be combined.

Flight Versus Fight

Let's start with some basic response possibilities to environmental stimuli. The fight-flight response is a typical and easy preference to see in yourself or others. *Flight* is the outer behavioral preference to move away from conflict—to reduce conflict by withdrawing, giving in, accommodating, or letting go of needs. *Fight* is the outer behavioral preference to compete—to contest or accelerate the conflict in a win or lose struggle to meet inner needs.[7] Examine the continuum displayed in Figure 3.1.

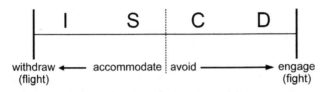

FIGURE 3.1 *Flight versus fight.*

The four dispositional patterns (DISC) are distributed along the continuum, from flight to fight. In Figure 3.1, the inner dispositional pattern most apt to fight is the "D," followed by the "C," who will tend to avoid the issue as a way of resisting or opposing an action. When the "C" can no longer avoid, he or she will directly engage. The inner dispositional pattern most disposed to flight or withdraw is the "I." The "S" disposition accommodates as long as possible, and then turns to flight. Please remember that no response mode is better or worse than the other. The response is functional or dysfunctional, depending on the situation.

Accept Versus Control

One of the most basic issues written about by psychologists is the individual's need to change or control the environment, rather than accept what the environment provides. *Control* is the tendency to act on the environment to change it, to meet one's inner needs. To *accept* is to take what the environment gives and use it to meet inner needs. To either *accept* or *control* what is given is a basic dispositional response.

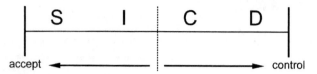

FIGURE 3.2 *Accept versus control.*

In Figure 3.2, the "D" disposition shows the strongest tendency to directly control situations, while the "C" prefers to indirectly control situations by focusing on process. The "S" disposition is most disposed to accepting the situation, followed by the "I" pattern. Although the "D" pattern is also capable of relating or accepting what is offered by the environment, it is not likely to do so as frequently as the "I" or "S" patterns.

For example, when people are first assigned to work as a team, some individuals may initially prefer to wait and see what happens, to let things unfold (accept), while other individuals may want to immediately get on with the task (control). Some individuals show a stronger preference to accept, accommodate, or show concern for others; other individuals demonstrate a preference to control, cause action, shape others' behaviors, or make things happen. The control or accept response mode usually becomes more intense and especially observable when an individual is in a stressful situation.

Extroversion Versus Introversion

A third basic response mode, which is easily identifiable, is that of *extroversion* or *introversion*. Some individuals may prefer to outwardly demonstrate their thoughts or emotions, while others may not prefer to show what they are thinking or feeling. The preference for extroversion not only implies the tendency to outwardly demonstrate inner thoughts and emotions, it also involves the tendency to want to continually be around other people. The preference for introversion, in addition to the tendency to not share thoughts and feelings, includes high needs for privacy and seclusion.

In Figure 3.3, the "I" disposition shows the greatest tendency to publicly exhibit feelings and thought. "I" and "D" are outwardly demonstrative and easily interact with others they do not know. However, the "I's" outward demonstration will first reveal feelings, while the "D's" outward expressions will first be concerned with results or tasks. It is as if the extrovert's energy is liberated when in the presence of others, while the introvert's energy is liberated when alone and quiet.

FIGURE 3.3 *Extroversion versus introversion.*

The "C" disposition shows the strongest tendency toward privacy, seclusion, and alone time. Both "C" and "S" minimally demonstrate inner thoughts and emotions. Both "S" and "C" can, at times, demonstrate a preference for extroversion, but the preference is infrequent in comparison to "I" and "D." The "S" and "C" will go to parties, work on teams, and be involved with group activities. However, they are less apt to volunteer and will behave more introspectively in the presence of others.

Were you recently asked to go to a party with a group of people whom you do not know? What was your reaction? If you thought, "Yes, it will be fun; I like to meet people and 'party it up,'" you might be more extroverted, with a "D" or "I" preference. This is especially true if you frequently go to or host parties just for the fun of it, rather than attending because you want to meet someone with whom to talk *business*. However, if you thought "No, parties are a bore; I don't mix well and I'll have more fun staying home reading or watching TV," you might be more introverted, with an "S" or a "C" preference.

The extroversion or introversion disposition is demonstrated through both nonverbal and verbal behavior. Placid facial expressions, infrequent direct eye contact, minimal or subdued body movements, and monotone voice projection are indicators of a preference for introversion and an "S" or "C" disposition. On the other hand, animated facial and body movements, frequent direct eye contact, and emotional vocal tones are indicators of a preference for extroversion and a "D" or "I" disposition.

Direct Versus Indirect

A fourth preference closely akin to extroversion/introversion is the preference for *direct* or *indirect* communication. People show a preference for how they want to give and receive information. One simple example is illustrated by people's preference for the amount of specificity or generality in speech patterns. Some individuals prefer brief, succinct statements; they "tell it like it is." Others lead up to what they want to say, delicately hinting at or inferring what is to come. Some individuals want others to say things directly, while some do not want that directness.

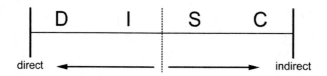

FIGURE 3.4 *Direct versus indirect.*

Figure 3.4 shows that in written communications the "D" and "I" patterns are quick to say or *tell* it, while the "S" and "C" patterns try to *show* it. A written report from an "S" or "C" will be detailed, specific, contextual, data based, and followed by qualified conclusions. A report written by an "I" or "D" may lead with conclusions, be brief and general in style, and contain little context.

For example, suppose two managers are responsible for conducting employee performance evaluations. One manager prefers indirect behavior, while the other prefers direct behavior. The indirect manager would tend to conduct his or her sessions by first setting the context for the meeting, describing the employee's job responsibilities, reviewing the criteria for evaluation, examining the data used for substantiating his or her conclusions, asking the employee's opinion, summarizing conclusions about the employee's performance, and then concluding the meeting.

The direct manager, however, would tend to call the meeting, welcome the employee to the meeting, and then say, "You didn't (or did) have a great year, so let's talk about next year and how you want to approach it."

The interesting thing is that the "D" and "I" tend to view the indirectness of the "S" and "C" as overdetailed, overjustified, and redundant with information they need to wade through. The "D" or "I" may view communication with an "S" or "C" as a waste of time. On the other hand, the "S" and "C" may view the "D" and "I" as providing incomplete and unsubstantiated communication, offering sweeping generalizations with little rationale to justify their conclusions.

When listening to an employee, do you ever think, "Just get to the point"? You may have "D" or "I" tendencies, while the employee could have "S" or "C" tendencies.

Perceive Versus Judge

Another basic response mode to consider is that of *judging* and *perceiving*. To *judge* is the tendency to qualify or test ideas and experiences of self and others against preconceived ideas of what "should" be. To *perceive* is the tendency to withhold judgment and allow input from a wider variety of people, places, or things.

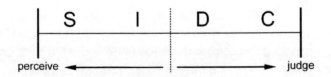

FIGURE 3.5   *Perceive versus judge.*

Consider the following example. You and your spouse go to an unfamiliar place for dinner with another couple. You notice that one of the other people in your foursome is rather critical. The valet is too rough as he drove away the car. The maître d' is too slow or too aloof. The group is not seated at the right table. The food is too hot, too cold, or not prepared properly. It is too noisy, too hot, too cold, and too expensive. The evening is filled with running commentary on all that is experienced.

This running commentary most likely reflects a "D" or "C" with a strong preference for judging. Of course, this may be an exaggeration for most of us, but the example is used to demonstrate the disposition to judge. Some individuals show a preference for judging much of what they experience. The "D" and "C" tend to judge, to evaluate, and qualify; while the "S" and "I" tend to allow events to unfold. "I" and "S" tend to accept events or people and flow with the differences that they perceive exist between themselves and others. Under pressure and experiencing a sense of lower self-esteem, this acceptance can range from criticism to overtolerance. Remember not to judge these preferences as good or bad, but to suspend your evaluation until the disposition is described within a context of functionality.

Risk-Taking Versus Risk-Assessing

When learning or trying something new, some people prefer to get actively involved. They need to get their hands *dirty* by *coming to know* through trial and error. Other people prefer to observe, to engage at a distance through studying the patterns and examining the possible consequences before acting.

In making decisions, for example, some individuals' natural tendencies are to go slow, gather data, examine alternatives, and reduce risk through careful consideration of the facts. Others prefer to learn as they go, trying some new things just to get to know the issues and see what they can discover. For the experimenter, risk-taking is expected and is a practical way to learn what the possible outcomes could be.

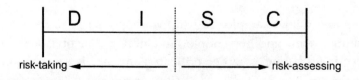

FIGURE 3.6 *Risk-taking versus risk-assessing.*

"D" and "I" tend to take more and greater risks, while "C" and "S" tend to assess even the smallest risk before taking action. Remember that one preference is not inherently *better*. Either preference can be functional or dysfunctional, depending on the situation and use over time.

Optimistic Versus Pessimistic

Someone who is an *optimist* tends to react as if the world is a friendly place, despite information or experience to the contrary. Some individuals see life events or environmental happenings as positive. They view the world as a generally favorable place and they can make lemonade from "life's lemons."

A *pessimist* is an individual who tends to react as if the world is an unfriendly, hostile place, despite information or experiences to the contrary. For a pessimist, the world is a less favorable place and poses potential hazards for *all* those in it.

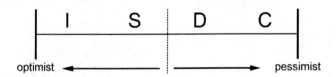

FIGURE 3.7 *Optimist versus pessimist.*

"I" and "S" tend to be optimists while "D" and "C" tend toward pessimism. This tendency does not imply that there are no threatening circumstances. Life events can be threatening to our economic, social, physical, or emotional well-being. With enough threatening circumstances over time, it would be reasonable to *assume* that the world is generally an unfriendly place.

An example is found in the story about two young boys who are placed in two separate rooms piled with horse manure. After some time elapsed, one boy was observed complaining and bemoaning the situation as terrible and unbearable, while the other was busily exploring the room saying, "There must be a pony in here somewhere!"

The point is that some individuals see the "*turns* of life" as someone picking on them. Others experience the same series of events and believe that "every cloud has a silver lining."

There are those who advocate optimism.[8] To debate the wisdom of preference is not at issue here. What is at issue is the proclivity to view life's events as either unfriendly or friendly, regardless of the context. It is almost as if each individual needs to cling to his or her own comfortable reality. People "need the eggs," even though the environmental circumstances don't warrant or require it.

Change-Oriented Versus Continuity-Oriented

Some individuals prefer a constantly changing environment that is filled with variety and newness. They expect change and become bored without it. Others prefer predictability and continuity.

FIGURE 3.8 *Change-oriented versus continuity-oriented.*

The "D" and "I" enjoy change, variety, and new experiences, while the "S" and "C" appreciate familiar surroundings and circumstances. "S" and "C" crave consistency and, generally, cannot function until things are settled. For example, some *continuity-oriented* people prefer to stay in the same work environment or cling to the same procedures or benefits, even if change would make things better. Change-oriented people prefer to embrace variety because it is natural to them and fun.

Summary of Basic Response Modes

The basic or primary response modes discussed can help you understand the DISC patterns described later in this chapter. To review, the primary response modes discussed thus far are as shown in Figure 3.9.

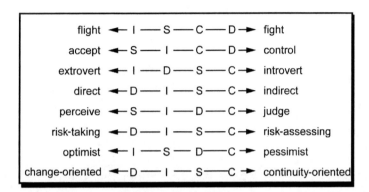

FIGURE 3.9 *Basic response modes.*

Bring your attention to the alignment of the "C" pattern consistently found on the right half of the list, in contrast to the "I" pattern shown most frequently on the left. As you may also note, the "I" and "C" patterns are on opposite "sides" in all of the comparisons. The "I" and "C" represent the most dissimilar dispositions.

If some of the basic response modes are combined, then interesting and distinct patterns begin to emerge. To visually represent some of what has been said, examine Figure 3.10.

This figure can help you remember and understand the fundamental DISC dispositions. You must seek a delicate balance between the response modes presented thus far *and* the central core mode presented in Figure 3.10. People are complex entities; when applying these ideas, do so gradually and try to add complexity to your diagnosis as you go.

Seek to understand the *mosaic* of disposition, not by just one or two response modes but by many. Use Figure 3.10 as a memory device, but add

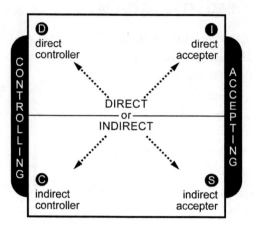

FIGURE 3.10 *DISC dispositions.*

to it as you move along. For example, remember that the "D" is not only a direct controller, but also a risktaker and a fighter who judges more frequently.

A central premise of this book is that you are *prone* to use certain behaviors and *disposed* not to use others. As you understand this model and incorporate it into your day-to-day living, remember your self-representation to others is both the frequently used behaviors and the absence of other likely behaviors. To change yourself, you must allow yourself the possibility of acting in ways other than your natural preference.

COUPLES

Felix Unger and Oscar Madison are well known, not only because of Neil Simon's brilliant play, *The Odd Couple*, and the subsequent television sitcom, but because the characters represent classic *archetypes* or patterns everyone has known. Simon hits a nerve by capturing the essence of two people whose ways of living drive each other to the brink of insanity.

Oscar represents the direct accepter (I) who cares little for organization, time, neatness, or tasks. He is more interested in poker parties, meeting

CHAPTER 3 ■ PREFERENCE AND DISPOSITION

women, baseball games, and caring for people. Felix, on the other hand, represents the indirect controller (C). He is the neatnik, the cleaner who leaves notes on Oscar's pillow about being out of corn flakes. He cooks and wants the pasta "al dente." He is more concerned with the smell of cigar smoke in the air, what to have for dinner, and leaving his wife a special delivery, return-receipt-requested note announcing that he is moving out of the house. He even went so far as to wash the playing cards with disinfectant before a poker party.

The four types of dispositions depicted in Figure 3.10 are classic patterns. Let's examine these *classic patterns* or dispositions in depth to understand the basis of the "odd couples" of the world.

The "D" Direct Controller

Let's begin to combine primary and secondary response modes to describe the classical types in detail. One of the more easily recognized behavioral patterns is that of the strong "D" pattern. The word "strong" is used to convey a high-frequency preference for response behaviors such as Control, Extroversion, Fight, Directness, and Judging.

The classic "D" disposition tends to be Directive or Dominant. If you are disposed toward "D-ness," you will prefer to be:

- Direct
- Judging
- Controlling
- Extroverted
- Risk-Taking
- Change-Oriented
- Pessimistic
- Fight-Oriented

Overview of a "D"

"D" individuals are dynamic, forceful, and results focused. They enjoy challenges, want to be creative, and show a strong will to achieve their goals. They tend to drive for concrete results, put in many hours doing so, and at times may pay a high price for success in their personal and social lives, because they choose getting results over developing relationships.

"Ds" tend to take control of tasks or outcomes. They like to be in charge of people and situations. They seek bottom-line results. They like to win and may challenge current expectations or rules to get their desired results. They can display impatience, aggressiveness, anger, and combativeness when stressed or thwarted.

"D" Strengths

"Ds" are driven to obtain results by shaping their environments and overcoming obstacles. They possess the drive to do what is necessary to reach their goals. They like leadership opportunities and prefer challenges that give them clear results by which they can judge their own self-worth. They also prefer to approach issues and problems from an overview perspective: They start from general concepts and move to specific information. This deductive approach suits them well when they take on their challenges. They display a high sense of personal worth, which leads to self-confidence that they can do the *impossible*. In their minds, they can do anything they set their energies to.

"D" Weaknesses

"Ds" can be aggressive, obstinate, and impatient when things are not going their way. They demonstrate a high need for autonomy and, therefore, naturally feel constrained by boundaries and procedures. They prefer to do it their way or no way at all. The "D" disposition may take control, even when they should not. They may show little sensitivity for the feelings of others and low tolerance for the inadequacies of others. They may also vent their inner tension on those around them, which can intimidate others with different dispositions.

"D" Decision Making

"Ds" prefer to make quick decisions based on the examination of limited alternatives. They may explore a single alternative that appears to give them the results they want. The choice is predicated on the desired results *they* have in mind.

"D" Evaluates Others

"Ds" prefer to evaluate others by how well they meet the standards and challenges set forth by the "D." The amount of work accomplished by others must meet the "D's" expectations. They tend to set demanding standards for themselves and will seek out those who do likewise. However, they can become even more competitive when people surpass them.

"D" Use of Time

"Ds" prefer fast-paced jobs or work in which there is fragmentation and brevity to what they do. They want just the *basic information*. Small talk is kept to a minimum. They like to be involved with many concurrent issues or projects of their own choosing. They prefer to delegate the details and concern themselves with the *big picture*.

"D" Goal

"Ds" prefer power and control, rather than tasks and people. They desire new opportunities and want to be able to lead. They might well subscribe to the motto "lead, follow, or get out of the way." They like to win. Their preference or goal is to accept challenges, take authority, and lead the way to produce results.

"D" Fear

The basic "D" fear is being taken advantage of. They don't like, or won't accept, the "fuzzy end of the lollipop." They dislike falling behind, boring work, and looking soft. They hate to lose control of situations, challenges, projects, and desired outcomes. They will go to extraordinary lengths to see that these fears are not realized.

Typical "D" Public Figures

Examples of "Ds" include the following: George Patton, Alexander Haig, Margaret Thatcher, Dan Rather, Barbara Walters, Vince Lombardi, Harry Truman, Madonna, Billy Martin, Hillary Clinton, Bette Davis, William Shatner as Captain Kirk, and Bea Arthur as Maude.

Typical "D" Comments

- "I don't care how you do it, just get it done!"
- "Winning isn't everything, it's the only thing!"
- "The buck stops here!"

Summary of High "D" Tendencies

"Ds'" preferences often result in their being a powerfully direct force in organizational settings. They may not always be right, but they will be out there in front leading. Their extroverted, direct need for control can be either a positive or negative influence, depending on the situation and other variables, such as values and adaptability, which will be addressed later in this book. "Ds" can be a tremendous asset to the organization because of their desire to take risks and reach creative solutions to new challenges.

The "I" Direct Accepter

Direct accepters are also easy to identify because of their outgoing manner. This classical disposition is people-oriented. The Interactive or Socializing disposition is typified by a need to be:

- Direct
- Accepting
- Risk-Taking
- Optimistic

- Perceiving
- Extroverted
- Change-Oriented
- Flight-Oriented

Overview of an "I"

The "I" dispositional type desires to be liked by people. They put relationships before tasks. They display an optimistic outlook about life and people. They find it energizing to be with others, almost without regard for the context. They seek frequent approval and affirmation from others, and will easily give it. A large amount of their psychic energy is used in understanding the emotional reactions of individuals and groups. The "Is" are concerned with gaining and giving interpersonal acceptance.

This dispositional type enjoys talking more than listening, but will observe the social norms enough to listen when necessary. They will strike up a conversation with almost anyone and often show a keen sense of humor. They influence others through their optimistic, friendly conversation in social or work environments. They establish a wide network of friends and build alliances in order to be included and accepted. An individual with an "I" disposition shows an expression of interpersonal warmth and down-to-earth congeniality.

"I" Strengths

The greatest strengths of the "I's" dispositional pattern are revealed in their optimistic, personal, and warm approach with people. Their outgoing enthusiasm and friendliness allow them to help others get caught up in their own dreams. They are energized by the opportunity to influence others and shape their environments by building alliances to accomplish results. Their playful, social, and talkative nature results in evoking feelings of care and empathy from those around them. They try to influence others by an optimistic focus on positive outcomes. They naturally show an energetic, fast-paced approach that puts relationships ahead of tasks. Because they like people, others around them *feel* the connection and reciprocate by responding favorably toward them.

"I" Weaknesses

"Is" can carry this direct accepter disposition to excess. In the extreme case, their natural weakness is to become too involved, too talkative, and too impatient with being alone. They may show a short attention span because of their outward focus on others. They can become easily bored. Life can become a playground, where attention is diverted to what is stimulating and at hand.

They tend to make sweeping generalizations with little data. They may not check everything out, assuming someone else will do it; or they may procrastinate if something they do not enjoy needs to be redone. When not fulfilled by accustomed relationships and ideas, they look for new stimulation and involvement again and again and again. When taken to extremes, their behaviors may be seen as erratic, superficial, undiscriminating, and *flighty*.

"I" Decision Making

"Is" like to make fast-paced decisions based on "gut feel." They talk out their decisions with anyone who will listen, from the custodian to the boss. They look for reactions as they brainstorm out loud. The decision may not be as important as the "charge" they get to their energy level through the conversations they have with others. The "Is" may be prone to group think and may tend to go along with the group's approach for the sake of social acceptance.

"I" Evaluates Others

"Is" tend to evaluate others by how well they verbalize feelings. They respect and like others who are expressive and optimistic. They prefer the term "opportunity" to the word "problem" and look for acceptance from those who want harmonious, easygoing work relationships.

"I" Use of Time

The direct accepter or interacter uses time as a "drunken sailor spends money." They like a friendly, informal atmosphere and large blocks of time for verbalizing and expressing themselves. Because connecting with people is important, they prefer socializing and *small talk*. They brainstorm out loud; therefore, a great deal of time will be spent *talking up* their ideas to elicit people's enthusiasm and feedback. The "I" disposition may show some tardiness for appointments because they are preoccupied with talking to those they are with at the moment.

"I" Goal

"I's" internal goals are oriented toward approval and acceptance as people. In a work setting, they seek companionship and social recognition. At work, they try to get to know as many people as possible on a first-name basis. They like to mingle and play as they work, learn, and go about life's business. "Doing the work and getting things done is not as important as doing it together in a fun way!" Because people are their business, they first seek out people to share the "here and now," with an eye on the future experiences they could share with them. Usually, those they seek to be with will be in power positions to meet their needs for popularity, social recognition, and possibly freedom from many details.

"I" Fear

"Is" tend to fear lack of inclusion, humiliation, or loss of social recognition. To appear uninvolved, unattractive, unsuccessful, or unacceptable to others, especially those in power, would be threatening to someone with high "I" tendencies. To be ostracized would result in the ultimate inner conflict for an individual with high "I" preferences.

Typical "I" Public Figures

Examples of "Is" include the following: Bill Cosby, Magic Johnson, Dom DeLuise, Hubert Humphrey, Will Rogers, Bill Clinton, Willard Scott, Dolly Parton, Zig Ziglar, Auntie Mame, Carol Burnett, Liza Minelli, and the Oscar Madison character.

Typical "I" Comments

- "Life is a banquet, yet there are beggars out there starving."
- "It's not whether you win or lose, it's how you look when you play the game."
- "Altitude is determined by attitude."

Summary of High "I" Tendencies

"Is'" preferences may *cause* them to become the *interpersonal glue* of the organization. They are sensitive to the emotional life of those around them and can be a *lightning rod* to the general feelings generated by organizational life events. Their extroverted, direct need for relationships can be either a positive or negative force, depending on the situation. They demonstrate tremendous value to the organization because of their optimism, enthusiasm, sense of humor, and ability to promote ideas, strategies, and products.

The "S" Indirect Accepter

The quiet, unassuming individuals with "S" preferences yearn for more tranquility and stability than the other three types. They prefer to be pleasant and cooperative, and to moderate their emotional extremes. They manifest a slower, steadier pace, relaxed disposition, and an appearance of approachability and warmth. The Stable or Steady preference tends to be:

- Indirect
- Accepting
- Risk-Assessing
- Optimistic
- Perceiving
- Introverted
- Continuity-Oriented
- Flight-Oriented

Overview of an "S"

This dispositional type is typified mainly by the behaviors of accommodation and steady-paced follow-through. They tend to care about people, but show that caring indirectly. They also tend to focus on building trust with the aim of establishing long-term personal friendships. They prefer a stable, constant environment that allows them to stick to what they already know. With the habitual environment, they can plug along, follow through at a relaxed pace, and earn the confidence and sincere personal attention of those around them. They have patience, staying power, and stick-to-itiveness. Indirect accepters commit themselves to and work hard at making relationships work.

"S" Strengths

The greatest strengths of the "S" dispositional pattern lie in their patient, steady follow-through and accommodation. They are great listeners and their calm reassuring exteriors complement their supportive manners. They plan and follow through on their own projects, and if they are working on a team, they may end up doing the work of others. They like to get along with others through helping relationships and predictable role relationships. They are less likely to "blow their own horns" or take credit, but they are appreciative when others sincerely acknowledge the contribution they make. In work settings, they prefer order and known, proven practices with concrete repeatable actions and roles. They lean toward teamwork, cooperation, and steady, long-term relationships.

"S" Weaknesses

When these indirect accepter tendencies are carried to extremes, individuals with "S" preferences can be sedentary, stern, and "stuck in their ways." They may display difficulty speaking up for themselves, seemingly going along with others or conditions while inwardly not agreeing. Assertive types may take advantage of the indirect accepter's tendency for accommodation and conflict avoidance. The "Ss'" need for a predictable, stable environment may result in a resistance to needed change or better ways of doing things. Because of the preference for indirect communication, they may not speak about what is on their minds, especially if they anticipate that conflict will result. They also tend to doubt themselves and their abilities, and often need to experience their success over and over before they will believe in themselves.

"S" Decision Making

"Ss" prefer to make slower paced decisions that reduce risk; they do not want to change what worked in the past. They want to confer with those who are affected by a decision, while they take time to think out the change logically to reduce the confusion or upheaval that is a natural by-product of change. The less time there is to make the change, the more apprehension may be produced for the high "S."

"S" Evaluates Others

"Ss" tend to evaluate others through a sense of compatibility that may or may not exist between them and the other person. If they feel they can earn the genuine inclusion and affection of another, then they base the relationship on the other's demonstrated commitment. They admire those who show a depth of contribution to the organization's or group's work.

"S" Use of Time

"Ss" prefer a slower paced, relaxed approach to work. They believe that work is best accomplished if an individual is organized and prepared; therefore, getting ready is necessary prior to doing. When in the process of doing, it becomes fun if those involved conferred and are in agreement as to the roles and goals. They are tolerant of the time it will take if the task is to be done through a group and with a minimum of conflict.

"S" Goal

The general orientation of the high "S" disposition is toward a controlled environment that embraces a minimum of changes or disruptions. With a stable environment, they can earn the confidence of a select group of people by using their follow-through and competency. Measured actions lead to stability and status quo, even if the status quo is not perfect. They demonstrate a strong need to be helpful, meeting people more than halfway to earn their confidence and affection. They like people and show it by competent, helpful actions and consistent follow-through.

"S" Fear

"Ss" tend to fear change, disruption, and conflict. If you want to create anxiety for an "S," borrow his or her stapler and don't return it. A stable environment gives "Ss" autonomy and productivity. Chaotic surroundings and constant change generates anxiety and apprehension for the high "S." Change requires more energy for the indirect accepter to become effective in earning the confidence of others.

Typical "S" Public Figures

Examples of "Ss" include the following: Tony Gwynn, Dwight Eisenhower, George Bush, Gerald Ford, Henry Fonda, Walter Cronkite, Mr. Rogers, General George Abrams, Mother Theresa, Mary Richards (of the *Mary Tyler Moore Show*), Elise Keaton (of *Family Ties*), Martina Navratilova, and Edith Bunker (of *All in the Family*).

Typical "S" Comments

- "Everything in moderation except tolerance."
- "It's not whether you win or lose, but how consistent your game is."
- "Actions speak louder than words."

Summary of High "S" Tendencies

"Ss" prefer low-key, relaxed, steady-paced actions that result in consistent, predictable follow-through on work tasks. Their value to an organization derives from producing consistent, predictable results over time. They may not be innovative, but they can incrementally improve what already exists. Their introverted, indirect need for relationships can be either a positive or negative force, depending on the situation. They can provide tremendous value to the organization because of their accommodating service and team orientation.

The "C" Indirect Controller

This quiet, controlling individual prefers to focus on task, process, details, and perfection. Because of their introverted preferences, they are sometimes hard to read. As a result of their judging and fight preferences, they hold strong opinions that lie below the surface of the indirect, introverted presentation of themselves. The Cautious or Conscientious preference shows a strong need to be:

- Indirect
- Controlling
- Risk-Assessing
- Pessimistic
- Judging
- Introverted
- Continuity-Oriented
- Fight-Oriented

Overview of a "C"

The "C" dispositional types are recognized by their introverted and controlling tendencies. They tend to look at the whole picture or system, while homing in on the main critical factors or issues that increase the efficiency or quality of the output. They like to solve problems through deductive, precise logic—in a true Sherlock Holmes fashion. They want products and services to be produced under specific, controlled conditions. They act as if subjectivity and emotions distort reality. They believe that there is a proper procedure or way for doing things. The way to improve outcomes is through logical, tested policies and practices, which eliminate risk and allow for further testing and improvement. Rationality and analysis in a nondemonstrative fashion, focused on the tasks at hand, is the order of the day.

"C" Strengths

The cautious "Cs" convey their essence by being accurate, independent, and organized. They often are careful, resourceful, and cagey. They will systematically approach work problems and make order out of chaos. "Cs" will follow policies and procedures to the letter, and if there are none, they will establish them. They are intuitive and will concentrate on making decisions in a logical, cautious way to ensure that they take the best available action. They tend to be comfortable as engineers, scientists, computer programmers, or accountants because of their preference for process and accuracy. They prefer to make things "go like clockwork." They prefer tasks to people, clearly defined priorities, and controlled procedures. They are also concerned with *why* something is done just so.

"C" Weaknesses

The "Cs'" need for accuracy, logic, and risk-assessing to control their environment puts a heavy requirement on being right. They can sometimes suffer from "analysis paralysis" as they seek to be perfect. They tend toward being overly critical of, and lack compassion for, themselves and others. Also, because of their preference for logic, they can often miss some of the joy and understanding that comes from an emotional experience. They seek to control their emotions to avoid the embarrassment of imperfection. Their indirect introversion leads them to keep their thoughts and feelings to themselves and prevents them from exploring or facilitating the feelings or emotions of those around them. They can often demonstrate a rather *Spock-like* manner that results in others viewing them as aloof, distant, or detached.

"C" Decision Making

In an almost *Dragnet* Jack Webb manner, they want *just the facts*. They deliberately gather data, and use proven, verified knowledge to evaluate alternatives and possible consequences. They prefer to determine the specific risks, margins of error, and other variables that significantly influence the desired results. Then they will take action. This thorough, risk-assessing approach takes the greatest amount of time of the four DISC patterns.

"C" Evaluates Others

"Cs" tend to naturally assess others. They do so by watching for evidence of cognitive ability, preciseness, and the quality of results. They place a priority on logical thinking and systematic overviews that are data based. They want people to do things correctly.

"C" Use of Time

"Cs" tend to equate the use of time with efficiency. They will be punctual and favorably assess others who show timeliness as well. They will sometimes sacrifice their timelines for the sake of thoroughness, accuracy, and refinement. However, if this happens too often, they will question the planning and procedures to allow for a more *realistic* picture in the future.

"C" Goal

The goal envisioned most frequently by the high "C" is correctness of process or procedures to obtain the most efficient outcomes possible. They prefer to act as if rational, logical thought can gain them the security they seek. Preparation and thoroughness are the way. The suppression of irrationality and emotion is preferred because it reduces the chance for mistakes and the embarrassment that comes with poor results. They prefer to retain information on a need-to-know basis, which allows for control as they ponder the *whys* and *hows* of a situation. They prefer a more formal, discreet set of relationships with a few select individuals, which are built over an extended period of time.

"C" Fear

"Cs" tend to fear personal criticism of their work efforts and invasion of their privacy. They often see the complexity in life and take themselves seriously. They can be perfectionistic and worried about the quality of their work. When "Cs" quietly hold their ground, they tend to do so as a direct result of their proven knowledge of facts and details. They dislike not having the data and resent any questioning of their conclusions once they have those facts. They think their emotional life is their internal business, and it should be analyzed on their own time in the privacy of their own space. Because emotionality does not serve efficient work outcomes, the display and discussion of it holds no place at work. They prefer not to get *bogged down* by somewhat trivial discussions of an interpersonal nature.

Typical "C" Public Figures

Examples of "Cs" include the following: Woodrow Wilson, Richard Nixon, Henry Kissinger, Larry Bird, Katharine Hepburn, Dick Cavett, Dustin Hoffman, Carl Sagan, the Mister Spock character, Ross Perot, Lawrence Welk, Meryl Streep, Barbra Streisand, Jacqueline Kennedy Onassis, and the characters Felix Unger and Sherlock Holmes.

Typical "C" Comments

- "It's not whether you win or lose, it's how you play the game" (the more perfectly competent the better).
- "In God we trust; everyone else bring data!"
- "An ounce of prevention is worth a pound of cure."

Summary of High "C" Tendencies

"Cs'" preferences may lead them to be the most technically proficient in their chosen field of interest because they perceive that power comes from the acquisition of systematically proven knowledge. With this knowledge, organizational work can be logically ordered and structured for maximum efficiency and output. "Cs" think that if the job is done according to the "book" yet the desired results are not forthcoming, then one could make the appropriate data-based modifications by logically examining where the breakdown occurred. Their introverted, controlling preferences can be either a positive or negative force, depending on the situation. The "Cs" offer tremendous worth to the organization because of their logical, data-based, systematic approach to the operation of organizational work. They seek to provide help in quality control and evaluation efforts.

CHAPTER 3 ■ PREFERENCE AND DISPOSITION

FUNDAMENTAL PRINCIPLES

The previous sections of this chapter provided you with a brief description of the classical preferences, although the "Ds" may not think it was so brief. As previously noted, these preferences or dispositions are not immutably expressed through each individual's behavior. Individuals may act in either an extroverted or introverted manner, based on the situation at a given point in time. The issue is one of frequency over time. The dispositional nature of an individual is demonstrated in combination with other preferences, such as preference for controlling or accepting, fighting or flighting, directness or indirectness, and so on.

It is the frequency, intensity, and unique combination of preferences within the self that can and must be understood. By understanding and acknowledging these preferences within yourself, you can also better understand others. You may discover yourself clearly defined by one of these patterns, although somewhat imperfectly.

You may find yourself saying, "Okay, but what can I do with this information?" (a common "D" response). You may react by saying, "I'm not comfortable labeling people and putting them in boxes" (a common "I" reaction). Maybe, as you read the pattern descriptions, you thought to yourself, "Am I really like that?" (a common "S" reaction). Or, perhaps, you thought, "This is too general; its more like a horoscope and needs to be more precise" (a common "C" response).

Given the descriptions thus far, you probably surmised that there are some basic principles encompassing all four of the basic disposition bases. As you more fully explore your preferences, consider the following principles.

DISC Principle #1

There is no best preference or DISC position.

A fundamental research finding[9] of leadership literature is that there are no universal leadership traits that typify good leaders. A major weakness of past research is that it did not examine traits in light of more specific role requirements. Researchers[10] are beginning to examine this relationship more fully.

A basic premise on which this book is based holds that certain roles in certain situations require certain behaviors. Behaviors originate partly in the dispositional nature of each individual (values being the other determining variable). *It is the preference in light of role requirements* that makes a preference *better or worse*. Your disposition will shape the "goodness of fit" between you and the position you hold. You must understand yourself, your core psychic needs, and the job requirements. With this understanding, you can choose your jobs or organizational positions more appropriately, and also develop latent dispositional aspects of yourself.

While there is no single *best* preference, each of the four DISC positions tends to fit best in different types of work (and leadership) situations. For example, if the role requirements call for direct, friendly, results-oriented communication and relationships, a "D" or an "I" preference will have the energy to handle the situation more effectively over time than the "C" or "S" disposition.

Figure 3.11 compares some of the obvious strengths of the various classical patterns.

Situations Requiring	most tendency toward			least tendency toward
self-initiative and risk-taking	D	I	C	S
enthusiasm and involvement	I	D	S	C
stability and follow-through	S	C	D	I
accuracy and thoroughness	C	S	D	I

FIGURE 3.11 *Disposition strenghts.*

What can be said about the four classic patterns, as shown in this figure, is that "D" and "I" dispositions tend not to enjoy or be "naturally" suited for roles that require follow through or accuracy over time. It can also be deduced that the "S" and "C" expend a great deal more energy in roles that require enthusiastic risk-taking over time.

Figure 3.12 describes the fears (or stresses) in each of the four classic patterns.

Situations Involving	most tendency to fear ◄···►		least tendency to fear	
loss of control	D	C	I	S
loss of approval	I	S	D	C
loss of predictability	S	C	D	I
loss of accuracy	C	S	D	I

FIGURE 3.12 *Disposition fears (stresses).*

In the case of "S" and "I," a job that denies opportunities for interpersonal expression and approval will be stressful for them over time. The "D" and "C" may find that a job in which they are unable to control the results ("D") or process ("C") is extremely tiring and unenjoyable over time.

DISC Principle #2

All people are motivated by their needs (goals and fears).

What is observed more often than not is that leaders try to meet their own needs through the job or role they play in the organization, rather than meet the requirements of the role. The organizational role becomes a vehicle for ego stimulation and enhancement. When the requirements call for something different, the individual is less equipped to recognize it, let alone behave appropriately to fulfill those new role requirements.

Goal and Fear Behavior Revisited

In Chapter 2, you learned that each individual can demonstrate either a positive or negative response to an experience. A heightened state of anxiety can result in a negative, fear-based response, while a heightened state of joy can result in a proactive, goal-based response. Examining Figure

3.13, you can see that the fear-based behavior of a "D" rests on the perception of being taken advantage of; the "I" fear rests on the perception of being rejected or disliked; the "S" fear rests on being asked to change; and the "C" fear rests on being criticized for poor-quality work. Within the shadow side of these dispositions are the *fear triggers* that impel the individual toward negative behaviors.

These negative responses are more short-term oriented, centered on predetermined conclusions, and more reactive. The fear-based behavior of the "D" results in others perceiving the "D" as *demanding* and *defiant*, while the "I" is seen as *impulsive* and *indiscriminate*. The "S" is perceived as *sedentary* and *stern*, while the "C" is seen as *callous* and *complaining*. Indeed, each disposition, when having a *bad day*, can be *off their feed* and dysfunctional. Operating from your fear base makes it difficult to lead others, and therefore, you lose credibility in the eyes of your employees.

The environmental experience that triggers the negative response may not be avoidable, but not recognizing when you are in your fear base *is* avoidable. Knowing when you are fear-driven can help you modify your behaviors before "you burn your bridges," and if necessary, it may help you mend your bridges afterward. This knowledge can also aid in understanding your shadow side. Why do you fear loss of control, rejection, change, or criticism? What is the worst that can happen if you "honored" that shadow by examination and experience? Recall the baseball coach who publicly reprimanded his player. It would have helped if he could have embraced the shadow within.

This principle also has tremendous ramifications for leaders' relationships with others. For example, the misalignment of needs between a "C" and an "I" can be enormous, because their natural energies lie in such different directions. Meeting the needs of others may require understanding parts of yourself that lie in the unaccepted shadow side of yourself. It could be the feeling side (or task side) of yourself that lies hidden for some forgotten reason. You, like every individual, have some capacity to demonstrate "I" or "C" behaviors. Without an inner awareness of self-preferences, and the strengths and *weaknesses* of those preferences, there can be little appreciation or acknowledgment of your differences or the differences of others.

CHAPTER 3 ■ PREFERENCE AND DISPOSITION

The leader must also understand the underlying disposition of those they seek to influence well enough to speak to their needs. While all needs cannot be met all the time, the forms of motivation, communication, and stress reduction can be. In other words, the understanding of self and others is a prerequisite (though not a guarantee) to long-term leadership effectiveness.

Figure 3.13 displays a summary of goals and fears for the classic patterns.

	Goal	Fear
D	power and control	being taken advantage of
I	popularity and prestige	being rejected or disliked
S	appreciation and sincerity	being asked to change
C	accuracy and precision	being criticized for poor quality

FIGURE 3.13 *Goals and fears summary.*

Please keep in mind that there are varying intensities in goals and fears. For example, most people share similar ends, such as economic security or success; many people fear being incapacitated or not getting the promotion for which they worked. While these ends and fears are real, they can be transitory and value based, in comparison to the deep-seated, core psychic needs and fears of these classic dispositions. If you want to be more effective in influencing others, then the central psychic dispositional themes around which your life rituals revolve and evolve must be understood and acknowledged in yourself. You must understand these core psychic needs and fears, as they are manifested in yourself and those you seek to influence. Without seeing yourself clearly, you distort the vision you hold of others.

Let's take an observed, actual example of an interaction between a high "D" president of a family-owned business and his high "C" chief financial officer. The topic of discussion was the profit-and-loss statement for the second quarter. The president's high "D" tendencies for directness and results were heightened by the CFO's reams of financial data in computer form, with which the CFO attempted to show how the figures were arrived at. The CFO worked hard at pointing out the variation, possible trends, and reasons for changes from the last quarter. The more precise the CFO was, the more impatient, angry, and dissatisfied the president became.

The president's focus was on what could be done to increase profitability and not on verifying the possible variations and conclusions. The CFO's tendency was to become quieter and less explorative; her body language left no doubt that she was talking to someone who did not understand the problem well enough to take any worthwhile steps to do something about it.

The president ended the conversation by saying, "Just give me the bottom line. Do we need to do something about this? If so, what?" The CFO sat back and said reflectively, "Ultimately, probably—but I'm not sure what."

This is a true story. What it illustrates is two patterns talking *past* each other, each pushing the other's *buttons*. Both are meeting their own needs for communication and ego stimulation; both are wondering how the other got to his or her position in the organization.

In this example, basic business issues were handled without knowledge of the participants' central psychic themes. The president and CFO did not understand each other well enough to communicate clearly. So, instead of two energetic, competent individuals who used their time to focus the organization's energies and resources, there were two irritated egos that found other people outside the meeting with whom to talk about their unmet needs.

DISC Principle #3

Eighty-five percent of the population demonstrates more than one DISC preference or DISC position.

While you may understand the primary types and acknowledge that you may demonstrate these tendencies to some degree, you may think that you possess some of each. The fact is, most people show tendencies toward more than one classic type. Most people display some degree of adaptability and exhibit a primary and secondary drive. Research shows that most people (85 percent) see themselves with tendencies that are combinations of these classic patterns. Those combinations are called mixed types. These mixed patterns are shown in Figure 3.14.

	SECONDARY			
PRIMARY	d	i	s	c
D	D	Di	Ds	Dc
I	Id	I	Is	Ic
S	Sd	Si	S	Sc
C	Cd	Ci	Cs	C

FIGURE 3.14 *Mixed-type dispositions.*

The capital letter signifies a primary tendency while a lowercase letter indicates a secondary, yet still frequent, preference in certain circumstances. As an example, examine the combinations of "Cd" and "Dc." At first, these two profiles would appear dissimilar. The combination of "D" and "C" would appear quite different from either the "D" or the "C" classical patterns.

In the case of a "Cd" or "Dc," remember that the main difference between these two individuals will be in the primary focus. The "Cd" will be less extroverted, less direct in speech patterns, less change-oriented, and/or will show less risk-taking than the "Dc." Both the "Cd" and the "Dc" will be controlling around tasks. The "Dc" will want to control the results, while the "Cd" will want to control the *hows* or process. Both types will be enduring in their outlook. They will be judges and competitive engagers (fighters), pessimistic, and have a high regard for their own opinion.

The "Dc" will tend to be outspoken, blunt, demanding, results-oriented, specific about how to obtain outcomes, and tend toward creative solutions for performance problems. The "Cd" will tend toward quiet, following procedures, and will want to work with tangible by-products from orderly, thorough routines. Results, to the "Cd," are important, but not at the expense of process and logical order.

"Wired" and "Acquired" Disposition Revisited

Recall that each individual usually develops a supplementary dispositional base, which results from upbringing and environmental requirements. Remember that the secondary disposition is generally supplementary, in the sense that it is not too far from the *wired* disposition. In Figure 3.14, the mixed dispositions show *both* the *wired* and *acquired* dispositions. That which is more dominant *behaviorally* is not necessarily what is dominant *psychically*. Some individuals may show their *acquired* disposition first, even though it may take more energy to do so. When they do show their *acquired* disposition first, it may be because they do not clearly understand themselves and do not comprehend the *energy* debt they are accruing. It could also be because role requirements are better met by the *acquired* disposition or because the individual's value base is overriding their *wired* disposition.

In certain mixed dispositions, the *wired* and *acquired* dispositional bases are less complementary and somewhat more complex. Those mixed types are "Ic," "Ci," "Ds," and "Sd." Let's examine the "Ic" mixed disposition. These two classic dispositions are quite different. The "I" is extroverted, direct, an accepter, a flighter, and a perceiver. The "C" is introverted, indirect, a controller, a fighter, and a judger. The individual with an "Ic" disposition may experience dissonance and energy deprivation in stressful times if they try to be both simultaneously. In quiet times of reflection, they may wonder who they are and what is really satisfying to them.

While mixed patterns in yourself and others may add complexity to the understanding of disposition, mixed patterns help explain the diversity within yourself and others. Don't be discouraged! Take your time and try to understand *your* pattern first. Then move to understanding others.

CHAPTER 3 ■ PREFERENCE AND DISPOSITION

DISC Principle #4

Two preferences cannot, at any one time, be equally strong under pressure.

With mixed patterns such as "Di," for example, there will be a tendency to act both for results *and* in response to people. In this case, the individual with a "Di" pattern wants to get results, is change-oriented, and takes charge because of the "D" preference base; at the same time, the "Di" individual wants to be liked by people, prefers an informal work atmosphere, and spends time getting to know and care about people because of the "I" preference base. These two preferences may be in conflict because of time demands, resource constraints, and competing interests of the parties involved. In a specific situation, the leader with "Di" preferences may need to choose between results and others' feelings of approval. The choice may create some sense of inner psychic discontent within this individual, as he or she is forced to meet one psychic need while leaving another unfulfilled at that choice point. Mixed patterns carry with them a potential for internal conflicts, which require self-understanding and realistic choices.

The value and beauty of mixed patterns lies in adaptability. Adaptability is important in situations where one of the preferences is especially helpful and is not in conflict with the other. Using the "Di" dispositions again, this pattern could be equally at ease in an initial sales call that requires the establishment of a social relationship with a customer (the strength of the "I" preference) and the subsequent requirement of closing the deal at a reasonable profit (the strength of the "D" preference).

With adaptability, individuals can show more natural energy, depending on the requirements of the job or situations in which they find themselves. Narrow preference bases, such as the classic patterns of "D," "I," "S," and "C," will experience less inner conflict because of simpler internal need patterns; but, when in multifaceted, complex environments, those individuals with a single classic pattern may require more energy to adapt to the incompatible requirements of the external world.

For example, the "D" preference, without the "I" preference as a backup, may be less effective in situations where they cannot control outcomes, take on challenges, take charge, or create change. Their *need* for an environment where control, challenge, and change are possible may result in inappropriate actions within environments that do not offer these aspects. They may show impatience, defiance, and passive aggression in an environment that does not meet their needs. The "D" need may result in resisting the "nonchangeable" environment, or in the case of assertive "Ds," in placing themselves in a different environment in which their needs can be met.

DISC Principle #5

Each personal preference has its own inherent strengths or limitations and, therefore, still undeveloped potentials.

Who you are and what you prefer does not *limit* how you choose to behave. In most cases, you are limited only when you are not aware of your alternatives. Without conscious awareness of your preference, you may act without understanding. You may act in ways that are limiting and dysfunctional to yourself and others. Through behavioral adaptability, you can respond to others in ways that *they* need to be treated. Behavioral adaptability is defined as *the willingness and ability to use a range of behaviors, not necessarily characteristic of your style, to deal effectively with the requirements of the situation or relationship.* This adaptability involves making adjustments to your way of communicating, based on the particular needs of the relationship at a particular time. It means going beyond your comfort zone to ensure that your message is heard.

Behavioral adaptability does not mean losing your identity and good sense. It is the willingness and ability to use behaviors not necessarily characteristic of your preference base. No individual type holds "a corner on the market" for effectiveness or functionality. Each disposition may be functional or dysfunctional in certain circumstances, depending on intensity and back-up tendencies. Your adaptability level affects the way others perceive you. Adaptability means adjusting your behavior to allow others to be

CHAPTER 3 ■ PREFERENCE AND DISPOSITION

more at ease and more apt to hear your message. It has to do with the way you manage your communication, solve problems, make decisions, and resolve conflict.

For example, when an "I" works with a "C" on a common task, one of the ways an "I" can adapt is by talking less, listening more, and focusing on critical tasks. A "D" could be more versatile by slowing down for an "S" or "C" individual. A "D" or "C" shows more versatility when he or she takes time to listen to a human-interest or family story told by an "I" or "S" individual.

Also notice that the *environmental requirement* for the "I" changes if they work with a "D" or another "I" instead of a "C." If the challenge is to work with the "D," then the "I's" natural disposition for relationships would be complementary to the "D's" results orientation. The "I" could help the "D" relax more but, on the other hand, would not be complementary to the "D's" need to delegate to someone who could follow through on details. Because the "I" is neither naturally disposed to be organized nor focused on details and concepts, the "I" would easily get along with another "I" on a common task, but may not bring the task to completion because of the tendency to enjoy the relationship aspect of the work.

By showing adaptability, you can build your undeveloped potential. Adaptability is not a goal in itself, but a means to the end of increased personal effectiveness with others. The key to adaptability is realizing what preferences you hold *and* what preferences you choose not to respond to. A second key is to sense the preferences *required* in the circumstance or relationship. Armed with these understandings, you can choose what you will and will not respond to.

If you do not choose to be adaptable, then a second option for self and others is to select work roles that build on your natural disposition. Research shows that the individual's field of interest is based more on values than on disposition. However, the implementation or way individuals perform their work *within* a particular job is based more on disposition than on values. For example, a computer programmer position, in most cases, will be better suited for someone with "S" or "C" tendencies. The position would require someone who enjoys working alone, seeks known procedures and processes, and wants accurate, systematic results.

If, on the other hand, you find it draining, tedious, and frustrating to focus on details, be tied down by procedures, and instead enjoy a *high-touch* work environment filled with fragmentation and variety, then your disposition is not well suited for a programmer's job. In other words, you must examine the organizational role you fulfill in light of your known disposition base. If you are not versatile, at least choose role responsibilities in line with your natural tendencies or disposition.

At this point in our discussion, a perfectly balanced onion looks like the one shown in Figure 3.15.

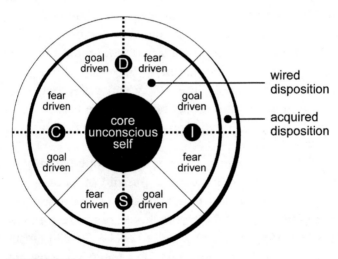

FIGURE 3.15 *A balanced onion.*

Remember that each individual includes both a *wired* and *acquired* aspect in his or her disposition. There will be a core "well of energy" and a developed tolerance for a secondary disposition. The developed base gives you more adaptability. The preferences of each individual would not look as balanced as depicted in Figure 3.15. A more typical scenario would show only one or two preferences highlighted, with other preferences more diminished.

CHAPTER 3 ■ PREFERENCE AND DISPOSITION

Your strength lies in your natural self's energy to act in certain ways. The "D's" natural strength lies in taking charge and organizing, the "I's" strength lies in interacting and caring, and so forth for "S" and "C" preferences. Additionally, the goal-driven "D" is different from the fear-driven or shadow-driven "D," who may become dictatorial and defiant. Acknowledging the shadow self, for the "Ds," resides in the willingness to admit when they are becoming dictatorial and defiant. Defiance is the key to knowing you are fearful; it is the key to becoming goal driven. Defiance is also the key to moving to other alternatives. Perhaps those alternatives lie in the unused, *lost* capacities to act and feel as an "I" or an "S" or a "C."

DISC Principle #6

People can become more versatile; other preferences can be developed.

People can build an understanding and acceptance of a range of behaviors outside their characteristic preference base. However, the development of adaptability requires a conscious awareness, at first, of what your preference is and what the alternatives are. Adaptability may require the use of unfamiliar behaviors outside of your comfort zone, or it may require you to be more extroverted. The situation may require you to be indirect when you prefer to be direct with your verbal and nonverbal communication.

To become more adaptable does not require you to hurt yourself or others by consciously violating promises or agreements. It should be made clear that you are not required to do something that is against your values and you are not being manipulative by *forcing* others to do something against their values. Being more adaptive means flexibly using a communication style that is more appropriate for those to whom you are speaking. In other words, speak the language *they* prefer.

Using and valuing preference bases other than your *natural* one is a way to appreciate diversity in yourself and others. Most people who fear their shadow do not appreciate what they are not. You must learn to embrace your shadow and learn from what you are not. You must not view other preference bases as weak, deficient, or inadequate; instead, view different preferences as your shadow self from which you can learn.

Adaptability results, first, from making a commitment to change, and then learning and using more effective behavior when the opportunity occurs. If the opportunity should pass, then you should commit to act differently at the next opportunity. Adaptability results from keeping your goals in mind and on paper, then revisiting those goals frequently.

Adaptability can be developed when people recognize that some of their behaviors or habits are counterproductive in certain circumstances. Sensing ineffectiveness, for most normal people, triggers a need for change. Remember that behavioral change may take more energy at first. However, if the behaviors are more appropriate for others around you, the change may ultimately result in saving you more energy and time.

The Platinum Rule

Throughout your childhood, you were probably asked to treat others as you wanted to be treated. The "golden rule" has been around a long time. As you think about this axiom, you should realize that it assumes all people are alike and they are all like you. Of course, this tenet was usually called into play around issues of fairness. While you would want to treat people fairly, the axiom should stop there. You can probably recall when you were a child and a parent or adult asked, "How would you feel if someone did that to you?" Reciprocity is a basic stage in moral development. Treating others as you want to be treated in values issues, such as money, opportunity, or possessions, would be quite different from nonvalue issues, such as information needs, time needs, or alone-time needs. Beyond the question of fairness, you make a critical mistake by assuming that how you would like to be treated is how others would like to be treated.

The *Platinum Rule* says, *"Do unto others as they want to be done unto."* This principle[11] holds great significance as you look at the role of leadership. Beyond the constancy of fairness, research suggests that people are naturally motivated to get *their* needs met, not necessarily to meet those of others. In fact, it seems that leaders spend a great deal of time shaping the behavior of others, but they appear unwilling or unable to change their

CHAPTER 3 ■ PREFERENCE AND DISPOSITION

own. Leaders must act on the premise that others are motivated and shaped by *their* own needs. Those needs involve basic issues such as speech patterns, interaction patterns, esteem needs, time needs, and psychic fears or goals.

Let's take an example of a high "I" interacting with a high "D." If the individual with intense "I" preferences approaches this discussion from the *golden rule* perspective, he or she would assume that the high "D" would want to spend time in casual, social interaction before, during, and after the business at hand was resolved. If the high "I" acted on personal needs, as a direct accepter, he or she would be right at home talking about himself or herself, the latest fad, news events, recent learnings, a recent emotional experience, or anything else that seemed spontaneous and social.

The "D" or direct controller's personal goals and needs are quite different; if the conversation goes on long enough, he or she may feel resentful of the misallocation of his or her time, focus, and energy. If the "I" observes the Platinum Rule, then the approach to communicating with a "D" is to remember that "Ds" require a results focus. They do not care *how* they play the game; they want results. "Ds" want to accomplish things for their own purposes, and they seek control over their work. They want directness in approach and conversation.

Given the need or focus of "Ds," the other preference bases should strive to do the following when interacting with them:

- Be brief, to the point, and focus on end results.
- Emphasize practicality and logic, not feelings.
- Outline actions for results.
- Be low-keyed about the hows, but make sure that everyone involved understands how results can be obtained.

There are more specific ways to communicate effectively with "D" tendency individuals, depending on the situation. For instance, in an organizational setting, if you are discussing goals, giving feedback, solving a problem, or holding an evaluation conference, the situation may require the general approach listed above, but with some variation.

When giving feedback to "D" individuals, remember that they want the information presented first and feelings later. They want the information presented briefly, directly, and with no frills. They want the real and ideal described. "Ds" are sensitive to criticism of their character. They prefer that you agree with the facts and not with them as individuals. They want to know how dealing with this feedback increases the chances of getting the desired results.

SUMMARY

The purpose of this chapter was to call your attention to your natural disposition base. The power of self-knowledge can enable you to better understand those of similar patterns, as well as others with difficult patterns of difference. Adherence to the Platinum Rule begins with self-understanding.

This chapter presented a framework for understanding your dispositional patterns. Briefly, these classic patterns are called D, I, S, and C. The following summary table shown in Figure 3.16 may be helpful.

	D	I	S	C
	Direct Controller	Direct Relater	Indirect Relater	Indirect Controller
seeks	control	recognition	acceptance	accuracy
strengths	leadership pioneering organizing	persuading entertaining cheerleading	listening teamwork follow-through	planning systematizing orchestration
weaknesses (growth areas)	impatient insensitive to others poor listener	inattentive to details short attention span low follow-through	oversensitive slow to begin action lack global perspective	perfectionist critical unresponsive
irritated by	inefficiency indecision	routines complexity	insensibility impatience	disorganization impropriety
under stress fear-driven	dictatorial defiant	impulsive indiscriminate	sedentary stern	critical callous

FIGURE 3.16 *DISC summary.*

Endnotes

1. Buffet, Dictionary of Quotations at *www.quotereference.com*.
2. Jung 1923, 1961.
3. Jung 1964.
4. Marston 1979.
5. Besides the DISC model, you might be familiar with the Myers-Briggs Type Indicator (MBTI model). See Keirsey and Bates 1978 or Kroeger and Thuesen 1988.
6. Research clearly connects disposition with the self's genetic and physiological aspects. The autonomic nervous system, limbic system, and hemispheres of the brain share a great deal with the individual's unique dispositional base. In many somatic, biological ways, much of the individual's uniqueness is shaped by its specific genetic configuration. See Ornstein 1993; Eysenck and Eysenck 1985.
7. Notably Lorenz 1966; and Montagu 1968.
8. Seligman 1990.
9. See Bass 1990 for an excellent overview.
10. Tett, Jackson, and Rothstein 1991.
11. For a more extensive treatment of this principle, see Alessandra, O'Connor, and Alessandra 1990.

CHAPTER 4

Beliefs and Points of View

"A society driven by responsibilities is oriented toward service, acknowledging other points of view, compromise and progress—whereas a society driven by rights is oriented toward acquisitions, confrontation and advocacy . . . at the most fundamental level, all conduct is individual so when you bring the moral dimension to individual actions, you bring integrity to the entire work environment."

— KESHAVAN NAIR[1]

BELIEFS

Beliefs as Building Blocks

In Chapter 1, we introduced the idea of a layered self and briefly discussed the disposition and values layers. In Chapter 2, we discussed how these two layers shape your views and behavior. In Chapter 3, we explored, in depth, the concepts of preference and disposition. Now, in this chapter, we explore the values layer.

While dispositions are instinctive, preconscious "would-do" behaviors, values are thoughtful, premeditative "should-do" behaviors. However, the notion of values, value systems, and points of view rests on a clear understanding of the concept of beliefs; beliefs are the foundation on which your values are built. As you will see, all values are beliefs, but not all beliefs are values. You form beliefs from your past and present experiences, which then shape your future experiences.

Importance of Beliefs

There are two reasons why you should examine and understand your beliefs: (1) to better know yourself, and (2) to provide a mechanism for self-change. Beliefs and values are a *cognitive structure*, "mental filters" by which you experience objects, people, and events. These filters influence your attitudes and intentions, and impact the way you interact with others.

The Power of Beliefs

A perceived similarity or dissimilarity between people's belief systems is the basis for rejection or acceptance of others.[2] Rejection of others on the basis of age, gender, race, or ethnic background is primarily based on perceptions of dissimilarity of beliefs. People who are racially different, yet embrace similar beliefs, are more likely to be compatible than are those of the same race who support different beliefs. More people are fair-minded about race than they are about beliefs. The principle of perceived belief similarity/dissimilarity holds direct implications for your influence approach with others. Leadership problems in organizations are not simply "miscommunication" problems, but clearly communicated differences in beliefs and values.[3]

Mechanism of Self-Change

You must begin to know and examine the beliefs that underlie your approach to yourself and the world. *It is not events that control your life, but your beliefs about what these events mean.*[4] You maintain beliefs about yourself, the world, and your "place" in the world. The beliefs you hold about yourself often require little or no consensus from others, and can be of a positive or negative nature. For example, "I am a reasonable person" versus "I am not attractive" are positive and negative beliefs, respectively.

Low self-esteem originates in your beliefs system; it is generated from negative beliefs about yourself. How do those negative beliefs limit you? What would happen if you lived with those limits the rest of your life? What price will you pay for those beliefs? How would you live your dreams, if those limits were removed?

Many beliefs are a misinterpretation of reality, which can restrict future achievements. Try this exercise. Identify one action you must do to further an aspiration, but postponed. Ask yourself why you have not yet acted. Then ask yourself, "What beliefs can be attributed to my lack of action? How do those beliefs contribute to not doing other things I want to do?"

The Concept of Belief

A belief is the *mental acceptance* that some idea or perception is true. A belief is not just the idea or concept, but also the *conviction* that the idea or concept fits a patterned reality. Sometimes the belief is not, or cannot be, verified. However, that which is regarded as "true" is usually supported by reason, facts, or evidence.

A belief contains an emotional, cognitive, and behavioral component. Most beliefs are forged in an emotional context or circumstance. This emotional context is then associated with intellectual thought about the self, the world, or the self's interaction in the world. The emotional context is, ultimately, either painful or pleasurable; the positive or negative emotion is "felt" whenever the belief is activated. In other words, this belief will trigger similar future emotional and intellectual reactions in similar contexts.

For example, if a child grows up in a household where one of the parents committed adultery, the child may believe that adultery is wrong. If the parent's adultery caused much unhappiness for everyone and resulted in a divorce, then the child's belief that adultery is wrong may be associated with the child's pain and grief. Thereafter, whenever discussions and actions associated with adultery arise, the child, now an adult, may experience grief or guilt if he or she acts contrary to the belief that adultery is wrong.

Beliefs are also cognitive; they exist within a conscious, logical framework of sequential thoughts. Beliefs include an intellectual quality of deductive thought by which you may apply the rules of logic and reasoning to what is assumed to be true or not true.

Beliefs may be psychologically organized, but not necessarily logically organized. You may activate an old belief simply because it is associated with a particular emotional event that occurred in the past. You hold countless beliefs that may be used at any point in time. However, not all beliefs are of equal importance. Some beliefs are more central, or core, to your everyday living, while others are more peripheral. For example, you may hold the belief that democracy is the best way to organize and govern a society. An associated, yet less central, belief may be that voting rights should be granted if a person is a citizen of a democratic society. If you do not believe that democracy is the best way to govern, then the issue of voting rights may be irrelevant. The greater the number of beliefs dependent on the core belief, the more central is the belief. The more central the belief, the more implications it holds for other beliefs.

BELIEFS AND VALUES

Beliefs are the basis of values and value systems. However, a point that needs repeating is that all values are beliefs, but not all beliefs are values. A value is a specific, single belief concerning an end or a mean. There could be other beliefs (called assumptions) that support the value, but the summary belief concerning the best end or mean is called a value.

What Is a Value?

A value is an enduring belief that a particular mean or end is more socially or individually preferable than another end or mean.[5] It is a belief that transcends a specific situation, object, or person, yet is applied across situations, objects, or people. A value is focused on a future end and/or the means to accomplish that particular end. It is a standard of better or best, versus what is not good or what is bad. Examples of *end* values include wanting to be rich or wanting a world at peace. Examples of means values include wanting to be honest, or doing unto others as you would want done unto you.

Consider the following story about Gandhi. A woman, concerned about her son's health, asked Gandhi to speak to her son. The woman shares with Gandhi how the sugar is affecting her son's teeth and liver. The woman asked Gandhi to tell the son to stop eating sugar. Gandhi quietly reflected for several minutes, and then said he would do as she asked. Gandhi told the woman to bring the son to him, but not before three weeks elapsed. Later, after Gandhi talked to the child and obtained the child's promise to stop eating sugar, the mother asked Gandhi why he asked her to wait three weeks before bringing the child to him. Gandhi quietly said that it took him three weeks to stop eating sugar.

Values Criteria

This story gives us the basis for values criteria. Consider the following criteria: (1) a value is chosen, (2) it is chosen from alternatives, (3) it is chosen with an understanding of the consequences, (4) it is acted on over time, and (5) it is prized or "publicly owned."[6] Let's explore these criteria one by one.

A Value Is Chosen

A value is a belief that is chosen. Coerced or forced behaviors are not considered values based. To act under the threat of punishment may be the result of a specific value, but not necessarily for the sake of the object of the act. For example, if an individual is required to either act in compliance with a company's values or be fired, then that does not mean the individual "values" the company's rules; instead, he or she "values" keeping his or her job. In the sugar story, Gandhi was not forced, but obviously chose, to speak to the boy.

Chosen from Alternatives

A value is chosen from alternatives. In other words, people believe that certain ends or means are better for themselves and/or others *in compari-*

son to other possible ends or means. To act on your values initially requires thoughtful reflection. It involves weighing what is better, what is right (or more right) against what may be worse or wrong.

Frequently, people make choices concerning what is good or bad for themselves and others with little consideration of the alternatives. For example, during the Korean conflict, most American GIs unquestioningly believed that democracy was the best form of government. However, soldiers fighting in Korea were directly confronted with the alternative ideology of communism. Some experienced a values conflict because they never previously reflected on the "pros and cons" of democracy and communism. But, to *choose* democracy over communism means to understand the pros and cons of both. We, of course, believe that the democratic way of life is the best alternative, but our belief should be based on our understanding the historical consequences of other alternatives such as fascism or communism.

People often act on a set of standards for right and wrong, but they may be affectively or emotionally connected to particular standards due to upbringing or association with significant others. People may act on these standards without examination of alternatives. These unexamined values are called *programmed values*; they are accepted social modes of behavior unquestionably acted on over time. They are values, because they involve sorting good or bad ends and means, but they are deemed programmed values because they are unexamined and based on derived beliefs.

Chosen While Anticipating the Consequences

A value is chosen while anticipating the consequences of the choice. In the sugar story, Gandhi understood that his choice to speak with the boy meant he must give up sugar before he could ask another to do the same. The anticipation of consequences is best done, in most instances, through direct encounters with the object of the value. Remember, beliefs (and, therefore, values) are either formed in direct experience or derived through authority.

A programmed value, poorly examined, is often formed without the direct experience that permits a full appreciation of the consequences. For example, if you think fascism is the best form of government, then to ensure that your belief is chosen rather than programmed, you need to examine the beliefs on which fascism is based. One belief inherent in fascism is that not all men are created equal. Another inherent belief is that the masses cannot understand or be made to understand the social implications of their wants. A third belief is that every society includes an elite who determine the best course of action for the masses. To *choose* fascism, you must examine the consequences of fascist beliefs, especially if you are one of the masses and can never be one of the elite.

A value (belief) formed through direct experience often facilitates the examination of alternatives *and* the anticipation of possible consequences. These examined values are called *developed values*.

Acted on over Time

A value is acted on over time. As previously stated, all values include a behavioral component. In Gandhi's case, he obviously did not want to ask the child to do something he could or would not do. While there may be exceptions, it is a major contradiction to say you value something, yet not act on that value over time.

A Value Is Prized

A value is prized or "publicly owned." Gandhi's quiet declaration of his three-week sugar abstinence let him make his behaviors known to others. By doing so, he tested his value choice in light of others' perceptions. Others can help you examine possible alternatives and unanticipated consequences. In most cases, public affirmation lets you test your emotional attachment or conviction. Do you really value something you wouldn't put in a newspaper or couldn't tell your loved ones? Of course, there are things you value but may not want publicized; however, most of your values should be able to "stand the light of day," if they are to be acted on over time.

Values Process

Developed values are shaped through a values process. If you choose certain values, then you choose among alternatives, after understanding the possible consequences. If you continue to make the same choice over time, then you are engaging in a values process. Obviously, over-time choices do not always involve such deliberate consideration, unless there is a great deal of variation in the choice that warrants more examination. After values are developed, they act as filters through which deliberation is reduced and a choice is made. For example, if you actively choose to believe that adultery is bad and previously examined the consequences of not being faithful, then the behavior to remain faithful will usually not require much further deliberation.

Types of Values

There are two types of values: *means* and *ends*. These distinctions are important to note because there are fewer end values than means values. Think of an end value as a goal state of existence for self or for others. These end values are either *social* or *personal* in focus. A world at peace, a satisfied customer, and family security are examples of *socially* oriented end values, while peace of mind, a prosperous life, and happiness might be examples of *personal* end values. If a value is social, then it will be concerned with how both the self and others should relate to others. Personal end values are primarily concerned with what is desirable for the self and include only indirect implications for others. In other words, end values can be either other- or self-focused.

Means values are also either *social* or *personal*. Examples of *social* means values include honesty, responsibility, and equality. These social means values, or modes of behavior, do not imply end states, but they do imply interaction with others. They are interpersonally focused and, when violated, cause pangs of guilt or conscience for the wrongdoer. The second type of means value is *personal*. A personal means is exemplified by values such as being logical, independent, and self-controlled. They are personally focused and do not seem particularly concerned with morality or social "shoulds" for others. However, failure to behave according to these values could lead to feelings of shame or personal inadequacy on the part of the individual. These end and means types are represented in Figure 4.1.

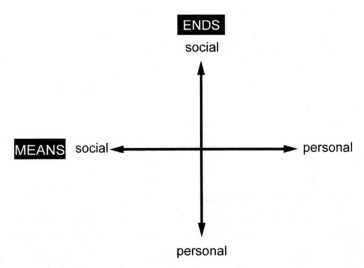

FIGURE 4.1 *End and means value types.*

Value Systems

Each person holds a unique combination of means and end values that are constantly used to sort experiences and make future choices. These combinations result in a cluster of interrelated values and beliefs called a *value system*. It is systemic, in the sense that certain beliefs and values depend on each other in a continuum from central to peripheral. It is not systematic, in the sense that well-organized priorities only occur with experience, application, and careful reflection.

All people have means and end values but, beyond that, a hierarchy of values for all people does not exist. Some people are personally ends driven and socially means driven. Others are oriented to social ends and personal means. It would be rare for an individual's behavior to be guided by only one value. Instead, a cluster of interrelated value beliefs, which may or may not be prioritized, guides most people. The priority of values, dependent on variables such as intellectual development, cultural stimulus, education, and gender, is developed with time and experience. In other words, a value system is a cluster of interrelated value beliefs that, when taken together, add stability to decision making.

There are topic areas where values are formed. People typically form values around issues such as politics, economics, aesthetics, morality, power, and social conduct. A well-integrated value system would include interrelated ideas and values that connect economics to power or to morality, and so on. Interestingly, means and ends are interconnected but not correlated. Ends do not "dictate" means. One mean might serve several ends, or several means might be used to serve one end.

For example, you and your spouse agree to raise your children to be honest; thus, you share the same end value. You may believe that the children must be punished every time they do not tell the truth; this is your means for raising honest children. However, your spouse may believe that the best way to raise honest children is to be completely honest with them and let them experience the consequences when they or others are not honest; this is another means to raising honest children.

The Value of Values

Values serve several important functions. To exemplify the major functions of values, consider the following story about Hank Aaron. In 1957, the Milwaukee Braves met the New York Yankees in the World Series. One of the Braves' most fearsome hitters was Hank Aaron, who would go on to become the all-time home run leader in Major League history. When he came up to bat, Yankee catcher Yogi Berra did what catchers often do with good hitters—he tried to rattle Aaron.

"You're holding the bat the wrong way," Berra said. "Turn it around so you can see the trademark." With his eyes steady on the pitcher, Aaron said, "Didn't come up here to read. Came up here to hit."[7]

CHAPTER 4 ■ BELIEFS AND POINTS OF VIEW

People use values for (1) ego defense, (2) presentation of self in a social context, (3) self-conflict resolution and decision making, and (4) motivation. Let's examine those functions, one by one.

Ego Defense

Needs, feelings, and actions that may be socially unacceptable can be recast into more amenable terms by a process of justification or rationalization. Values, of course, are not "ready-to-wear" notions that can be conveniently used. But values can be called on to explain or justify past actions, even though those values may not always be responsible for those past behaviors. Values let an individual rationalize certain actions that are unacceptable to others so that he or she can still maintain feelings of morality and competence, which are essential to self-esteem.

In the baseball story, Aaron wasn't necessarily called on to defend his actions to an opposing player, but he was "defending" against Berra's attempts to rattle him.

Presentation of Self

Values are the "social grease" by which personal interaction between a group and an individual is smoothly conducted. Values allow people to take a particular position on the social, economic, legal, political, ethical, and aesthetic issues encountered in everyday living. They are guidelines for how to manage the self in light of others' expectations (values). Conversely, each individual uses his or her values to judge, evaluate, praise, or blame others. Values can also be used to persuade and influence others through the connection made with common beliefs or values.

The values held by Aaron and Berra, not to mention all the players and fans at the time, were defined by "the game." Most sports have particular values (means and ends) that define "the game." Rules, customs, and rituals are values; they define the context for the presentation of self. The fascination people hold with playing and watching sports lies in watching individual effort within defined rules and boundaries, or *clear means and ends*. If the organizational "game" was that clear, do you think people could display as much fun and energy?

Self-Conflict Resolution and Decision Making

Value differences stand at the base of conflict or strife throughout the history of human beings. The resolution of value conflicts between nations, groups, or individuals goes beyond the scope of this book. However, an understanding of values can help you explain and resolve some of the inner self-conflicts you might experience. Because a certain type of situation can activate more than one value, conflicts often arise *within* your value system. Many times it will be difficult to behave congruently with all the values within your values system.

The acquisition of a value can sometimes occur in isolation from other values, in an all-or-nothing form. People are not taught to be "a little honest" or "a little happy," nor are they taught to be honest sometimes and not at other times. As people mature and develop, they begin to weigh and choose one value over another. They begin to place one value before another and integrate isolated absolute values into an organized set that places values in an order or priority. When a decision is made to act on one value over another, the "behavior will be the result of the relative importance of all the competing values that the situation has activated."[8]

In the Aaron story, Hank is clear about the value on which he wants to act. He is there to hit, not read. He is not distracted by Berra's remark. A value system is a learned set of beliefs or values that help one to choose between alternatives and conflicts and decide on a course of action.

Motivation

Values also serve as means for self-motivation. End values are most often future oriented and serve as a long-range expression of your desires. The ends and means of attainment represent your reasons for living, beyond immediate biological needs. They keep you striving, and ultimately provide you with a sense of self-esteem along your life evolution toward personal

CHAPTER 4 ■ BELIEFS AND POINTS OF VIEW

fulfillment. End values become a purpose—a focus for future action. They tell you what "business" you are in as a human being.

Adherence to end values liberates energy. Motivation is the expression of the interest, excitement, or enthusiasm to produce some end. In the Aaron example, Hank's motivation is clear. His performance, over time, also shows the clear end he had in mind. Motivation is manifested in consistent, focused behavior toward a desired end; it is a purposeful action. Without end values, purposeful action is limited to transitory adaptation to the environment. You must own a sense of purpose that exceeds the sense of task.

Like Aaron, you are frequently "at bat" in your life and in organizational settings. What purposes do you carry into those times at bat? Your success and motivation are intimately connected to your values. As a leader and/or follower, your actions and those of others are ultimately determined by the clarity of "the game." A major emphasis of your leadership behaviors lies in making "the game" clear for those you wish to influence so they can motivate themselves. Your definition of what "the game" should be is greatly shaped by your point of view or *value system*.

POINTS OF VIEW

You know from experience that people hold different points of view. The main premise of this chapter is that enacted beliefs result in self-selected choices of ends and means for self and others. Different points of view are the result of different beliefs about what are desirable ends and means. The ends and means of each individual are organized into a somewhat prioritized value system of interrelated beliefs. A set of patterned enacted values (beliefs) is called a *point of view*.

Research shows that there are four general points of view.[9] The letters T, I, C, and S will be used to designate these four points of view. The letters TICS bear absolutely no connection to the DISC model presented in Chapter 3. As discussed in Chapter 3, disposition is instinctive, nonpremeditative behavior, while values are much more rational, deliberate behavior. Before naming and fully describing these values-related points of view, notice how the letters appear on the means and ends axis of Figure 4.2. Social means and social ends drive the "T"; the "S" is driven by social ends and personal means; and so on. These four points of view are related to the ends and means types displayed in Figure 4.1.

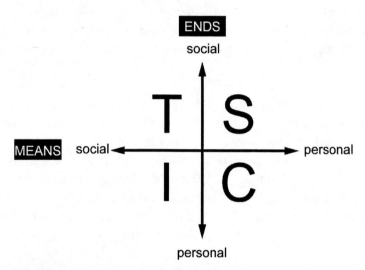

FIGURE 4.2 *Ends and means points of view.*

Self/Other Focus

Each of the values types (ends and means) maintains a different focus. For example, a *social* end focuses on what future end state is best for all human beings (e.g., a world at peace). The concept of social end implies a good or best for all people concerned. When acting on a social end, you are acting on behalf of *others*.

Suppose, however, that you hold a comfortable life as your end state. This end value is more focused on *self*. By advocating a comfortable life, you don't imply the inclusion of others. You may or may not want all people to enjoy a comfortable life, depending on whether others' comfort infringed on yours. When acting on a personal end, you are acting on behalf of yourself (see Figure 4.3).

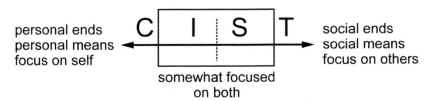

FIGURE 4.3 *Self and other focus.*

The C point of view is most focused on ends and means that are oriented toward self. A comfortable life, satisfaction, wealth, security, and self-respect are examples of self-oriented ends and means.[10] A desire to be logical, brave, thrifty, or imaginative and adages such as "do unto others *before* they can do unto you" or "all's fair in love and war" are examples of self-oriented means.

The T point of view mostly focuses on ends and means that are socially oriented. A world at peace, a world of beauty, equality, and national security are examples of socially oriented ends. To be honest, fair, or loving are examples of socially oriented means. As you can see, the C and T are quite opposite in viewpoints.

To truly understand these points of view, suspend your judgment about good or bad and right or wrong as you initially begin to analyze these concepts. Otherwise, you may reject before truly understanding.

Rights/Responsibility Focus

A second major consideration when examining valuing points of views is the locus of control. For the rights-oriented individual, control of the ends and means lies with *the person*. Values held by the rights-oriented individual must allow maximum freedom and discretion for the individual. A rights orientation supports self-assertion and self-preservation. A rights orientation supports the individual's claim to certain prerogatives (or rights), self-initiatives, and results in self-acquisitions.

In contrast, a responsibility orientation places the definition of goodness in the hands of *the group*. A responsibility orientation is concerned with what the group requires from the individual, and what is "better" for the group rather than for a given individual. A responsibility orientation fosters the orientation of service, acknowledgment of other points of view, and compromise for the welfare of the group. Priority is given to the group's well-being, and then the individual's responsibility and role in support of the group's collective thinking (see Figure 4.4).

For example, when discussing abortion, a pro-choice position may be supported by a rights orientation that "no one is going to tell me what to do with my body." A pro-life position could be supported by a responsibility orientation in which "it is not a right, it's a human being" and "thou shalt not kill."

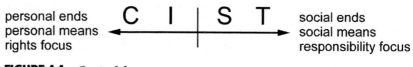

FIGURE 4.4 *Control focus.*

The C and I viewpoints are most oriented toward the personal rights inherent in the means and ends chosen. Examples are satisfaction, pleasure, or a comfortable life as ends or imaginativeness, logic, or competency as means.

The T and S viewpoints are more oriented toward values that are inherently responsibility oriented. Ends such as a world at peace or equality are examples. Means are illustrated by being forgiving, helpful, or cheerful. A logical combination of these focuses is illustrated in Figure 4.5.

The letters T, I, C, and S symbolize the names for the points of view. The T stands for the *traditionalist*, I for *inbetweener*, C for *challenger*, and S for *synthesizer*.

CHAPTER 4 ■ BELIEFS AND POINTS OF VIEW

social ends social means others focus responsibilities focus **T**	social ends personal means others and self focus responsibility of self and others focus **S**
personal ends social means others and self focus rights of self and other focus **I**	personal ends personal means self focus rights focus **C**

FIGURE 4.5   *Points-of-view matrix.*

Before you examine the descriptions of these four points of view, keep in mind that (1) no values point of view is perfect or inherently better than another in its ability to guide an individual's actions; (2) the points-of-view framework may not predict an individual's specific position on a given values question, because the individual may lack the experience to integrate the specific position into his or her value system; (3) experience, socialization, and significant life events may result in a shift of point of view through reconsideration in a direct encounter with the "object" of value; and (4) just the observation of an individual's behavior is not enough to identify the underlying point of view. How someone acts may give more insight into his or her disposition. Asking someone to explain what particular belief or value led to a behavior will be predictive of his or her point of view. The answer will easily reveal the beliefs that drive his or her value system.

THE TRADITIONALIST POINT OF VIEW

As shown in Figure 4.5, traditionalists are oriented toward social ends and social means. They focus on responsibilities and expectations that others define as the "goods and bads" of life. They care about responsibilities—their *and* others' responsibilities. Traditionalists seek to understand the rules, laws, customs, and beliefs of the group to which they belong; and they view themselves as truly dedicated to those understandings. For an accurate understanding of the traditionalist-specific beliefs, you also need to know a great deal about the group to which he or she belongs. For example, you need to consider whether they are Catholic or Buddhist, republican or democrat, doctor or lawyer, and so on.

Key End Values—Social Ends

The key end value for traditionalists is responsible living. Their quest is for a state of continuous "responsible living," whether at work or at home. They are geared to what is best for the family, organization, church, or other special reference group with which they identify. They are motivated to contribute to others and their society. They want to be of service—to make their world a better place. They believe in the traditions of the past and will try to preserve age-old standards and values in keeping with the views of "the group."

Traditionalists take a "we" orientation, once the appropriate authority or process determines the group's goals and courses of action. They take a great deal of pride in meeting those obligations or standards. They value being "role players" who contribute by "keeping their nose to the grindstone," because together people can accomplish more. They don't mind giving more than they get and see it as their duty to work for a better future as a legacy to pass on to the next generation.

Key Means Values—Social Means

The key means values of traditionalists are devotion, loyalty, and dependability. The value of *devotion* involves the commitment to work hard for their goals. They will work diligently to make a responsible contribution to their identity groups. They make commitments to others and are devoted to keeping those commitments. Some traditionalists dedicate themselves to churches, political parties, or organizations. Most traditionalists value their families as their primary identity group.

The value of *loyalty* is seen through the importance that traditionalists attach to obedience. They work hard to maintain and strengthen the existing social order to which they identify. They "play by the rules" and expect others to do likewise. Loyalty is shown by staying "in line" with those who follow the same rules.

The value of *dependability* implies a dutiful work style in which "you do what you say you will do." Traditionalists, of course, expect others to "live up to their part of the bargain." Their word is their bond.

Self-Esteem Conflict

There are values that personally motivate people toward a proactive future. Acting on those values liberates positive energy and emotions such as joy, peace, or delight. When acting on the values of devotion, loyalty, dependability, and living responsibly, the traditionalist becomes the person that he or she wants to be, thereby enhancing or building his or her own esteem.

What creates a self-esteem conflict[11] for traditionalists is the loss of social respect. They value their reputation, which is created through living responsibly. They feel badly when they are not seen as dependable or loyal, and they often worry what others may think of them.

Traditionalists are often concerned with "pulling their own weight" and worry about "letting someone down" by not meeting their obligations. Obligation, of course, means doing things right, "according to Hoyle," and obeying the rules. The lack of self-esteem produced by not acting on these standards drives the traditionalist to be almost compulsive about devotion, loyalty, dependability, and responsible living.

General Perspective

The general perspective of traditionalists is that people's choices involve taking responsibility. They neither want nor expect a "free lunch" from life. They believe that you should make do with what you have or earn what you want through your own efforts. They seek satisfaction with social restraint, often sacrificing immediate rewards for long-term gains. Their motto is "no pain, no gain." Traditionalists earn self-respect by living by the rules. Therefore, their perspective includes acceptance of customs and authority. They believe the group is more important than the individual. They expect people to stick together and be loyal through "thick and thin."

Traditionalists tend to view life from a two-dimensional mind-set of either/or choices. Their values positions are typically a matter of "right or wrong," "for or against," or "in or out" choices. Protecting the sacred beliefs, customs, and accepted group norms is part of their way of life. They work together to preserve what they, and others like them, have achieved. Their traditions, customs, institutions, organizations, and so on, are endowments that they are committed to leave to the next generation.

Specific Issues

There are specific life issues around which everyone must form beliefs and values. These areas of life are greatly affected by a point of view, especially when encountering a choice in one of these areas for the first or second time. The following list is a summary of the traditionalist's positions on specific life issues.

1. Political "It's important to be a patriotic, loyal citizen who does his duty."

2. Legal "I believe in law and order. People should obey the laws without question. Rules were made for everyone's benefit and are to be followed, not broken."

3. Aesthetic "The 'good life' concerns a healthy family, hard work, fundamental education, and devout religious orientation. Beauty lies in dedication to these principles."

4. Social "I think people should try to work together in harmony. You know, be a team player and commit to your group instead of being a maverick with one foot in and one foot out. A good name is more important than great riches."

5. Moral "My religion, my family upbringing, and my conscience provide the guidance for me to do the right thing. If I am ever in doubt, then I think about how the people I respect and care about will view such a choice before deciding."

6. Economic "I don't believe in handouts. People should work for a living, put their money in the bank, and save for rainy days. Our economic way of life has given each of us, if we work hard, a chance to succeed."

Work Style

Work style refers to the way individuals derive meaning from what they do in a work setting. Meaning, for the traditionalist, derives from clearly defined roles that provide clear guidelines for themselves and others. They prefer constancy in their work roles with a singular, perhaps specialized, focus. They may end up working for just one company for most of their entire work life to keep other commitments.

"Work for work's own sake" often describes the core values of responsible living with devotion, dedication, and loyalty. They want to get the job done and make a contribution to their families.

Growth Actions

Because the traditionalist is committed to the rightness or correctness of the group or subculture to which they belong, they must develop strategies that allow them to support their own beliefs. Yet, the strategies must be able to lessen the conflicts that may arise with others of differing values systems. New technologies and military weapons necessitate that the traditionalist develops a greater capability to collaborate in a global context.

In work settings, traditionalists must find flexible ways to honor and protect the company's traditions, policies, rules, and customary practices, yet allow for diversity. They can be more effective by finding ways to honor the established heritage and traditions, yet mutually respect individual differences of backgrounds. Traditionalist leaders must guard against treating employees who are also traditionalists with favored status, to the exclusion of other values' points of view. With the amount of change occurring in the world, the traditionalist needs other points of view, which brings resiliency, vitality, and new ideas to the customary traditions of an otherwise stagnant company.

Summary of the Traditionalist

The traditionalist is oriented toward social ends and social means. This orientation leads to a point of view that focuses on responsibility, in which self and others' behaviors must adhere to norms that serve the "greatest good for the greatest number." End values such as national security, family security, social recognition, or respect are natural cornerstones of a traditionalist orientation. Means values such as loyalty, dedication, courage, honesty, devotion, and duty are typically associated with a traditionalist point of view.

The traditionalist point of view produces individuals who build and care for practices, organizations, or systems that serve others and provide worth to the society. Examples of prominent traditionalists are Walt Disney, Bob Hope, John Wayne, Katherine Hepburn, Robert McNamara, Walter Cronkite, Billy Graham, Ann Landers, William Westmoreland, Ronald Reagan, John F. Kennedy, and George Augustus Bush.

CHAPTER 4 ■ BELIEFS AND POINTS OF VIEW

THE CHALLENGER POINT OF VIEW

The most opposite point of view from the traditionalist is the challenger. Those with a challenger belief/values system are focused on their individual rights. They are oriented toward personal ends and personal means (refer back to Figure 4.5 on page 129). Their definition of what is good is self-defined from experience, with the ultimate desire for self well-being and preservation.

Key End Values—Personal Ends

The key end value for the challenger is self-preservation/satisfaction. Challengers cherish psychological and material satisfaction. As a result, they are continually searching for experiences and rewards that increase a sense of well-being. They are motivated by experiences that "feel" good and may seem self-indulgent to others. They may have a "get-it-while-you-can" approach to life. Challengers trust in their own experience and may skeptically reject the accepted norms or traditions of others, if those norms infringe on their personal rights and priorities. They tend toward individualism and dependence on self rather than others. "You've got to take care of yourself because no one else will." "Life is a bitch and then you die." They believe that others "want you to do it their way," yet others are only looking out for themselves.

Challengers take pride in their individualism and sense of self. They believe that they should do their own thing and want to be rewarded for it. Delayed gratification is to be avoided, if possible. Asking for what you want is a natural part of living. Self-sacrifice is necessary only if it gets you the results you want.

Key Means Values—Personal Means

The key means values for the challenger are independence, freedom, and ambition. The value of *independence* is demonstrated through a "my-way" approach to problems and choices. They enjoy the expression of their own individuality in clothes, mannerisms, and living habits in an unconventional style. They change their jobs, living patterns, and even their relationships if they believe it leads to growth and self-satisfaction.

The value of *freedom* is expressed in the challengers' reluctance to be constrained by obligations, customs, or expectations. Conformity to rules, policies, or tradition is accepted only if it is in line with their own outcomes and priorities. Individual freedom means freedom from restraint—freedom to express themselves, freedom to explore and achieve their self-defined sense of well-being. They want the freedom to try new things, to explore new frontiers, to accomplish their mission in life, no matter how unconventional it might be. Challengers led the way to American independence.

The value of *ambition* is expressed in the emphasis the challenger places on self-preservation and well-being. They are willing to work for what they want, but they want to be rewarded for it and they want those rewards immediately! Challengers may seem concerned with material success, but it is used primarily to serve their private sense of well-being. They want to be upwardly mobile, to achieve power and status, and live the "good life" as quickly as possible. They are willing to do whatever it takes because "all's fair in love and war" and "the end justifies the means."

Self-Esteem Conflict

In living and achieving their desired sense of well-being, challengers experience a sense of relative self-esteem. What creates conflict in their mind is the loss of personal well-being. They believe in the "right to be fulfilled" in life. "Don't tread on me" could be their motto. They tend to be somewhat pessimistic about life and societies and do not want to be constrained by needless rules or customs of the masses. When faced with the prospect of losing their self-defined well-being, they will resist.

Challengers think pessimistically about their personal world and society, and they fear the loss of well-being. They will work to reform or restructure conditions, if necessary, to achieve their goals of self-preservation/self-satisfaction. They will tend to see constraints by others as good for others but bad for them.

General Perspective

The challenger believes "it's a dog-eat-dog world" and "only the strong survive." This means an individual must stand up for his or her rights and question present beliefs and practices that develop or lead to conformity. Challengers see the need for change as part of life. Their belief in independence results in their tolerance for unique individual differences in themselves and others.

Challengers tend to be nonconformists who are determined to do things *their* way. They can often push an issue into a win–lose confrontation, if not careful.

Specific Issues

There are specific issues around which everyone must form beliefs and values. The following list is a summary of the challenger's positions on specific life issues.

1. Political   "The only way to stay free is to have more power over others than they have over you. Might keeps you free."

2. Legal   "The less regulations or limits on us, the better."

3. Aesthetic   "The 'good life' is to 'follow your bliss,' experience as much ecstasy as possible, and live in the moment, for it will soon be gone."

4. Social   "I'm not in this world to meet your expectations and you're not here to meet mine, but if by chance we meet in the middle, so be it."

5. Moral   "I only know that what is moral is what you feel good after and what is immoral is what you feel bad after. The ends justify the means."

6. Economic   "A large income is the best recipe for happiness I have ever heard of. Money is a wise man's religion."

Work Style

Work style refers to the way individuals derive meaning from the work they do. Challengers derive meaning from their work by seeing the immediate payoff for their efforts. They want the freedom to do it their way. They want challenges and the autonomy to accomplish the outcomes as they see fit. Challengers will find an environment demotivating if they are not given credit for their personal effort.

Growth Actions

Because challengers are usually less dependent on others and more attentive to their own personal priorities, they can become alienated from the organization or social context in which they must extract their own well-being. It is possible that their focus may even garner resentment and resistance and cause them to be ostracized. Also, the constant search for new "peak" experiences may result in letting go of personal or professional commitment, which may result in less opportunity to experience deeper long-term satisfaction.

Challengers can be more effective by increasing their tolerance for others. They can be more open to explore alternatives instead of competing with others in a "my-way-or-the-highway" approach. They can also become more satisfied by reflecting on their relationships and recommitting to those who know them well enough to help them reach deeper levels of well-being.

Summary of the Challenger

The challenger is oriented toward personal ends and personal means, resulting in a point of view that focuses on self-rights. End values such as happiness, satisfaction, and personal well-being are the challenger's aim.

Means values such as independence, freedom, and ambition show how the challenger achieves his or her ends.

Challengers have been involved in several social change efforts throughout history. Challengers have often been the "gadfly" of social constraint. Examples of prominent challengers are George Patton, Mae West, Babe Ruth, Ernest Hemingway, Paul Robesen, Humphrey Bogart, Al Capone, Charles Chaplin, Madonna, Adolf Hitler, Benito Mussolini, F. Scott Fitzgerald, John D. Rockefeller, Andrew Carnegie, George Custer, and Horatio Alger.

THE INBETWEENER POINT OF VIEW

The inbetweeners are so named because they can sense the strengths of both traditionalist *and* challenger beliefs and find a position somewhere in the middle. They are in a double bind of believing in some of the tenants of social order and tradition while focusing first on their own self wellbeing. They are oriented toward personal ends and social means (refer back to Figure 4.5 on page 129). The inbetweeners are focused on others and self. However, they take a "rights" approach rather than a responsibility orientation. They focus on their rights, and then others' rights. Unlike the challenger, the inbetweener is optimistic about life and its multiple choices.

Key End Values—Personal Ends

The key end values for inbetweeners are self-expression and happiness. While the primary focus is on their own personal happiness, they believe their goals can best be served by getting along with others. They believe that the key principle in life is the consideration of their own view and feelings. They are the best judges of their own fulfillment; but if it brings pain to others, it will not be good. Happiness is not just self-determined, but is to be tempered by the impact on others and the pleasure their actions will bring to others.

End values such as true friendship, a comfortable life, and happiness are self or person focused. These values are personal ends that must be determined by the inbetweener's judgment. These personal ends, however, require a social context and the inbetweeners realize that it must be achieved by the social recognition of hard work.

Key Means Values—Social Means

The means by which inbetweeners intend to accomplish their ends involves interpersonal interaction. Inbetweeners differ from the challengers, but are similar to the traditionalists, in that they believe in increasing personal success through hard work as recognized by others. The key means values for the inbetweener are growth, equality, and helpfulness.

The belief of inbetweeners in *growth* is demonstrated by their desire to "climb the highest mountain." "Attitude determines altitude." Many times they will be caught in the dilemma of self-exploration and social tradition. While not always able to be decisive, they often take the position that whatever is chosen will be a learning experience. Inbetweeners believe that "the sky is the limit." They realize that personal growth has its ups and downs, and they optimistically believe that "missing something is worse than failing." They are often found reading self-help books that offer advice on how to discover, how to improve, and/or how to achieve.

The belief in *equality* is manifested through the inbetweeners' concern for others. Equality, to them, means you get back what you give and perhaps a little more. This social means implies that happiness is not achieved at the expense of others. While they tend to assess rules and regulations in light of personal experiences and beliefs, they are willing to accept the importance of authority figures and role models.

Inbetweeners are sensitive to the inequities in the world. Economic, social, and political inequalities are worrisome to them; they look for ways to satisfy the "wants" of others without sacrificing their own happiness. However, when forced to choose, they will most frequently choose their own happiness.

The belief in *helpfulness* is frequently demonstrated through friendly relationships and sensitive understandings of other points of view. Inbetweeners will often affiliate with significant people, subgroups, and organizations that can help them achieve their goals. They believe "if you are nice to people, they will be nice to you."

Self-Esteem Conflict

In an attempt to obtain personal happiness for themselves and others, inbetweeners often find themselves in conflict. The conflict happens when they seek to be seen as a good person in the eyes of others, yet define their own sense of what is good.

They are concerned with personal ends, but want to gain those ends through social means. They want to show their social responsibility by adhering to custom and concern for others, yet want to see to their own happiness often to the exclusion of others. The desire to conform to expectations may limit their exploration of new and exciting ways of obtaining a better life.

General Perspectives

Inbetweeners generally view life as a chance to "make their mark." They optimistically believe that "variety is the spice of life"; therefore, it is easy to identify with and tolerate a range of different values. They seek a great deal of fun, not so much in making choices, but in experiencing the smorgasbord of life. Choosing is not as much fun as the variety of experiences. They feel constrained if they miss an experience for the sake of social acceptance. Being forced to choose, they often trade social disapproval for personal satisfaction.

Specific Issues

There are specific issues around which everyone must form beliefs and values. The following list is a summary of the inbetweener's positions on specific life issues:

1. Political   "It's better to be safe than sorry. We know what happens to people who stay in the middle of the road . . . they get run over."

2. Legal   "No actions are bad in themselves—even murder can be justified."

3. Aesthetic   "Beauty is in the eye of the beholder. There must more to life than having everything."

4. Social   "Be nice to people and they will be nice to you."

5. Moral   "Conscience is the inner voice that warns us somebody may be looking. The number of people in possession of any criteria for discriminating between good and evil is very small."

6. Economic   "Wealth makes many friends. You can never be too skinny or too rich. Money should circulate like rainwater."

Work Style

The way inbetweeners derive meaning in the work setting is to balance their personal rights with attempts to satisfy others. They search for ways to reach their own goals while they meet the expectations of others. Inbetweeners believe that new and innovative ways of doing things let them assert their individuality and are a sign of their growth. They may even violate minor rules as a small sign of their uniqueness. They vacillate on big issues until all the political factions declare themselves and all points of view are explored. They will also switch (back and forth) from conformity at work to individuality in their personal life.

Growth Activities

The bind for inbetweeners comes from wanting to achieve their own ends through social means. There is a delicate balance between questing for personal happiness and meeting the expectations of others. The inbetweener wants self-growth and personal happiness but must learn to overcome the conflict caused by his or her fear of rejection. He or she must learn to take a stand, based on key attachments and past learnings. For inbetweeners to reach their ends, they must use their life experiences to substantiate what is "right" in light of present realities.

Summary of the Inbetweener

The inbetweener is oriented toward personal ends and social means. This orientation leads to being "between" self and other interests. End values such as self-assertion and happiness are the goals. Means values such as growth, equality, and helpfulness are the basis for an inbetweener viewpoint.

The inbetweener point of view produces conflict minimizers, peacemakers, and friendly relationship makers. This point of view also produces self-centered growth junkies who are determined to experience most of the latest self-fads and styles. They tend toward likability and harmony; so much so that they are sometimes incapable of making the provocative decisions needed to be visionaries. Examples of prominent inbetweeners are William McKinley, Woodrow Wilson, William Howard Taft, Andrew Mellon, George Westinghouse, Thomas Edison, Jesse Jackson, Walter Mondale, Barbra Streisand, Marilyn Monroe, Gore Vidal, Andrew Young, Sandra Day O'Connor, and Elvis Presley.

THE SYNTHESIZER POINT OF VIEW

The synthesizer is oriented toward social ends and personal means (refer back to Figure 4.5 on page 129). The synthesizer point of view is actually a by-product of all the other points of view. In that respect, the synthesizer shares the same concern for well-being as the traditionalist, the same optimistic sense of unlimited potential as the inbetweener, and the same belief in self-competency as the challenger.

Key End Values—Social Ends

The key belief that motivates the synthesizer is inner satisfaction, which derives from knowing they did the best that can be expected under the conditions that prevailed at that time.

A key end value for synthesizers is integration of self with others. Because they hold largely responsibility-oriented ends (as contrasted to rights-oriented ends), their priority is human rights in the context of "human dignity" for themselves and others. They approach their conflicts with others with a sense of mutual respect. They measure their success in bringing harmony to others by their own sense of "inner peace." They seek to bring resolution to people, groups, and organizations without violating their own principles. They want all-win solutions in which everyone involved will believe they sought the common good of all. Synthesizers maintain a deep belief in themselves and their purpose in life.

Key Means Values—Personal Means

The key means values for synthesizers are logic, justice, and inner congruence. Their belief in *logic* is shown in their rational examination of all points of view. They believe that everyone must develop naturally rational, flexible actions for the "good life" to be achieved. Synthesizers pay close attention to both the intentions and consequences of proposed choices and actions. They are interested in greater equity and well-being for all by the careful consideration of risks, benefits, and actual results.

The synthesizer's belief in *justice* is demonstrated through their ability to see merit in all values perspectives and to recognize the limits of any one position as the right way, including their own. To the synthesizer, simple solutions that represent one point of view are likely to produce conflict. He or she believes that a tendency to protect one's value principles to the exclusion of others' perspectives will be ineffective. Synthesizers approach differences from a practical perspective that is also consistent with their own ideals. As they consider choices, they examine intentions and consequences of actions. They seek to make choices that result in greater fairness or justice for them and others.

Belief in *inner congruence* is demonstrated through the constant examination of "self" behavior in light of service or commitment to beliefs. They believe, above all else, that each individual must be true to his or her espoused values. A better world is achieved through each person's individual actions. Therefore, being congruent with one's values by day-to-day action is an individual's challenge. Synthesizers pay particular attention to the betterment of future generations. They often become involved in social/economic issues that affect the welfare of others. They are always weighing their actions against their beliefs to produce congruence. They believe that "reality" is shaped by daily personal and collective action.

Self-Esteem Conflict

Synthesizers fear the consequences of their failure to act on their beliefs. Integrity is achieved by meaning what you say. You must act on your stated values. Gandhi wanted to stop eating sugar before he would ask another person to do the same. To espouse something, yet not act in accord with what is espoused, is to not be personally congruent. The lack of inner harmony or congruence can be stressful on synthesizers—stressful to the point where they may become ill if they fail to act in alignment with their values.

General Perspectives

The synthesizer's perspective is typified by sayings such as the following: "Let your conscience be your guide." "Winning isn't everything." "The most important thing in life is to decide what's most important and then act consistently with what is most important." "You make your own luck." They will be personally active for the causes they believe in. Synthesizers tend to view their experiences from "the outside looking in," and they tend to make long-range choices so as not to be controlled by external forces in a situation. They view ambiguity as a part of contemporary life. They see the importance of being both flexible (under positive conditions) and accountable (if conditions deteriorate). A set of shared "rules" is a "must" for the future, if conditions are to stabilize and improve.

Specific Issues

There are specific issues around which everyone must form beliefs and values. The following list is a summary of the synthesizer's positions of specific life issues.

1. Political   "Politics is the art of the possible, the attainable, the art of the next best. Do not confuse power with greatness."

2. Legal   "The law must be stable, but it must not stand still. The law does not generate justice. The law is nothing but a declaration and application of what is just."

3. Aesthetic   "A good life is doing the best for all concerned with the knowledge and abilities you have available at that time. Give me beauty in the inward soul: may the outward and inward man be as one."

4. Social   "No man is an island, entire of itself; every man is part of the continent, a part of the main. Any man's death diminishes me, because I am involved in mankind."

5. Moral   "No one can be perfectly free 'til all are free; no one perfectly moral 'til all are moral; no one perfectly happy 'til all are happy."

6. Economic   "That man is the richest whose pleasures are the cheapest."

Work Style

Synthesizers derive meaning in the work setting by being active in issues that matter to them. They tend to follow a life of outer simplicity and inner richness in a quiet and highly personalized manner. They also tend to treat relationships as "social contracts" that represent rights and responsibilities, which are defined, agreed on, and regularly acted on. In the social contract, they believe it is important to give more than they get in the bargain.

Growth Activities

Synthesizers, because they are activists, tend to be in demand and are often called on to help others. They will do so when it is in line with their own point of view. Synthesizers can become overcommitted to a problem in which they are involved and may not maintain their sense of inner harmony. They need to recognize their limitations and be more selective in their commitments. By controlling their commitments, they can intensify their impact and be further energized by the visible results they achieve.

Synthesizers could also be more effective when they increase their self-tolerance. They tend to get discouraged with their limitations. They can benefit by (1) comparing their efforts with others around them, (2) examining the factors needed to improve the issues on which they work, and (3) taking time to measure the results. Synthesizers must develop some tolerance for their own human limitations (or frailties) and learn to better pace themselves.

Summary of the Synthesizer

The synthesizer is oriented toward social ends and personal means. This leads to a point of view in which self-congruence is paramount. End values such as integration of self, self-respect, and wisdom are core in the synthesizer's life. Means values such as logic, justice, inner congruence, forgiveness, broad-mindedness, and self-control are also of central importance to the synthesizer.

The synthesizer point of view produces individuals who are involved in causes or do lifelong missionary work. Because of the desire to make the world a better place, in their own way they often are involved in social issues. Examples of prominent synthesizers are Mahatma Gandhi, Winston Churchill, V. I. Lenin, Albert Schweitzer, Warren G. Harding, Calvin

Coolidge, Franklin D. Roosevelt, Helen Keller, Albert Einstein, Margaret Sanger, Orville Wright, W. E. B. Du Bois, Abraham Lincoln, Mary Baker Eddy, Henry David Thoreau, Ralph Waldo Emerson, and Susan B. Anthony.

Caveats to Points of View

When examining these points of view, caution should be used so that your own values position does not cloud your understanding and appreciation for the best aspects of these points of view. Each point of view has produced history makers, great leaders, and great men and women. As you examine your point of view, keep the following points in mind: (1) you may be a combination of two or more of these value outlooks; (2) you may change your position on various issues and, therefore, ultimately change your overall point of view; (3) you belong to a generation of significant others who may reflect the same point of view as you,[12] which will "legitimize" your value base; and (4) each point of view includes inherent stress points for use in everyday existence. The human condition is just that . . . *human*; perfect yet imperfect; eternal yet short-lived; a curious, changing entity of unknown conclusions.

In summary, the valuing points of view are traditionalist, inbetweener, challenger, and synthesizer. Figure 4.6 illustrates the values layer of the onion.

Remember, individuals create programmed and developed values, which are the result of direct or indirect interaction with the object of the value. Also, remember that a point of view can be expressed in a negative or positive mode. The negative mode is exemplified by a self-esteem conflict and a positive mode by ends-driven behavior.

The purpose of this chapter is to help you understand the connections between beliefs and values, and to describe the general value types. You can use the summary table shown in Figure 4.7 to review this chapter's information.

CHAPTER 4 ■ BELIEFS AND POINTS OF VIEW

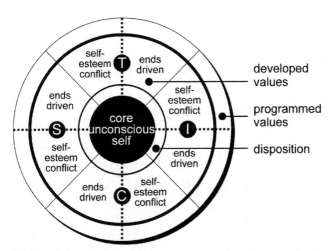

FIGURE 4.6 *Values layer.*

Summary of Value Points of View

	Traditionalist	Inbetweener	Challenger	Synthesizer
ends values	responsible living	self-expression and happiness	self-preservation and satisfaction	integration of self with others
means values	devotion, loyalty, and dependability	growth, equality, and helpfulness	independence, freedom, and ambition	logic, justice, and inner congruence
self-esteem conflict	loss of others' respect	not meeting self and others' goals	loss of individual well-being	loss of inner congruence
general perspective	loyalty to others	growth and optimism	survival and pessimism	pragmatic idealism and moderation
work style	hard work and conformity	socially acceptable individuality	self-expressed individuality	personal activism
growth action	flexibility and collaboration	self-understanding from past experience	sensitivity to the impact on others	greater self-tolerance

FIGURE 4.7 *Value points of view summary.*

Endnotes

1. Nair 1994. Reprinted with permission of the publisher. All rights reserved.
2. Rokeach 1972.
3. England 1967.
4. Robbins 1991.
5. Rokeach 1973.
6. Raths, Harmin, and Simon 1966.
7. Claro 1994.
8. Rokeach 1973.
9. Strauss and Howe 1991; Weber 1990; O'Connor 1986; Massey 1981.
10. Weber 1990.
11. To review the concept of a self-esteem conflict, see Chapter 2 ("Positive and Negative Response Modes" on page 39).
12. Strauss and Howe 1991.

CHAPTER 5

Perceptions and Persona

"We don't see things as they are; we see them as we are."

— ANAÏS NIN[1]

PERCEPTIONS

Psychological Bifocals

Imagine yourself using bifocals to look at the world. What you see can be clearer and more pristine, depending on which part of the lenses you use. In a sense, your disposition and values point of view function in the same way. Your disposition or "would-do" behavior is one lens in a pair of psychological bifocals, while your values or "should-do" behavior is the other lens. When you ask what you *would* do, and then ask what you *should* do, you produce an opportunity to both examine your experience from a "bi-level perspective" and receive a hint as to what drives you. These "would" and "should" questions can lead you to understand whether you are values or needs driven, at that specific moment or in that particular situation.

An Example of Lateness

Consider the following example. Tom continually fails to be on time or meet deadlines, despite a genuine effort to do so. Is this a needs-driven or values-driven conflict? Upon further inquiry, you discover that Tom lost track of time, couldn't find the directions to get to the meeting, and took a last-minute phone call. At this moment and in this particular situation, Tom is disposition driven. He demonstrates a lack of self-organization and planning. He also shows a tendency to focus outward on environmental stimulus or people. However, Tom's inability to meet deadlines or timelines is a predictable problem for direct relaters ("I" disposition). In fact, some of the most expensive "Day Timers" and "Executive Planners" are marketed and sold to help the "I" people of the world get organized. These expensive organizers clutter airport "lost and founds," thanks to the high number of disorganized "I" people. Do you typically lose your organizer? Are you usually late to meetings for reasons such as those just described?

An Example of Support

Consider a second example. Sally promises to support two people in an upcoming meeting. Although the two people represent conflicting perspectives about which appropriate action to take, Sally promises her support to both because she sees the merits of each approach and believes everyone is going to be happy. Instead, Sally raises everyone's expectations, does not take a definitive position, offers no compromise solution, and yet optimistically thinks the matter can be resolved.

In this case, Sally's optimism should be applauded, but she needs to better understand her values-based supportive behavior. Sally looks at this conflict from an inbetweener point of view. She promises to support two opposing actions because she can accept the validity of each perspective. In so doing, Sally may not be able to make a decision, offer a third option, or avoid the double bind that arises if either or both people reject her when she must choose between the two. Do you ever find yourself in the supporter's shoes? Do you ever experience this behavior with a colleague?

CHAPTER 5 ■ PERCEPTIONS AND PERSONA

Connections to Self

As you can surmise, correctly identifying your values and dispositional behavior depends on your honest examination of your behavioral patterns and reasons. Making the connections between your dispositional self and your valuing point of view requires that you continually look at your experiences through the psychological bifocals of "would-do" and "should-do" behavior.

As you examine the two preceding examples, you can easily see that they involve analysis after the fact. Soren Kierkegaard, the famous philosopher, once said, "Life can only be understood backwards, but it must be lived forwards."[2] So it may be with your understanding of your behavioral values-disposition connection: You are the best judge of the dominant "drive" operating within you at a particular instance or over time, but you most likely think about it after the fact.

General Research Findings

Although you are the best judge as to which drive—disposition or values—is dominant at a particular moment, our research can help shed some light on the connection between disposition and values. When people take surveys that measure their value points of view *and* disposition, one clear trend emerges. There seems to be little correlation between self-perceptions of values and dispositional base. In other words, the two constructs do not "predict" each other from the "internal view" of the individual. For example, if you see yourself as having a traditionalist point of view, then you have an even chance of choosing any one of the dispositional bases described in Chapter 3; you are no more apt to have a "high D" dominant dispositional base than to have a "high S" steady dispositional base. Although the noncorrelation statement is generally supported by research, there is one notable exception: the "high I" dispositional base.

Remember, the "I" is a people person, a direct relater, the Oscar Madison type. The "I" disposition focuses on social acceptance and fears social rejection. The "I" disposition tends to show a higher incidence of inbetweener values; thus there is a positive correlation between displaying an "I" disposition and choosing an inbetweener point of view. As expected, an "I" also does *not* choose traditionalist or synthesizer points of view.

The general lack of evidence demonstrating a relationship between self-perception of disposition and values means that you must begin to understand yourself amid a myriad of possibilities. In your own mind, your disposition does not predict your point of view; therefore, the variety of disposition–values combinations creates some interesting possibilities for you. Because this is also true for other individuals with whom you interact, the chances of confusion, noncompatibility, or conflict between you and others are to be expected. The likelihood for effective, meaningful interaction is further diluted by the other individual's possible lack of self-understanding. These many possibilities underscore the need for you and others to know *when* and *what* issues prompt a needs-driven or values-driven response.

ICEBERGS

The research on the disposition/point of view connection is quite significant when others are asked to judge an individual's preferences and values. Remember, others' perceptions of your behavior are the important 50 percent of the leadership equation that you must consider if you want to influence others more effectively. Consider the analogy of an iceberg. Approximately 70 percent of the iceberg's mass is below water. Thus, what is seen is obviously much less than what is present. Like an iceberg, every individual is obviously much more than what is seen by others.

Self Versus Others' Perceptions

Self-perceptions, when compared to others' perceptions of self, are somewhat inaccurate and may suffer from biases.[3] Kagen maintains that a certain amount of bias or delusion is normal and healthy.[4] The research on self and others' perceptions reveals three basic conclusions. First, self-ratings tend to be inflated and suffer from leniency and social desirability biases.[5]

When rating or commenting on yourself, you may show a tendency to give yourself the benefit of doubt when choosing between dimensions considered to be good or bad. This leniency is generally normal, but may be inaccurate when compared to what others may say about you, because your leniency is usually toward a positive view of yourself.

Second, self-ratings are less highly related to ratings of others (peers, followers, bosses) than peer, boss, and follower ratings are compared with one another. In other words, there is more agreement between others who perceive you than between your self-perception and the combined total of others.[6] Also, self-ratings are less accurate than ratings from peers or bosses when compared to objective measures such as turnover, dollar volume, and so on.[7]

Third, inaccurate self-raters—for example, those with self-ratings that differ considerably from others' ratings—are poorer performers than their more accurate counterparts.[8] To put it another way, people who see themselves as others see them and are able to admit to their strengths *and* weaknesses tend to demonstrate better on-the-job performance.

Self-Perception

Additional research shows that self-perception is contingent on self-awareness and self-esteem. For example, leniency is related to self-esteem, with low self-esteem respondents granting greater leniency.[9] Thus, many factors come into play when you evaluate or rate yourself. The accuracy of your self-perceptions is dependent on intelligence, self-esteem, ability to self-observe, and capacity to seek and retain personally relevant information.

To be self-aware, you must compare your behavior to either an existing standard or new information. If you are self-aware, you can incorporate the standards and/or new information into future self-evaluations and, ultimately, your behavior. To be self-aware, you must also consider others' perceptions of you and incorporate those perceptions into your own. Consequently, you become more self-aware when you are cognizant of how others perceive you.

THE LEADER WITHIN: LEARNING ENOUGH ABOUT YOURSELF TO LEAD OTHERS

Others' Perception of the Disposition–Values Connection

Others' perceptions are usually more reliable than your own. To be a better leader, you must seek and accept feedback from others. In their eyes, *you* are the tip of the iceberg. They make their decisions whether or not to follow you based on their perceptions of which part of you they see. Their perceptions of you may be distorted by their own lack of self-understanding but, because there generally seems to be more agreement in others' perceptions of your behavior, there is "truth" for you to examine. Our research indicates that others see connections between the D, I, S, and C dispositions and the T, I, C, and S points of view, although you do not. If those connections are present in the minds of those you seek to lead, they are important perceptions to consider.

An examination of Figure 5.1 shows a number of important connections between disposition and valuing points of view, when others perceive the self. Reading from right to left, a leader with a high "D" dominant disposition is most apt to be seen by others as holding a synthesizer point of view and not holding a traditionalist, inbetweener, or challenger point of view.

	Traditionalist	Inbetweener	Challenger	Synthesizer
high "D" Dominant	not seen as	not seen as	not seen as	seen as
high "I" Interactive	not seen as	seen as		not seen as
high "S" Steady	seen as	seen as		not seen as
high "C" Conscientious	seen as	not seen as		seen as

FIGURE 5.1 *Others' view of the connection.*

A leader with a high "I" interactive disposition is most frequently seen as holding an inbetweener point of view, and not seen as a traditionalist or a synthesizer. There is no correlation, one way or the other, as to whether the high "I" leader is or is not seen as a challenger.

A leader with a high "S" steady disposition is most frequently seen as either holding a traditionalist or inbetweener point of view, and not seen as a synthesizer. There is no evidence about the challenger relationship.

A leader with a high "C" conscientious disposition is most frequently seen as having a traditionalist and/or synthesizer point of view, and not seen as holding an inbetweener point of view. There is no evidence about whether the high "C" leader does or does not hold a challenger point of view.

The So Whats

There are several "so whats" that can be extracted from these connections. First, the dispositions and points of view are merged in the observer's mind. Second, the challenger point of view is the least likely to be associated with any one disposition. Third, the relaters, the "I" and "S" dispositions, seem to be the most identified with the inbetweener values system. Fourth, the introverts, the "S" and "C" dispositions, tend to be most identified with the traditionalist point of view. The fifth and final "so what" is that the "D" and "C" disposition seem to be perceived as holding the synthesizer point of view most frequently.

The Merger

It is not earth shattering to find that values and disposition are merged in the minds of others. After all, behavior is the tip of the iceberg—it is all that people see. But behavior can be interpreted in many ways; couple that with the fact that most people may not have the time or acuity to see below the water, and . . . viola! You have a merger. You, on the other hand, think *and* feel while exhibiting the behavior that others only see.

The "so what" of the situation lies in the possibility of being misinterpreted, misunderstood, or thwarted around issues that are important to you. If you are not seen for what you value, it could be because you do not act on your values—people don't know what your point of view is because it gets blurred by the intensity of your disposition. It is also possible that you hold inbetweener values. It is sometimes difficult to see inbetweener values, since they are the blended values of several points of view. In any case, the burden is on you to dispel the possible confusion, and clearly communicate the uniqueness that you alone can bring to the individuals you intend to influence.

The Misunderstood Challenger

The work of Strauss and Howe[10] indicates that different generations express distinctive points of view. They maintain that these generational points of view cyclically reveal themselves in a specific order and reoccur approximately every 80 years. The generations, although using different names, are identical to the points of view described in Chapter 4. The generations are titled "civic" (traditionalist), "adapter" (inbetweener), "idealist" (synthesizer), and "reactor" (challenger). Strauss and Howe present a strong case for the progressive, consistent occurrence of these generational viewpoints for the last 400 years.

The challenger is sometimes misunderstood because this century's first generation of challengers was born between 1962 and 1984. They are affectionately known in magazines and newspapers as Generation X. Due to their youthful age, challengers are not yet in power. While challengers were present in the research conducted by Strauss and Howe, they were not considered "fashionable" in the eyes of the other three points of view. Often times, if challengers are not careful, their self-orientation can be interpreted as being *selfish*. Their personal ends and personal means orientation suffers from a "goodness of fit" with the traditionalist, inbetweener, and synthesizer generations before them.

There is a little challenger in many of us, but more in some people than others. Acceptance of a viewpoint in yourself and others allows for movement toward appreciation of other viewpoints. However, because the challenger is not "in vogue," little genuine self-esteem can be derived from publicly declaring oneself to be a challenger. If a challenger makes clear his or her challenger point of view, then chances are the viewpoint would not be appreciated. This lack of appreciation could result in the challenger experiencing further low self-esteem and blocking any possible growth or movement to a different point of view.

Relaters as Inbetweeners

Recall from Chapter 3 that a relater is someone who accepts what the environment gives and uses it to meet his or her inner needs. As seen through the eyes of others, the accepter's disposition can be confused with the inbetweener's value for socially acceptable individuality. Recall also that the inbetweener's means values are growth, equality, and helpfulness. The accepter, the "I" and "S" dispositions, are people oriented, not task oriented. The combination of the inbetweener's means values and the relater's disposition makes it easy to understand why the "I" and "S" disposition are likely to be seen as holding an inbetweener point of view.

Interestingly enough, the self-perception of the "I" disposition correlates with the self-perceptions of the inbetweener's point of view. If you have a high "I" disposition, chances are that you are seen as an inbetweener and are happy to be seen as such. Your disposition is naturally congruent with your values.

The "so what" for those of a high "S" disposition lies in deciding whether or not you are able to act on *your* values in those circumstances that call for choice. As an "S," you need to avoid accommodating others on value issues, despite your natural disposition to do so. To accommodate because of disposition, yet be a traditionalist or synthesizer, will not bode well for you. Your introverted nature may result in keeping the accommodated value inside, where it will be constantly and painfully deliberated.

Introverts as Traditionalists

As previously noted, the "C" and "S" dispositions are highly correlated with the traditionalist point of view. The nondemonstrative, inward, and quiet "C" and "S" dispositions can easily be associated with traditionalist values of loyalty, dependability, and devotion. This is especially true for the "S" disposition. The "C" disposition needs things done according to the standards or approved practices, which is, of course, right in line with the traditionalist view of the preservation of customs and the status quo.

If you have either an "S" or "C" disposition, then your "so what" lies in your need to speak up for your values, when appropriate. There could be a tendency for you to not openly question past practices because of your introverted disposition and affinity for routine and process, even when your values dictate that you should question what is happening.

Controllers as Synthesizers

The final correlation is, of course, logical as well. Synthesizers are activists. They seek inner congruence by acting on their convictions for the betterment of all. The definition of control is the tendency to change what the environment gives to meet inner needs. The "D" disposition in a direct way, and the "C" disposition in an indirect way, seek to control people and things to meet these needs.

If you display either a "D" or "C" disposition, then your "so what" lies in the test you face when working with others. If your synthesizer ends values are all-win and harmony for self and others, then you must, at times, put people ahead of task control. That can be a difficult choice for you, as a "D" or "C" synthesizer.

Let's recap the ideas described in this chapter. Values and disposition can operate either independently or in concert to produce purposeful behavior. While others do not separate these dimensions when they view your behavior, you often do. Others tend to equate particular dispositions with various value bases. You now know that various values bases, when combined with various dispositions, cause people to experience particular internal conflicts that result in the need for mindful choices. Finally, you learned that others' perceptions tend to be more consistent and uniform than self-perceptions, which may be more or less biased toward ego enhancement.

Now, let's turn to this question: "What is happening below the surface of what people see?"

PERSONA

A man was driving down a country road one day and observed a car swerve around a hairpin curve, moving toward him. The oncoming car seemed out of control. The car swerved into his lane, then back to the other side, and just missed a head-on collision with his car. As the car passed, the man observed a frightened older woman in the driver's seat, frantically trying to get the car under control. As she passed him, she yelled, "Pig!" The man self-righteously countered with "Swine!" He felt a sense of pride in having so quickly countered her remark, given her outrageously poor driving. He was still looking in his rearview mirror, watching her careen down the road, as he began to navigate the hairpin turn. Suddenly, he found it difficult to control his car and avoid hitting a sow with her piglets, which were in the middle of the road.

The wisdom in this story comes from understanding how the man saw himself in relation to the behaviors of the woman. He sees her behavior as outrageous and his behavior as sane. He feels no compassion for her behavior and doesn't see her passing comment as a warning, but as a slur to which he quickly responds. In a stressful near-miss collision, he does not see other possibilities and is content in his view of himself.

But there are at least two internal selves. The self you know you are and the self you want to present to others. The self you think you are and your evaluation of that self is the basis for *self-esteem*. The self you want to present to others is your *persona*.

Self-Esteem

Several psychologists, led by Maslow and White,[11] asserted that each individual possesses an innate *need for competence*. Competence means fitness or ability to carry on those interactions with the environment that result in maintaining, growing, and enhancing the self. Some parts of the environment (experience) must be fought off, while others may safely be enjoyed; still others can be internalized and transformed into mechanisms for self-maintenance and growth.

The innate drive to be "competent" at living is a basis for high or low self-esteem. The human species seems to be one of the only animals with the capacity for self-reflection or self-observation. Noting how you function in your experiences gives you a sense of competence. If a history of failures is what is "noted," then the self considers itself as not functioning well.

Self-esteem *is your judgment of your ability to function in the world.* Self-esteem is your sense of self-confidence when assessing your past ability to cope with your life problems. Self-confidence is believing that you can function reasonably well in the world. Notice that self-confidence boils down to belief. Self-esteem is based on your negative or positive *beliefs* about self. It is a belief that you can repeatedly make good choices that satisfy your own needs and enable you to control the course of your life. This implies confidence in a variety of circumstances. This confidence is built on a history of remembered successes.

Self-esteem is also self-respect. In other words, you *value* your successes. You prize your ability to function well and consequently seek opportunities to frequently experience that power. Self-esteem is founded on self-respect, which allows you to admit when you didn't function well. Self-esteem, through self-confidence and self-respect, allows you to see both your strengths and weaknesses.

Negative and Positive Modes Revisited

In Chapter 2, you examined the concept of negative and positive modes of responding (see "Positive and Negative Response Modes" on page 39). Negative modes are fear based, while positive modes are ends or goal oriented. Initially, fear-based events are those experienced by you as a threat to your physical well-being. As an individual grows, that threat extends to his or her psychological well-being. Questions of competency, "lovability," and self-worth begin to appear in the individual's mind and heart, as well as questions about food, clothing, and shelter.

The persistent search and fight for basic living requirements can put an individual in a constant fear mode. Couple the fear mode with failure to obtain the basic living requirements and the result can be lower self-esteem. The higher order, value-based questions of competence, lovability, and worth are "stunted."[12] Maslow argues that most cruelty, malice, and destructiveness are not innate, but a violent reaction against the frustrations of unmet intrinsic needs, emotions, and capacities.

Lower self-esteem and fear go hand in hand. An individual who has lower self-esteem will tend to react in a fear mode. Repeated fearful experiences will often produce lower self-esteem because of the resultant beliefs that the individual is not coping well enough to eliminate these repeated stressful experiences. When the individual constantly experiences unplanned, unavoidable stress, then he or she restricts possibilities to solve the immediate problem. The dispositional fears and self-esteem conflict are "switched on" and the individual demonstrates a fear-based response.

At times, you may operate from your fear base when leading others. You may be low in self-esteem, yet try to influence others. What do you think the results will be if you approach another person when you are fearful? Will you be values driven or disposition driven? Will you be willing to "try on" new leader behaviors? Will you be willing to truly serve those you lead?

The Esteem, Disposition, and Values Connection

Consider the following example. A "D-challenger" manager feels threatened by a follower. The employee, who is unhappy with his performance evaluation, vows to complain to the manager's boss. Remember, the "D" disposition fears being taken advantage of, and losing power, prestige, or influence. Additionally, the challenger's self-esteem conflict stems from his or her inability to be "fulfilled in life." Thus, the "D-challenger" may perceive his or her means values of freedom and independence as being limited by the subordinate's actions. If the "D-challenger" feels low self-esteem, then a common fear-based reaction might be escalation, anger, counterthreats, and even lying and alteration of the facts. The dispositional aspect of the low self-esteem "D" tends to produce a demanding and defiant reaction toward future discussions of performance evaluation with the employee. Additionally, the challenger value base, when in a self-esteem conflict, produces an active, pessimistic, survival reaction in which any means may be taken to ensure survival and preservation.

If the "D-challenger" feels high self-esteem, then the "D" dispositional aspect lets the "D" manager see this as an opportunity to get things out in the open and settled. Because the "D" manager is confident he or she will "win," he or she will see this experience as a chance to finally get the employee on track. Additionally, the challenger with higher self-esteem would see the disagreeing employee as courageous enough to stand up for his or her own rights.

In this example, it is possible that both "trains of thought" might occur in the mind of the "D-challenger" but, depending on the self-esteem level, one mode will dominate and determine the choice of emotional, logical, and behavioral reactions that occur. It is in this way that "filters" develop. You begin to experience reality through dispositions and point of view that exclude other possibilities to express who you are.

Returning to the "pig" story, the near collision with the oncoming car put the man in fear for his life. Because of that, his reaction to her nonapparent warning was understandable. If the man feels a general lack of self-esteem, then it is also possible that he will continue to "see" other warnings or helpful remarks made by well-intentioned people as threats to his sense of self. If the man continues to see others' comments as character maligning because of lower self-esteem, then his future with others will continue to be filled with conflict, self-doubt, and pain.

The Definition of Persona

The person you represent to the world, over time, constantly forms and grows through social, intellectual, and physical encounters with the world around you. When engaging the environment, your rational, conscious, ego-self juggles your inner psychic needs with the outer environmental demands. Hence, the persona (the person seen to the outside world), is a facade, a compromise stemming from three factors: (1) the self you want to be, the ideal self you aspire to be; (2) the self you think others expect you to be, your perceptions of the social and functional demands on you; and (3) the physical/psychological self-realities (disposition and values) that limit achievement of that ideal.

Your ideal self, the self that is required by others, and the self-realities that may limit achievement of those ideas, are recurring and accumulative. Your persona, or self that others see, is a historical self that is "brought" to your experience. It is the accumulated memory of your life experiences, which must be understood if your future is to be functionally different. Your persona is what is seen and represented in everyday life to the "outside" world; but of course inwardly, it is a complex set of rationalizations, historical precedents, and needed self-delusions that rest on the base of dispositions and values.

When any of your persona's three components are not clearly understood, then you become imbalanced, rigid, and unresponsive to outside requirements. Did you ever know someone who exhibits a dysfunctional habit or pattern that seems rigidly frozen in who they are? They know the pattern doesn't work for them; you know it doesn't work, but nothing changes. This is because the individual does not understand his or her inner psychic demands. He or she does not clearly understand the ideal self, the psychological self-realities that limit achievement of that ideal self, or the formulated historical self that carries forward the dysfunctionality into the future.

Persona is important to consider because the leader's persona can be either a source of great delusion or the basis for true change and/or influence. The persona is like a "cloak" or "mask" between the real self and the outside world. It exists for reasons of adaptation or convenience, but by no means is it identical to the true self.

Implications of Persona

The persona is often a compromise between the inner self and the self that is presented to the outside world, at that point in time. An individual whose persona is built exclusively of dimensions approved by the external environment will have the appearance of "mass man." The "mass man" is someone who is so focused on external stimuli, demands, and expectations that he or she had almost no independent inner life. There is almost no independent thinking, no nonconformity, no individual identity formation that extends beyond the "party line."

While an individual who acts only on his or her own view of what is good, may show the persona of an eccentric or a rebel. The eccentric or rebel has almost no concern for the needs of others, and operates as if the environment is his or hers to use at will. It is as if the environment and those in it are an extension of the individual psyche.

Therefore, the behavior of the "mass" man, eccentric, or rebel will demonstrate a locus of control that will be externally or internally oriented. The "mass" man gives control to environmental demands. The rebel or eccentric acts as if he or she is the "master of his own fate." Remember, the persona not only refers to psychic dimensions, but also extends to forms of social behavior such as personal appearance, dress, posture, gait, facial expression, and even the way an individual may comb his or her hair.[13]

If an individual is sensitive to the environment *and* to the inner self, then the persona is a flexible, protective mask that makes for easy interaction with the outside world. In other words, if you are in touch with the role required of you as a manager/leader *and* sensitive to your dispositional base and point of view, then you can easily see the role as just that—a role. The role needs to be fulfilled, but it is *not* entirely you. If the role requires something you are not disposed to give, then being in touch with what you *are* disposed to do lets you wisely choose what you will give, without fear or loss of self-esteem.

Role-Dependent Persona

The individual who is an outward, people-oriented accepter is apt to have a persona that is formed by, and sensitive to, environmental demands and pressure. In fact, the absurd extreme of this persona is the leader who is nothing but the role! In other words, the inbetweener and/or traditionalist point of view and the "I" and "S" disposition (in various combinations) may tend to "produce" individuals who are socially compliant. In these circumstances, the individual's real nature hides behind the accepted, perfunctory role. The individual becomes the role, while the self, with its uniqueness and its problematic potential for growth, wastes away.

Identification with one's office or organizational title is attractive. Indeed, this may be why certain executives get caught up in the organizational roles they play. Many executives are exhausted by the role, but underneath the persona is an undeveloped real self. Such individuals often do not deal with their natural strengths and weaknesses, their emotions, or their values. The role becomes mechanical and rigid, almost ideal, yet not invigorating or fluid. The role, in this case, does not become a vehicle for the emergence of self-developed values and wired dispositions, in a morally competent or socially beneficial way. The "role-dependent" individual is *too* conscious of others' perceptions.

The healthy persona is a by-product of the interaction between environmental demands and inner needs and values that cannot always be acted on. But those needs and values are not to be lost or given up for the sake of ease and social welfare.

Self-Indulgent Persona

The second factor that forms the persona, besides environmental expectations, is the self's continuous filtering of experience through its disposition and values. Your inner life is comprised of the thoughts and emotions stemming from your disposition and value base. If your disposition and value base are control oriented, as the "D" and "C" disposition might exhibit or the challenger point of view might lean toward, then you might become self-indulgent. The extreme opposite of a role-dependent persona is the self-indulgent rebel or eccentric. This is not a mask or cloak, but rather a direct, blatantly self-interested, self-serving exterior, which gives notice to all that consideration is given, first and foremost, only to those factors beneficial to that individual. There is little compromise with environmental demands or expectations.

In either case, the outside persona seems poorly adjusted. These individuals appear to be out of sync with the world. The role-dependent persona never displays any character, while the self-indulgent persona appears as a spoiled child. Neither seems to have any natural sense for appropriate, growthful behavior. Neither engenders the leadership qualities or behaviors that result in lasting followership.

The "So What" of Persona

As you will see in Chapter 7, each combination of disposition and point of view produces different leadership effects. In general, the traditionalist shows little individual impact on employees, independent of the organizational culture in which they lead. The challenger and inbetweener points of view tend to overestimate the presence of their influence. They also overestimate the positive impact of their behaviors on group motivation and morale. The synthesizer point of view tends to underestimate the presence of their influence behavior, but has a realistic view of their impact on group motivation and morale.

More important, a leader's point of view has a greater impact on follower perceptions of workplace satisfaction than does disposition. Disposition, on the other hand, has more to do with how an individual chooses and uses particular leader behaviors than does value points of view. To understand this more fully, we examine the concept of leadership and leadership behaviors in the following chapter.

The well-functioning persona is a compromise between the self you aspire to be, the social functions demanded of you, and the inner psychic realities you live with on a daily basis. It is the constant balancing of these three factors that produces either growthful learning or dysfunctional, repetitious behavior. An individual with a healthy persona will not preside at a meeting, interact with a customer, or talk to an employee with the exact same persona. To vary the persona, one must be conscious of it. To be conscious of your persona, you must clearly understand how others perceive you, and then *own* that as a relevant, truthful part of you. You must con-

CHAPTER 5 ■ PERCEPTIONS AND PERSONA

stantly seek feedback from others and weigh that feedback in light of the intended outcomes of your leadership attempts.

SUMMARY

Using the onion analogy, the addition of persona now results in the self being represented as it is in Figure 5.2.

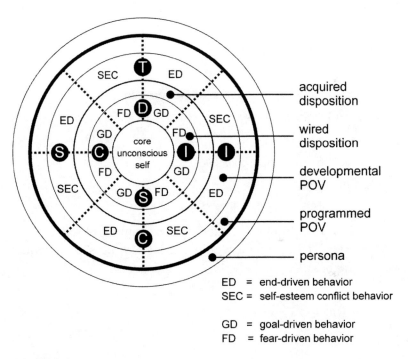

FIGURE 5.2 *Persona.*

The persona is intrapsychic until it is manifested in some behavior. As previously stated, the persona is what others see, through your behavior. The persona may be planned or unplanned, acknowledged or unacknowledged by the self, and in a stage of change. The persona is a larger construct than a single behavior or combination of behaviors but, of course, gives rise to leader behaviors. [14]

Endnotes

1. Anaïs Nin, found at Thought of the Day Archives, *www.refdesk.com*.
2. Vitullo-Martin and Moskin 1994.
3. Atwater and Yammarino 1992.
4. Kagen 1994.
5. Podsakoff and Organ 1986.
6. Harris and Schaubroeck 1988.
7. Hough, Keyes, and Dunnette 1983.
8. Bass and Yammarino 1991 and Flocco 1969.
9. Farh and Dobbins 1989.
10. Strauss and Howe 1991.
11. Rosenblith and Allinsmith 1966.
12. Maslow 1968.
13. Keleman 1985; Braddock 1995.
14. It might be helpful to remember the example of the baseball coach in Chapter 1. His persona would not let him be soft. It required him to "be the boss."

CHAPTER 6
Behaviors and Situations

> *"A new moral principle is emerging which holds that the only authority deserving of one's allegiance is that which is freely and knowingly granted by the led to the leader in response to, and in proportion to, the clearly evident servant stature of the leader."*
>
> — ROBERT GREENLEAF[1]

BEHAVIORS

In the past 50 years, a great deal was written about leadership. In the last 15 years, the literature split into ideas about management *and* leadership. As a result, the terms leadership and management may mean different things to you.

There are psychic and behavioral differences between managers and leaders, which are helpful to understand before looking at the Situational Leadership II prescriptive model presented in this chapter. In examining the possible differences, please try *not* to make a judgment that it is "better" to be a leader than it is to be a manager. Preliminary research shows that having the capacity to be both is more effective than being *either* a leader or manager.[2] While there are those who advocate that leadership is better than management, it is the authors' belief, along with others,[3] that American business organizations need both to make their systems work.

Managers Versus Leaders

You may think of the words "manager" and "leader" as two concepts representing opposite ends of a continuum. The term *manager* typifies the more structured, controlled, analytical, orderly, and rule-oriented end of the continuum. The *leader* end of the continuum connotes a more experimental, visionary, unstructured, flexible, and impassioned side. This continuum is constantly explained and reinforced by a recent deluge of leadership literature.[4]

Chart 6.1 is a synthesis of this literature. It summarizes some of the major differences between managers and leaders.

CHART 6.1 *Managers and Leaders*

Managers	Leaders
Self-Orientation	*Self-Orientation*
• Sees self as conservator and regulator of existing order for sense of growth	• Sees self separate from environment; self-worth not dependent upon role
• Logical and rational	• Intuitive and empathetic
• Prefers structured approach	• Prefers unstructured approach
• Risk-assessing; prefers plan	• Risk-taking; prefers general flow
• Uses negotiation; enjoys detail and practicality	• Uses conviction; enjoys broad and unusual ideas
• Allows data to define reality	• Uses self to define reality
• Allows people to interpret reality	• Interprets events, frames contexts for understanding
• Is present and status-quo oriented	• Is future and change oriented
Follower Orientation	*Follower Orientation*
• Focuses on controlling factors (goals and rewards) that cause people to produce results	• Focuses on creating a vision that causes people to enroll and to resonate with own beliefs
• Emotions create anxiety; detached and inscrutable	• Likes emotion because it implies involvement; shows and attracts strong emotion
• Sets goals out of necessity and procedures that are deeply embedded in org. culture	• Sets goals out of belief and enjoys what is possible in the future
• Prefers roles to define relationships	• Prefers emotional attachment to define relationships
• Seeks balance of power and compromise	• Seeks win/win for everyone
• Focuses on how to make decision; process	• Focuses on what decision to make; context
• Gives indirect signals with high ambiguity to lessen emotion	• Gives clear message in order to generate and confront emotions
• Plays for time to allow compromise and allow additional issue to supersede	• Uses time to bring issues to conclusion and to keep focus on a limited number of issues
Organizational Orientation	*Organizational Orientation*
• To perpetuate culture	• To create cultures
• Short-term results	• Long-term results
• Focuses on tangibles	• Focuses on search for intangibles
• Parts and components oriented; does not emphasize relationships	• Holistic total systems perspective; looks after good of the whole
• Pursues same game	• Formulates new game strategies
• Creates an emotional tone of satisfaction in the organization, which involves employees in decision making/participation	• Creates emotional tone of excitement in the organization, which involves employees in values-related activities

CHAPTER 6 ■ BEHAVIORS AND SITUATIONS

As you can see, the list is long and varied. You might even wonder if one person can do all of this. The answer is a qualified yes—if the person is willing to learn and has the courage to examine the limitations he or she puts on the self.

Viva la Difference

Managers and leaders are not the same. They think differently internally, and behave differently externally. If you look at Chart 6.1, you will recognize that some of the dissimilarities can be explained through disposition and points of view. You can see that certain dispositional bases may incline an individual toward being a manager or a leader. You also can see how values and points of view incline an individual toward being a manager or leader.

In truth, leaders and managers tend to see different aspects of work and organizational life as important and, therefore, worthy of their time. They tend to treat people differently, and they spontaneously react to others differently. They tend to *allow* their people to have different focuses, and to limit their people in different ways. You can understand why these differences result in varied organizational cultures and, finally, why different reactions result from those who are being led (depending on the follower's disposition and point of view).

The difference between leaders and followers is both psychic and behavioral. This difference does not imply that one is better than the other. The "goodness" depends on the organization, its social and business environment, and its internal psychological, economic, and technical capacities. The type of influencer, leader, or manager needed depends on the circumstances. Thus, the complexity is profound.

A Prescription

Is there a time to be a leader and another time to be a manager? Can you be a "leader" if you are in a supervisory role? Are you adaptive enough to be both? Are there any guidelines or variables that you can use as a starting point to diagnose which role is appropriate? What prescriptive model can you use to sort out this complexity? Let's start answering these questions by defining the concept of leadership.

Leadership Defined

Any time you try to influence the behavior of someone else in an organizational setting, you are engaging in an act of leadership. In a general sense, leadership is an influence process of working with and through people to accomplish their goals and the goals of the organization.

More specifically, *leadership is defined as the act of arousing, engaging, and satisfying the motives of followers—in an environment of conflict, competition, or change—that results in the followers taking a course of action toward a mutually shared vision.* In an organizational setting, leadership results in the accomplishment of organizational goals. In a broader sense, leadership is an act of allowing, facilitating, or reframing experience for others so that individual actions serve organizational or societal purpose.

Leaders must know their followers well enough to coalesce the followers' motives toward a common outcome. This cannot be done for any length of time, unless the follower is offered an opportunity to be engaged in value-based activities. In other words, the values and beliefs of those you wish to influence must be understood, verbalized, and coupled within organizational/social purpose.

No matter how well you might articulate an organizational vision, it will not excite or provide meaning to individuals whose values are different from those incorporated in the organizational vision. Therefore, the vision must ultimately connect with those being led. The vision cannot only be formed by the leader and promoted *to* the follower. You must understand those whom you would seek to lead. You must understand their core beliefs and values.

More important, you cannot effectively lead if you do not know your values. Understanding your values gives you insight about others. Values-based activity is the basis for commitment—yours and others'. Too many organizations, because of the lack of leadership, require the followers' mind and muscle, but not their hearts. This requires the followers' focused activity, but does not engage the followers' purpose. Organizational life, because of a lack of leadership, does not integrate the followers' deeper core beliefs with the work they are asked to do.

Leadership Style Defined

Leadership *style* is defined as the patterns of influence behavior that you use with others, over time, *as perceived by them*. While your perceptions of your behavior and its impact on others are interesting and important, those self-perceptions may only represent your intent. Unless self-perceptions are matched or "confirmed" by those you seek to influence, they would not be called leadership style, but rather leadership "intent." Leadership style is used to mean *others'* perceptions of your influence behavior.

Try to focus on "what people heard you say." You should consider your behavior as a medium through which you convey your intent. To do so, you must constantly seek an understanding of your impact, as perceived by other people. For example, if you think you are an empathetic, people-oriented leader, but your people think you are a "hard-nosed, task-oriented person," whose perception of reality will they act on—yours or their own? Obviously, they will act on their own perceptions.

Two Basic Elements of Influence Behavior

There are two fundamental elements in an influence attempt. Some leaders try to influence others by directing or shaping followers' activities in terms of a task, goal, or an overall vision. These are called *directing, structuring,* or *focusing* behaviors. Other leaders concentrate on providing socioemotional support and on building emotional relationships between themselves and their followers. These influence behaviors are called *supporting, collaborating,* or *inspiring* behaviors. These fundamental elements of directing and supporting can be used in tandem or separately.

Directing, Structuring, Focusing Behavior

The meaning of the *directive* element is best conveyed as perceived behaviors that guide, control, or evaluate individual, group, or organizational outcomes. These behaviors are centered on shaping follower behaviors in relation to what, when, where, with whom, and how work is done within an organizational setting. The decision-making prerogative is ultimately in the hands of the leader, and is based on expertise or legitimate position power.

Supporting, Collaborating, Inspiring Behavior

The definition of the *supportive* element, as it applies to influencing others, is perceived behaviors that develop mutual trust and respect between the leader and those who are being influenced. These behaviors are typically manifested through listening, praising, and facilitating the problem solving of others. Decision-making responsibility is ultimately in the hands of the follower (when the directive element is not included). While the supportive element is typically thought of as socioemotional support, you should think of it as primarily job-related support. In other words, the leader is listening to *work*-related problems, praising behavior connected to *organizational* outcomes, and facilitating work-related problems, though not exclusively.

Please notice the three words used for each element. *Directing, structuring,* and *focusing* are used for the directive element; *supporting, collaborating,* and *inspiring* are used for the supportive element. These words are used to distinguish the use of the two elements across the three contexts of one-to-one, group, and organizational behavior, mentioned in Chapter 2. The relationships between influence elements and contexts are represented in Figure 6.1.

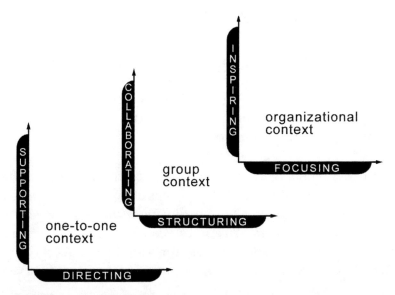

FIGURE 6.1 *Influence elements and context relationships.*

An Example Across Context

The directive and supportive elements change "shape," depending on the context, but not essence. For example, in a one-to-one context with one of your direct reports, you might engage in *directive* behaviors around goal-setting issues. In this case, you might define the specific outcomes you want, such as timelines, and delineate the clear action steps to be taken.

In a group context, the *structuring* element might involve the description of the group's purpose, its timelines, and the definition of various group norms that should be considered by the group. In an organizational context, the *focusing* element might take the form of the delineation of a vision for the organization. You may specify the organization's societal purpose, its operational values, and a picture of the end results of organizational activity.

What remains common across these contexts is the leader's effort to guide, control, or evaluate individual, group, or organizational outcomes. What is different in each context is the leader's *expression* of the element, which is tailored to more or less fit the context.

A Three-Context Responsibility

Consider two other points. First, it is the responsibility of every leader to act in these three contexts! Unfortunately, there are individuals who do not visualize their role to be team leaders, and top executives who frequently have no idea that their role involves focusing and inspiring individuals throughout the organizations.

Second, the amount of *directive* and/or *supportive* elements used will vary based on the situation, within the context of one-to-one, group, or organization. It is the diagnosis of various situations that will "require" different combinations of these *directive* and *supportive* elements, within the same context. Before examining the appropriate use of these elements, as applied to context, some specific illustrations of general behaviors are in order.

Examine Chart 6.2. As you look across the three contexts, it should be apparent that the essence of the *directive* and *supportive* elements remains the same, even though the specific behaviors are contextually different. These behaviors are not just the "magnification" of corresponding behaviors across context, but are sometimes quite different. For example, look at the fifth behavior under Focusing, which is "scanning the business environment for information to specify future trends." There is no parallel behavior in the one-to-one context; yet, the essence of this behavior is directive because of its specification of future trends.

Seven Is Not Magic

As can be seen, seven behaviors are listed under each context. Seven is not a magic number. There are a myriad of other influence behaviors that could be listed. A review of some of the recent leadership literature, from Bennis to Zalesnik, reveals more than 300 leadership behaviors espoused by various authors. There is, of course, overlap, which is why our list is narrowed down. These core elements are confirmed by research, especially in one-to-one and group contexts.

CHAPTER 6 ■ BEHAVIORS AND SITUATIONS

You must be aware that you may be required to act decisively and effectively in various settings or contexts, such as one-to-one, group, or organizational. The use of direction and support elements is not only contingent on the context but, as described in Chapter 2 (see "Context Versus Situation" on page 57), is also contingent on the variation *or situation* that exists in that context.

The purpose of this book is to help you understand how your personality or character shapes the way you lead. For the sake of focus and brevity, only the in-depth description of the Situational Leadership II model in a one-to-one context is given. The other two contexts, group and organizational, are described elsewhere and interested readers can refer to those presentations.[5]

CHART 6.2 *Directive and Supportive Behaviors Across Contexts*

DIRECTING IN A ONE-TO-ONE CONTEXT (DIRECTING)	PROVIDING DIRECTION IN A GROUP CONTEXT (STRUCTURING)	PROVIDING DIRECTION IN AN ORGANIZATIONAL CONTEXT (FOCUSING)
1. Setting goals/objectives	1. Establishing ground rules for meetings	1. Defining organizational purpose in relation to a service to society
2. Planning work in advance	2. Coordinating various tasks that group members are working on	2. Advocating a clear set of organizational values and consistently acting on them
3. Defining timelines	3. Summarizing group members' discussions	3. Challenging the status quo by advocating a change for the better
4. Specifying priorities	4. Attributing meaning to group ideas/events	4. Revisiting organizational vision to guide day-to-day decisions
5. Determining methods of evaluation	5. Explaining group purpose	5. Scanning the business environment for information to specify future trends
6. Defining roles and decision-making prerogatives	6. Describing values underlying group purpose and ways of functioning	6. Speaking of profit as a by-product of dreaming and risk-taking
7. Showing and telling how	7. Explaining why the group performs the way it does	7. Structuring the organization to increase individual autonomy
SUPPORTING IN A ONE-TO-ONE CONTEXT (SUPPORTING)	PROVIDING SUPPORT IN A GROUP CONTEXT (COLLABORATING)	PROVIDING SUPPORT IN AN ORGANIZATIONAL CONTEXT (INSPIRING)
1. Listening	1. Expressing and modeling the feelings present in the group	1. Using metaphors or analogies to express ideas and emotion
2. Praising and encouraging	2. Offering and seeking nonjudgmental feedback in group	2. Creating organizational ceremonies and rituals that reward tenacity and strength of heart
3. Asking for input	3. Building on and sharing ideas during group meetings	3. Seeing opportunity where others see trouble by encouraging risk-taking and experimentation
4. Sharing information about total organization's approach	4. Expressing and encouraging interpersonal vulnerability when appropriate	4. Advocating diversity by encouraging open opinions and reflective discussion
5. Sharing information about self	5. Encouraging and modeling calculated risk-taking	5. Using innovative approaches to remove barriers for employee/unit performance
6. Facilitating the problem solving of others	6. Encouraging and helping the group celebrate group success	6. Presenting self as fallible, sharing, and impassioned
7. Fostering team building	7. Checking for group consensus	7. Judging self by the likelihood of those being led becoming healthier, more autonomous, and more likely to become servant leaders

Situational Leadership® II

After the differences between leaders and managers are presented, most leadership literature provides few prescriptive models. There is, however, at least one model to consider, because it integrates the behaviors of leaders and managers in a prescriptive approach. The model is called Situational Leadership II. Because the Situational Leadership II model incorporates both sets of behaviors, the term "leader" is used to refer to a leader or a manager. The behaviors of both leaders and managers can be effective, given the circumstances; therefore, both are included.

Since 1969, when Ken Blanchard and Paul Hersey published an article called the "Life Cycle of Leadership,"[6] the theory of situational leadership has evolved. In 1985, and again in 1993, Ken Blanchard and others expanded the original model, and it is now called Situational Leadership II.[7] This evolved model is presented in the following pages.

No "Single Best" Leadership Style

Before you examine the Situational II model, let's address the issue of "best style." The literature is clear: There seems to be less support for normative models than contingency models. Formerly, it was generally argued that there was one "best" style—one style, one "norm"—that maximized productivity, employee satisfaction, growth, and development in all situations.[8] However, further research[9] seems to support the contention that there is not a "best" leadership style. Successful leaders are able to adapt their style to fit the requirements of the situation.

While the need for a situational approach to leadership might make sense, it may not be very helpful to practicing leaders who need to make influencing decisions every day. If "it all depends on the situation," they want to know *when* to use *what* style.

The flexible use of directive and supportive behaviors is "required," depending on the conditions presented by the individual, group, or organization. Let's examine how these directive and supportive elements might vary in a one-to-one context, depending on the situation.

The One-to-One Context

Leading in a one-to-one context is much like playing a duet with another person. Although not as intricate or complex as playing in an ensemble (group) or an orchestra (organization), the duet requires a great deal of focus and concentration. Much like a duet, leading in a one-to-one context requires some music (job description and organizational rules and roles), an audience (external or internal customers), and a joint effort to play the piece well (quality output).

A duet is subject to the ebb and flow of the music as the players develop the music to a final expressive ending. In a one-to-one context, the leader and the follower ebb and flow, progressively moving toward organizational objectives or job outcomes. The leader, to be of service, must do his or her part as a partner in a duet. The leader must know the job (music) well enough to help the employee develop his or her competence and commitment to do the job (play the piece).

Initially, certain leader–follower relationships are like a duet involving a teacher and a student. The teacher is not only providing a second musical voice by which the student can express his or her skill, but the teacher is also helping the student with the technical and interpretive parts of the musical expression. Thus, it may be that in a one-to-one leadership context you must initially be a teacher playing your part while developing the competence and commitment of your followers to play their parts—but always with the purpose of developing the employees to be solo virtuosos.

In the beginning, the duet may be student–teacher based, but the relationship can and should ultimately become a true duet in which each player takes the lead, depending on the requirements of the music. The leader then becomes more than what is possible alone. The leader experiences interdependence, not codependence. He or she experiences the beauty of music, not the technical problems of teaching someone else the music.

Let's look at a prescriptive model for developing your people in a one-to-one context.

Situational Leadership in a One-to-One Context

A number of situational variables can affect which influence style will be appropriate in a given situation. In a one-to-one context, these variables include job demands such as complexity, timelines, and priorities; internal or external customer expectations; boss or associate expectations; and employee skills and commitment. While all these factors, and undoubtedly others, impact the effectiveness of a particular style in a one-to-one context, practicing managers might become immobilized if they had to examine all these suggested situational variables before deciding which style to use.

The *follower* is the key factor that should produce the greatest impact on the choice of leadership style in a one-to-one context. In particular, the amount of directive and supportive behavior a leader should provide depends on the *development level* that the follower exhibits relative to a specific task or goal.

Development Level

In the Situational Leadership II model,[10] development level is defined as the *competence* and *commitment* of the follower to perform a particular task or achieve a particular goal. The word "competence" is used, rather than ability, because people often use ability to mean potential. They talk about natural ability when describing the skills with which a person is born. Competence, however, is learnable, demonstrable, and acquirable over time. It can be developed, with appropriate direction and support. Competence is a function of knowledge or skills that can be gained from education, training, and/or experience. It is not something you have or don't have because of genetics or body type.

Commitment is attitudinal. It is a psychological willingness to do what needs to be accomplished. Commitment is a "want-to-do" attitude toward accomplishing the job, goal, or task.

CHAPTER 6 ■ BEHAVIORS AND SITUATIONS

These dimensions of competence and commitment are the key factors for determining appropriate amounts of directive and supportive leader behaviors. Therefore, to help you understand and use these concepts, further explanation follows.

Subdivisions of Competence

The idea of competence is subdivided into task knowledge and transferable skills. *Task knowledge* is defined as the task-relevant information, education, or experience necessary to complete a specific job. *Transferable skills* are defined as the skills or behaviors that could be used to produce results, and they could also be used to accomplish several other tasks. These definitions can be illustrated by the following example.

Suppose you just finished saying that you were recently in an auto accident. While no one was hurt, you must find someone to advise you because you will soon need to go to court. A friend then tells you that he has a longtime friend who is one of the best lawyers in the state. He says his friend is well known in the tax field. Would you want to call him? You would probably say "Thanks, but no thanks."

Why? Because in situational leadership language, the lawyer friend has no task knowledge, even though he may have transferable skills. In other words, he knows tax law, not state insurance liability or vehicular codes. He does not have the *task-relevant* knowledge, education, or experience necessary to defend you.

On the other hand, what do all lawyers learn besides billable hour ratios? This lawyer may have transferable skills to help you defend your case, because all lawyers learn about brief preparation, research, logic, effective argument in front of a jury or judge, and the American judicial/legal system. These skills could be helpful to you in your court appearance. These transferable skills contribute to this lawyer's competency level, but without *both* transferable skills and task knowledge, this lawyer is probably not competent to aid in your defense.

Subdivisions of Commitment

Commitment is a combination of confidence and motivation. *Confidence* is a measure of one's self-assuredness. It is the "faith" one has in being able to do a task well without much supervision. *Motivation* is defined as the desire, excitement, or enthusiasm to be the "best" or to get ahead. It is the achievement ethic. A lack of commitment is a very different management problem if it stems from a lack of confidence rather than motivation. An employee who lacks motivation could show all the confidence in the world but still perform poorly because of a low motivation level.

Given these dimensions of competence and commitment, there are several possible combinations that can be used to define employee development levels. These combinations are represented in Figure 6.2.

high competence	high/moderate competence	some/low competence	low competence
high commitment	variable commitment	low commitment	high commitment
D4	D3	D2	D1

developed ←———————————→ developing

FIGURE 6.2 *Competence and commitment combinations.*

Development Levels Are Somewhat Sequential

Situational leadership theory advocates that as the development level of an individual increases from D1 to D4, his or her competence and commitment fluctuates. When first beginning a new task for which an employee possesses little or no prior knowledge or experience, most individuals are enthusiastic and ready to learn (D1—high commitment and low competence), but they may not be competent to do so.

As they begin to become involved with the task, people often find it is either more difficult to learn to perform the task than they initially thought, or less interesting than they first anticipated. This disillusionment decreases their commitment (D2—low commitment and low/some competence). If people pass through this level of development and learn to perform the task with help from others, most will then go through a self-doubt phase in which they question whether they can perform the task well *on their own* under slightly new circumstances (D3—variable commitment and high competence). Others may think the D3 is competent, but the fact is that they themselves doubt their competence. These alternating feelings of competence and self-doubt cause the varied commitment associated with D3—commitment that fluctuates from excitement to insecurity.

With proper support, individuals can eventually become peak performers (D4—high commitment and high competence) who demonstrate a high level of competence *and* commitment. In other words, given appropriate leadership, people can progress to peak performance.

The development level sequence described thus far is "progressive" in nature. Most people move beyond the initial level required to learn a new or different task or goal. They typically begin with the commitment, but not the knowledge, skill, or experience. Then they progress to competent and committed performance, if given the right circumstances. An individual who is at the D3 level of high competence and variable commitment in the progressive cycle presents a different leadership need than a previously good performer who now shows a drop in commitment.

In the progressive cycle, variable commitment is "caused," more often than not, by the individual's initial lack of confidence that he or she can do the task or accomplish the goal. In this case, the leader needs to listen, problem solve, and provide encouragement to help the follower develop the necessary confidence.

Regressive Cycle

Another possibility for the D3 "condition" could be that the individual was a good performer (D4), but now shows a lack of good performance due to variable commitment. In this case, performance regresses. What now lies at the base of the variable commitment is a drop in motivation, not confidence. The follower may be "demotivated" by either on- or off-the-job issues. On-the-job issues, such as the organization's practices, your leadership style, or other job-related factors, could be the source of demotivation. Off-the-job issues, such as family illness, divorce, birth of a child, and other personal factors, may also cause demotivation. In either case, a responsive leader in a one-to-one context would use supportive behaviors to listen, problem solve, and ask for input to help the follower rekindle his or her motivation (not confidence).

Development Level Is Task or Goal Specific

When considering someone's development level, it is important to remember that people are not either "fully developed" or "underdeveloped." Development level is not a global concept; it is a task- or goal-specific concept. In other words, people tend to be at different levels of development, depending on the specific task, objective, or function that they are assigned.

For example, let's say that an engineer might be highly developed (competent and committed) to handle the technical design work assigned to him or her. The individual may be a D4 with design work, but may display a different level of commitment or competence when it comes to estimating contract costs for the client. The engineer may even be at a third level of competence or commitment when working with subcontractors on the project. Development level is different for different people, and it also varies for different tasks for the same individual.

In summary, the situation varies within the one-to-one context, based on the competence and commitment of the individual being asked to carry out a particular task, goal, or function. This variability in competence and commitment creates the need for leaders to use differing amounts of directive and supportive behaviors. Let's now examine the various possible leadership styles that are based on combinations of directive and supportive behaviors.

STYLES

As previously noted, the two basic elements of an influence attempt in a one-to-one context are directive and supportive behaviors. Refer to Figure 6.3.

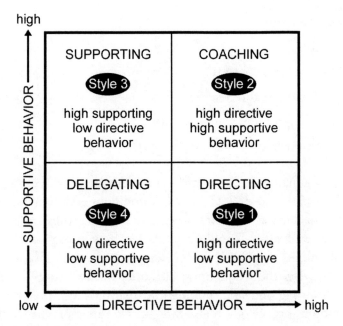

FIGURE 6.3 *Combinations of direction and support.*

Remember, leadership style is the pattern of influence you use with others, over time, as perceived by them. Also recall that directive behaviors in a one-to-one context are as follows:

1. Setting goals
2. Planning work in advance
3. Defining timelines
4. Specifying priorities
5. Determining methods of evaluation
6. Defining roles and decision-making prerogatives
7. Showing and telling *how* outcomes will be accomplished (see Chart 6.2 on page 179)

Supportive behaviors in a one-to-one context have been described as follows:

1. Listening
2. Praising and encouraging
3. Asking for input
4. Sharing information about the total organization's operation
5. Sharing information about self
6. Facilitating the problem solving of others
7. Providing rationale (see Chart 6.2 on page 179)

Figure 6.3 shows that leaders can vary on the amount of directive and supportive behaviors they use. If a leader frequently uses directive behaviors, he or she will be seen as high on directive behaviors. Infrequent goal setting, planning, evaluating, showing or telling how something should be done will, of course, result in a leader being perceived as low in directive behaviors. Likewise, the frequent or infrequent use of supportive behaviors, such as listening, praising, sharing information about the organization or self, or mutual problem solving, will lead to an individual being perceived as high or low in supportive behaviors.

The frequent and infrequent use of directive and supportive behaviors gives rise to four basic leadership styles, as seen by others. Research shows that, while there is no absolute finite point where one style stops and another begins, these styles are substantiated in general use.[11]

A General Concept of Style 1—Directing

In a one-to-one context, Style 1 (S1) is comprised of high amounts of directive behaviors and low amounts of supportive behaviors. In Style 1, the leader defines the roles of the follower and specifies what, how, when, where, and with whom tasks are to be done. The leader initiates problem solving and decision making. Solutions and decisions are announced, communication is largely one way, and implementation of the "hows" by the follower is closely monitored.

Research[12] indicates that most managers do not feel comfortable with frequent use of Style 1. Unless the company culture fosters a high directive/low supportive style (such as with military or paramilitary organizations), most managers reflexively accept the voguish messages of empowerment or "participative" management now being promoted in today's leadership or managerial literature.

Sometimes Style 1 behavior becomes unattractive because it is viewed as a dictatorial, noncompassionate, power-hungry "macho" style that resembles something close to the character of Attila the Hun. Other times, Style 1 behavior is not used because managers do not want that style directed toward them and, therefore, will not use it with others.

People who are competent and successful tend to forget that they wanted or needed direction when they first started and were probably frustrated when they did not get the needed direction. The issue here is not the needs of the leader, but rather the needs of the follower.

Style 1 does not need to be delivered harshly, insensitively, or in a patronizing manner. In fact, if used in the appropriate circumstances, it can be seen as a strong, helpful, informative style that aids in employee skill development and output.

To temper some possible objections to the effective and timely use of Style 1 directing, it is important to remember the "micro" behaviors (see page 188) that shape the employees' perceptions of Style 1 use. Style 1 represents the frequent use of directive behaviors, with the infrequent use of supportive behaviors. The leader's listening behavior does not include asking open-ended questions, asking for the employee's input, or facilitating the employee's expansion of alternatives. Information about the "big picture" is not shared. Some supportive behaviors could be used, but they are infrequent compared to the use of directive behaviors in this style of interaction.

The seven directive microbehaviors are clearly not of equal importance in shaping an employee's view of Style 1 use. In other words, some behaviors are more meaningful and prominent to the "receiver." What drives the employee's perception of frequent Style 1 use are the behaviors of (1) setting goals, and (2) telling and showing *how* goals are to be accomplished.

The prominent, important microskills, which must be used to be seen as a Style 1 manager, are the "whats" and the "hows." The remaining skills of planning, establishing timelines, setting priorities, and so on, are "lesser" skills—not in terms of importance to task accomplishment, but in terms of shaping the employee's perception of the manager's use of high amounts of Style 1 directive behavior. Surprisingly, when managers are seen as "negatively" using Style 1 by their followers, these managers often overdo the planning, timelines, and priorities without providing the clear "hows." This often leaves the employee confused and angry.

The conclusion that can be drawn from this research is that you must continually communicate *what* the goals are and *how* those outcomes are to be achieved, if you are to be seen as a Style 1 directing manager. Of secondary importance to employee perception of Style 1 use is the when, with whom, how much, and other supportive behavior skills. (This is assuming infrequent use of supportive behaviors.)

Sometimes managers mistakenly think that describing the "what" is sufficient for Style 1. However, to only describe what goals are to be achieved, without the related "hows," may frequently result in employee perceptions that the manager uses Style 4 delegating (low direction and low support).

In summary, research indicates that employees see Style 1 managers as short-term oriented. Such managers do not explain the big picture or present the long-term, overarching strategies necessary for goal accomplishment. Instead, they focus their followers around tactics, not strategies; on "hows," not "whys"; and on activities, not global functions.

An Example

As an example, suppose you manage a sales force. In a discussion with a salesperson, you must set goals and specify how those goals are to be accomplished, if you are to be seen as high in Style 1. You might say to the salesperson, "I think a reasonable goal for this quarter would be to close on approximately 100–125 units, with an average pretax profit of 7 percent. That goal can be obtained by scanning the business directory to make six cold calls per week. The cold calls should be made using our call-reports format."

Let's assume the goal in this example is attainable. Let's also assume there are other activities that could help obtain the results wanted, such as a bid process. The important point in this example is your specification of *what* and *how*.

You will soon learn when Style 1 should be used, but first understanding the nature of Style 1 should reduce your "aversion" to it.

Style Is in the Delivery

The nonverbal, as well as verbal, aspects of management behavior shape others' perceptions. If the sample statement concerning a reasonable sales goal was delivered by a manager whose mannerisms included hands on hips, standing over a seated salesperson, words spoken rapidly in a sarcastic tone with furrowed brow and a loud voice, how do you think it would be perceived by the employee? The fact of the matter is, for reception to be clear, the picture must be clear. What is the manager's intent? Is it to serve or to be better than?

There is one last point about Style 1 managers. Research[13] shows that when managers justify the use of Style 1 to themselves, they do not think they use coercive power to get adherence to directives. They believe they hold the legitimate authority to ask for employee compliance. This could explain their lack of sensitivity in delivery.

A General Concept of Style 3—Supporting

The style most in contrast to a Style 1 (high direction and low support) is a Style 3 (high support and low direction). To help you clearly understand Style 3 (S3), let's explore it before discussing Style 2, which is a blend of direction and support.

Interestingly, both manager self-perceptions and employee perceptions indicate that a majority of leaders use Style 3 (high support and low direction). It is estimated (variations in professions aside) that between 65 and 70 percent of managers see themselves as Style 3 managers, while 55–65 percent of their employees perceive their managers to be in the Style 3 category. This can, in some ways, be explained by the social acceptability of Style 3 behaviors, in light of current cultural and business values.

The spectrum of writings such as *The Servant as Leader*,[14] *The Leadership Challenge*,[15] *Stewardship: Choosing Service over Self-Interest*,[16] and others, espouse a set of behaviors and attitudes that "fit" well with the Style 3 behaviors of the Situational Leadership II model. It is also "easier" to be a Style 3 manager because the style minimizes interpersonal conflict and promotes employee self-focus; but, if used inappropriately, it tends to put employee needs above the needs of the organization.

To better understand the appropriate use of this style, you must clearly appreciate the microbehaviors inherent in Style 3 high supportive and low directive behaviors. Those microbehaviors, previously listed in Chart 6.2, are as follows:

1. Listening
2. Praising and encouraging
3. Asking for input
4. Sharing information about the total organization's operations
5. Sharing information about yourself

6. Facilitating the problem solving of others
7. Providing rationale

Style 3 supportive behaviors are frequently used with a concurrent, *infrequent* use of directive behaviors. Some directive behaviors, such as the discussion of timelines or priorities, could be used, but these behaviors would be infrequent in comparison to the supportive behaviors.

Research shows that these seven supporting microbehaviors are not of equal importance in shaping an employee's view of Style 3 use. Some of these behaviors are more meaningful and prominent to the "receiver." The two key supporting behaviors that influence employees' perception of frequent Style 3 use are listening and facilitating employee problem solving.

In other words, for *mutual* trust and respect to develop between you and the employees being influenced, you must actively listen to them about work-related issues and seek to help them reach *their* answers to work-related issues. Facilitating work-related problems means asking the critical, open-ended questions that assist employees in finding their own solutions, not promoting your solutions. In assisting employees with their own work solutions, you also give them the prerogative to decide for themselves how something is to be accomplished.

An Example

Let's return to the imaginary discussion between you and a salesperson about the goal to close on approximately 100–125 units, with an average pretax profit of 7 percent. Using Style 3, the discussion might go something like this:

"As you know, your goal for this quarter is for you to close on 100–125 units, at a pretax profit of 7 percent. How are you feeling about that goal and what kinds of things are you planning to do to reach that goal?"

In this discussion, you are soliciting the salesperson's thoughts about how to accomplish the goal and seeking his or her feelings or commitment. Your intention is to listen and ask questions that allow the employee to think out his or her approach. It should be the employee's ideas and final choice as to the action steps taken.

A word of caution: If you previously opened the door for employees to think out their ideas, and then slammed the door hard on their faces by telling them you do not think those are appropriate ideas, their perceptions of your initial probing questions, as described in this example, will not seem supportive. These questions will, because of the past history, seem invasive and controlling. Therefore, you must understand your true intent. You must know yourself well enough to convey your intent.

If the importance of the task or goal is so crucial that you cannot afford failure, then maybe Style 3 is not appropriate. If the employee did not demonstrate skill on this task or goal in the past, then Style 3 should not be used at this time. In addition, if the employee accomplished the task or met the goal in the past, then the individual will look on your solutions as evaluative, controlling, and unnecessary.

Past history aside, if an employee expresses doubt or confusion, then problem-solving questions are in order. If the employee in the sample leader–salesperson interaction said, "Well, I'm a little uneasy about the goal for this quarter, because my sales region was reorganized and I haven't yet developed the face-to-face contact with my customer base that I want," a good Style 3 problem-solving behavior would be to ask, "What is completed?" The ball is now in the employee's court. The individual may spend 20 minutes telling you what he or she accomplished. Based on what the employee says, you could then ask, "What alternatives do you see?"

The key leader behaviors that define a Style 3, in the mind of the follower, are mutual problem solving and listening. The remaining skills of praising, asking for input, sharing information about total organization and self, and rationale building are no less important for task accomplishment, but they are lesser in terms of shaping the employees' view of a leader's use of high amounts of Style 3 supportive behavior.

If you want to be seen as a Style 3 manager, then you must listen *and* facilitate employees' thinking about task or goal accomplishment. And, of course, you must allow them to implement those actions that they think will be best for the outcomes you and they want.

Style 3 is the most frequently used style of the four. This is true for a number of reasons. First, most individuals in leadership roles are interested in maintaining an interpersonal connection with their employees. They want to be seen as reasonable, caring people. Second, they think that "ownership" of outcomes and personal motivation to achieve them are increased when the employee can help define and control how the outcomes are reached. Third, managers may not possess the technical expertise to specifically tell the employee how to do something. Fourth and finally, the leader may not be thoughtful or knowledgeable about how to handle the employee. Because some individuals are not skillful leaders, they fall back on this disposition or value point of view that guides their actions. Those dispositions or points of view may lead to inappropriate leadership behaviors. Given certain dispositions and points of view already described, you can understand why some leaders may not provide the high supportive, but low directive, leadership styles.

A General Concept of Style 2—Coaching

Style 2 (S2) is the least instinctive style of the four. Style 1 is natural to some individuals because their disposition and/or point of view "leans" them toward control, which is the essence of Style 1. Style 3 is also natural to some individuals because their disposition and/or value base "leans" them toward accepter behaviors, which are basic to an effective Style 3. However, Style 2 requires understandings and behaviors that combine directive and supportive behaviors to both "push" and "pull" the follower toward goal accomplishment.

A comprehensive Style 2 results in employee input and involvement, but the leader controls final decision-making power. Style 2 is the delicate balance of self and others' expertise and enthusiasm. The delicateness resides in your maintaining control over the what and how, yet staying open to using employee suggestions. The ultimate test is whether the employee feels heard and feels positive about the "givens" of your decision making.

Style 2 is the judicious use of listening and asking for input, yet setting goals and defining action plans. Style 2 uses *both* high directive and high supportive behaviors. This balancing act is time-consuming, which explains why many managers don't use it often. However, Style 2 seems to be the most frequent backup style, as perceived by most employees.

A General Concept of Style 4—Delegating

Style 4 (S4), delegating (low directive and low supportive), is the least understood style of the four. Many managers use Style 4 to "dump" unwanted work on unsuspecting followers. Style 4 also "happens" because the leader possesses neither the time nor technical knowledge to do anything else. Lastly, it is also typical for leaders to use Style 4 as a way to "test" the employees' ability to work. The "test" is, of course, warranted if the employee has the competence and commitment to handle the desired outcomes.

Most people do not use Style 4 because they are afraid to lose control, afraid that "if you give them an inch, they will take a mile," and afraid that their image will suffer if they are not intimately involved in all phases of the work. Interestingly enough, employees seldom perceive Style 4 as a positive statement of their bosses' faith in them. Employees frequently view the repetitive, delegating leader as "out to lunch."

If you plan to frequently delegate to your employees, then you must understand that low direction does not mean *no* direction, and low support does not mean *no* support. To delegate well means that you must establish ways of staying informed about the work progress and outcomes. If you delegate without ongoing, updated information about outcomes, you increase your chances of being caught unaware.

While D4s will already do the majority of their work without much direction, remember that, as the leader, you will still delegate *something*. That *something* will be more generally stated in Style 4 than in Style 1; nonetheless, you still will shape the focus of the employee's activity and energy.

The word "shape" is used because the goal may be a product of the employee's perception rather than that of the leader. In fact, a D4 may bring an innovative idea or goal that needs only the leader's okay. Delegation could range from giving an employee a generally defined *what*, but not *how*, to giving an employee the power to act in the leader's place.

Delegation means the leader transfers to the employee the appropriate *responsibility* and *authority* for goal and task accomplishment. The leader communicates the responsibility and authority that is required for the employee to feel empowered to get the job done on his or her own. Appropriate *responsibility* means the communication of a mutually agreed-upon *obligation* for goal and task accomplishment. The employee must feel it is *his* or *her* obligation to accomplish the goal and its related tasks. When an employee comes to the leader for permission, this signifies that the employee already feels an obligation to accomplish the goal.

Appropriate *authority* is the legitimized capacity to act in the leader's place when using resources to accomplish a goal and its related tasks. The leader allows the employee to use personnel, spend money, or make decisions that the employee feels are necessary to accomplish goals he or she deems important.

Delegating responsibility without authority frustrates an employee quickly—especially a D4 with a proven track record. A leader may assign the obligation, but not the power necessary for goal accomplishment. This is because he or she does not trust the employee, given the importance and scope of the goal. Effective delegation requires a leader to understand the *scope* of the delegated goal and the related subtasks *before* delegating. Clarity of scope enables the leader to assign the appropriate responsibility and authority.

Remember that delegation is goal or task specific, based on the employee's competence and commitment. Your leadership role may also require you to set goals for your unit, or even to set goals with one employee differently from another. However, you still remain responsible for your unit's evaluation process or for managing the consequences of individual or unit performance.

SITUATIONS

By now it should be fairly evident that appropriate leader behaviors are based on employee competence and commitment. The diagnosis of employee competence and commitment should be done in dialogue with the employee. Situational leadership is not done *to* the follower; rather, it is done *with* the follower. Development level is task specific. It is possible that a person could be a D1 on one task, but a D4 on another. Therefore, you must use "different strokes for different folks" and "different strokes for the same folks," depending on the task or goal to be accomplished. Development level, or competence and commitment, changes and moves forward or backward, depending on the circumstances.

A change in jobs, or a change in technology while on the job, may cause competence to change. Commitment may change based on job-related or non-job-related factors. Boredom, lack of recognition, organizational politics, a change in marital status, long-term illness, and a lack of organizational vision are examples of factors that reduce employee commitment.

To be a situational leader (as depicted in Figure 6.4), you must diagnose the competence and commitment level of those with whom you work in a one-to-one context and then use the appropriate level of direction and support. You must match leadership style to development level.

When to Use Style 1 in a One-to-One Context

As previously noted, an employee's development level is an important factor in selecting the appropriate leadership style. For example, a D1 is depicted as someone who shows high commitment to accomplish a particular task or goal, but low competence to do so. In the salesperson example, if you want to help a D1 employee meet sales goals, then your appropriate behavior is to describe "what" and "how." A D1 employee's competence develops through transference of the knowledge and information necessary to accomplish goals that serve the organization. To emphasize deadlines, priorities, and evaluations, without specifying what and how, would only frustrate the learning employee.

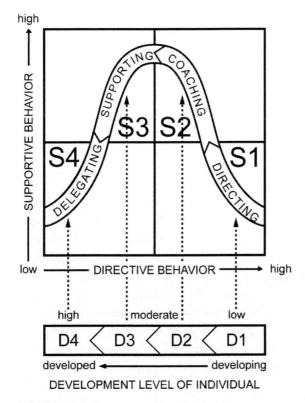

FIGURE 6.4 *Situational Leadership II.*

Although your interpersonal delivery may be low-key, kind, and friendly, the task's goals and action plans are not open for much discussion or modification when you are using Style 1, nor should they be. The D1 follower does not have the task knowledge and/or transferable skills necessary to accomplish the task. The best way to help him or her build the necessary knowledge and skills is to be very clear about the what, how, when, where, and with whom to get the goal or task accomplished.

To use frequent supportive behaviors, such as asking for the input of someone who does not have knowledge, would also frustrate the learner. Sharing the "big picture" might also overwhelm someone who wants a limited view of a discrete, "hands-on" solution to the assigned task. The follower who is high in commitment, but low in competence, brings a certain naive optimism to the situation, which is best served by assisting him or her with specific directions. Supportive behaviors should be used when the follower is more experienced with the assigned goal or task.

An Example

Imagine you hire Sally and want her to become skillful in the use of your voice-mail system. Sally is not experienced with phone-mail systems, but is enthusiastic about its use because she can see how it will save her time. The most appropriate style with this committed, yet incompetent, follower is to pull out the manual and slowly go through the steps necessary to explain the phone system's functions and options. In this situation, using Style 1 behaviors, while also checking for understanding as you direct Sally, is most helpful.

For the Style 1 to be complete and most effective in the voice-mail system example, you would show Sally *how* to use the system by demonstrating each feature, giving her an opportunity to replicate the behavior, and staying with her during her initial use of the system.

To simply give the manual to Sally and tell her to go through it at her leisure would be Style 4 delegating, which may not ensure Sally's skill development. Instead, Style 4 delegating may force Sally to go to someone else to get the knowledge you could—but did not—give her. In addition, to use supportive behaviors, such as asking for her ideas on the phone-mail system, may reduce her commitment. Further, to ask her what should be done to program her own greeting or clear her messages, at this point, is not helpful and, worse yet, may reduce your credibility as a helper or facilitator.

As previously stated, Style 1 directing has a "bad reputation" because of the normative voguish swings in the leadership literature. However, few writers would deny that the functions of setting goals and defining "how-tos" must be served if work is to be accomplished by the employee. The question then, is who initiates, explains, and executes the "whats" and "hows." The Situational Leadership II model advocates that initiation and explana-

CHAPTER 6 ■ BEHAVIORS AND SITUATIONS

tions of the whats and hows is contextually dependent on the employees' apparent competence and commitment. Do not be afraid to execute a directive Style 1 because "participative management" is "in." Use Style 1 because it meets the needs of a committed, but as yet unskilled, employee.

The style most in contrast to a Style 1 (high direction and low support) is a Style 3 (high support and low direction). To help you clearly understand Style 3, let's explore it before discussing Style 2, which is a blend of direction and support.

When to Use Style 2 in a One-to-One Context

The most effective use of Style 2 is with followers who display low-to-moderate competence and low commitment. In most D2 situations, the employees possess some experience with the task or goal, but are discouraged by their lack of progress. Most D2s (low/moderate competence and low commitment) know that they need to learn more to be more productive, yet may be discouraged that they can't get the knowledge fast enough. There are many reasons for their discouragement, including: (1) it is harder than they thought; (2) it is boring; (3) the more they learn, the more they need to learn; or (4) they did not receive needed help from their leader.

An important point to remember is that the D2s' skill level, as well as their commitment level, is not sufficient for task or goal accomplishment. They need task information, problem exploration, and generation of alternative ways of attacking the problem; they also need to hear rationales for certain choices that you make.

At the same time, D2s need to be listened to and encouraged to keep trying. They need to explore their own ideas about what can be done to achieve their goals and incorporate their ideas into the final action plan, when appropriate. D2s need more refinement of their skills and ideas, which emerges from joint discussion and "what-if" thinking.

An effective Style 2 should be prefaced with clarity about who will make the final decision concerning goals and action plans. As soon as decision-making responsibility is clear, the leader should ask for employee input and suggestions.

An Example

In the salesperson example, a Style 2 leader might say, "As you know, your goal for this quarter is to close on 100-125 units, at a pretax profit of 7 percent. I can recommend some action steps that I think you should take to reach your goal. I'd like to share them with you and get your thoughts and feelings so I can modify the approach, based on your input."

When you are using Style 2, you define the goals and initiate the action plans. The goals are usually not "up for grabs," while the action plans are to be modified by you after hearing the concerns and suggestions of the follower. This is appropriate, because D2s will possess some experience with the goals and action plans, and therefore they will hold some opinions and ideas that can contribute to the approach to be taken.

Remember that the D2s' discouragement about not reaching or making progress in their goals can be reversed with the appropriate direction and support. Many times, the discouragement or commitment aspect of the problem should be handled first. This can be done by leading with questions of commitment such as, "I've noticed, Bill, that you seem a little discouraged about this quarter's sales goals. Would you be willing to share with me what's going on so I can help you?" In this approach, the specific steps Bill could take will come after discussing issues of motivation or confidence. In Style 2, the leader may renegotiate the goals or timelines because of unforeseen circumstances that are not the fault of the employee.

Style 2 is the most neglected of the styles because it takes time and is not "instinctive"; instead, it is a learned style that requires a delicate balance of both directive and supportive behaviors. Style 2 requires a sensitive use of control and relationship behaviors—as seen from the employees' viewpoint—if you are to successfully aid such employees in developing competency and answering their commitment questions.

When to Use Style 3 in a One-to-One Context

The appropriate use of Style 3 is based on the combination of competence and commitment demonstrated by the follower. Style 3 should be used with people who show competence in reaching the outcomes desired, but may not display either the confidence or motivation to do what is needed.

Frequent use of directive behaviors would not be needed, and perhaps might be demotivating, with employees who already know *how* to get the job done. Their issues are attitudinal, not competency based. Telling them what and how to do something that they already demonstrated they know, would, over time, produce feelings of anger in them and result in disrespect toward you.

When you sense a commitment problem, you must determine if it is based on confidence or motivation issues. Either case will require a highly supportive listening style. A confidence issue requires your revisiting past instances of success, lowering the stakes through examination of possible consequences for failure, and re-examining the strategies chosen to accomplish the employee's outcomes.

A commitment problem due to motivation issues requires you to ask questions that get at the employee's lack of motivation. The drop in motivation could be the result of your past leadership; the organization's procedures, rules, or constraints; or it could be because the task/goal is routine, boring, and unchallenging; or just the opposite, too difficult. The use of Style 3 in the instance of low motivation requires a great deal of nonjudgmental listening at first, and creative problem solving as the one-to-one meeting goes on.

An Example

In the sales example used earlier, suppose Bill never previously sold 125 units at a pretax profit of 7 percent. Instead, for two quarters in a row he sold 95 units at a 6 percent profit. Bill's hesitancy and reluctance could be a confidence issue, which must be explored if you are to sustain his commitment. As additional information, you know that last quarter five other salespeople achieved the required outcome in territories that are the same size as Bill's territory. How you share this information in a supportive way, yet maintain his motivation, lies at the heart of using Style 3 well.

In another example, suppose Bill is one of the five who previously sold 100–125 units at a pretax profit of 7 percent, but now seems to be "dragging his feet" on the challenge for this quarter. Again, the issue seems to be one of motivation. This will require that you delicately explore the reasons, which may be either job-related or non-job-related. Suppose Bill shares with you that he is tired of being a salesperson and wants to be promoted to a district manager's role, and that last quarter he was passed over for an opening for which he applied. To regain Bill's commitment for the sales goal, you will need to discuss how you can support his development of the skills needed to move into the district manager's role. However, to support him means that you may lose one of your top performers. Therefore, Style 3 would then involve a discussion of the alternative ways he and you can work together to develop his management skills while he sells 100–125 units at a pretax profit of 7 percent.

In Style 3, the action plan is open for negotiation, but the outcomes are not. The final decisions concerning how something is accomplished, when, with whom, and what resources could be used, are mostly left up to the employee. The final decisions are in the hands of the employee, with frank, open discussion concerning the alternatives and possible consequences being facilitated by both the leader and the follower.

Remember, Style 3 involves high amounts of support, but low amounts of direction. Many times that low direction is in the form of reminding the employee of the organizational expectations under which you both operate. As previously explained, for work to be accomplished, the processes of goal setting and action planning must be served. Who initiates that and executes those "whats" and "hows" is situationally dependent on the competence and commitment of the follower. In Style 3, the action plans are left up to the employee, after a dialogue with the leader.

When to Use Style 4 in a One-to-One Context

The Style 4 delegation style is, of course, to be used when you work with an employee who is both committed and competent to handle the outcome you both want. Reluctance on your part to properly delegate can be frustrating and demotivating to a D4. This is especially true if you delegate the responsibility, but not the authority, for goal accomplishment.

A leader who truly delegates gives to the follower the responsibility and authority to decide what is to be accomplished and how it is to be accomplished. The obligation to keep you informed could also reside with the follower. However, with important "high-stakes" issues, you might want to set some dates in your calendar as to when you and the follower can meet to discuss his or her progress.

Low support does not mean *no* support. Your role is to acknowledge, affirm, and empower the D4. The goal, evaluation, and reward focuses of Style 4 center on appreciating the effort the D4 gives and outcomes he or she obtains. The support is still low, in that you do not need to listen, problem solve, or share information about yourself or the total organization's operations to the D4. They can do that on their own. What they should *not* do alone is celebrate their victories or accomplishments. You should help them recognize their efforts.

Does Situational Leadership Work?

If you become adept at diagnosing the situation and using the appropriate behavior, then the payoff can be well worth the effort. Studies [17] show that the appropriate application of leadership style to development level can do wonders for the motivation and morale of employees. In five separate studies[18] researchers found connections between selected climate measures in the workplace and the ability of managers to match leadership styles to development levels. Each time you are about to influence someone, ask yourself, "What is this person's competence and commitment to accomplish this goal or task?" This question should help you diagnose the situation and can result in a more appropriate leadership style.

Development and Regressive Cycles

An individual's commitment and competence are constantly changing around a particular goal or task. Therefore, you must continually examine whether or not you may need to change your leadership style. Hopefully, individuals will progress in competency and commitment, if given the right direction and support. The development cycle is used to describe the sequential progress through the four development levels, while the regressive cycle is used to describe the decline in performance that is due to a drop in competence and/or commitment.

The four development levels, when matched with the appropriate leadership styles, are predictable and sequential. While there is no guarantee, using the appropriate leader behavior for the development level should allow the follower to progress more quickly to high levels of performance.

Development Cycle

In developing self-reliant achievers, D4s, the factor that triggers a change in leadership style is performance. Improvements in performance prompt forward shifts in leadership style from S1 to S2 to S3 to S4, one style at a time, as represented on the bell-shaped curve in Figure 6.5.

Usually, an individual undertakes a new task as a D1. In some cases, however, an individual may enter the development cycle as a D2. This situation can be the result of an involuntary transfer or other job- or non-job-related issues. Because both competence and commitment are low, Style 2, with an emphasis on active listening, would be appropriate.

Regressive Cycle

Just as improvements in performance call for forward shifts in style along the bell-shaped curve, decreases in performance require a backward shift in leadership style. This is called the regressive cycle, as depicted in Figure 6.6 on page 208. In other words, whenever an individual performs at a

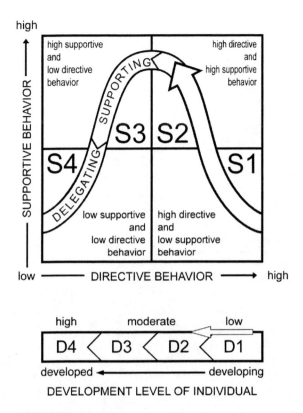

FIGURE 6.5 *The development cycle.*

level lower than previously demonstrated, the leader should adjust his or her behavior to respond to the individual's current development level.

For example, a highly experienced individual is falling seriously short of his production goals. Rumors of a buyout or perhaps a family crisis begin to affect this person's performance. In this situation, shifting from a delegating style to a supporting style is appropriate.

In both the development and regressive cycles, changes in leadership style should be made, either forward or backward, one step or style at a time.

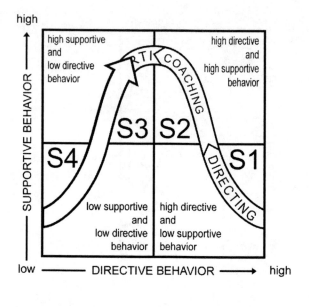

FIGURE 6.6 *The regressive cycle.*

Using Situational Leadership Theory

As you can see, the challenge for you, as a leader, is to make skillful *diagnoses* of situations in which you act. You must diagnose, and then be *flexible* enough to use the needed directive and supportive behaviors. As you will see in the next chapter, your value base and disposition will make this process either easy or difficult, unless you are committed to explore parts of your shadow self. You must be committed to all the behaviors available to you, regardless of your extrovert or introvert preferences, and your inbetweener or traditionalist point of view. *Diagnosis* and *flexibility* are the keys to using the Situational Leadership II model. Your competence and commitment to do so are based on your disposition and point of view—your character.

SUMMARY

Leading in a one-to-one context is probably the most important and most frequent context in which you lead. This context provides you with reduced complexity and narrows your focus for maximum impact. You must use it wisely by matching your leadership style to the perceived competence and commitment of the follower. Remember, competence and commitment are task or goal specific. It is highly probable that you will use several different styles (combinations of direction and support) with the same individual, depending on the goal or task. Shifting leadership styles is greatly enhanced when both you and the follower understand the Situational Leadership II model, and use it as a common language to ask for what you both want.

Endnotes

1. Greenleaf 1991.
2. Stoner-Zemel 1988.
3. Sashkin 1986; Stoner-Zemel 1988; Kouzes and Posner 1987.
4. Burns 1978; Kotter 1990; Hickman 1990; Williamson 1984; Bass 1985; Tichy and Deranna 1986; Stoner-Zemel 1988; Sashkin 1986; Kouzes and Posner 1987; Zalesnik 1977.
5. For the group context see Carew, Parisi-Carew, and Blanchard 1990; Blanchard, Carew, and Parisi-Carew 1990; Woodring and Zigarmi 1997; Lacoursiere 1980. For the organizational context see Adizes 1988; Greiner 1977; Hall et al. 1977; Hall and Hord 1987; Loucks et al. 1975; Newlove and Hall 1976; Blanchard, Zigarmi, and Zigarmi 1994.
6. Hersey and Blanchard 1969.
7. Others who contributed to the expansion of this model were the founding associates of the Ken Blanchard Companies: Drea Zigarmi, Pat Zigarmi, Don Carew, Eunice Parisi-Carew, Fred Finch, Laurie Hawkins, and Marjorie Blanchard.
8. For example, Blake and Mouton 1964.
9. For example, Bass 1990; Fiedler 1967; Korman 1966; Reddin 1970.

10. Blanchard, Zigarmi, and Zigarmi 1985.
11. Zigarmi, Edeburn, and Blanchard 1997.
12. Zigarmi, Edeburn, and Blanchard 1997.
13. Sonkin 1991.
14. Greenleaf 1991.
15. Kouzes and Posner 1987.
16. Block 1993.
17. Zigarmi, Edeburn, and Blanchard 1997; Blanchard, Zigarmi, and Nelson 1993.
18. Lobben 1988; Wilkinson 1990; Birden 1992; Stoner-Zemel 1988; Zigarmi, Edeburn, and Blanchard 1997.

CHAPTER 7

Vision and Learning

"We need a new heroic ideal: the brave, truthful, non-violent individual who is in the service of humanity, resists injustice and exploitation, and leads by appealing to our ideals and our spirit."

— KESHAVAN NAIR[1]

VISION

The "vision thing," as George Augustus Bush used to call it, is ever more prominent, as people realize its value and writers explore its implications in a business setting.[2] The concept of vision can seem mysterious and difficult to grasp; but vision, and its connection to leadership, is not magical. Many leaders are capable of creating a compelling vision and working with followers to bring it to reality. When leaders and followers create and share a common vision, then enormous amounts of focused energy, effort, productivity, and satisfaction can result.

Dimensions of Vision

A *vision* is a picture of a possible, ongoing future you intend to create, one that illuminates your guiding values and beliefs.[3] A compelling vision focuses on end results; it concentrates on where you are going, not on how you are getting there. The closer you are to achieving your vision, the clearer it becomes.

A strong vision crystallizes the needs, desires, beliefs, and values of followers. It excites the minds *and* hearts of those you lead by clarifying the *purpose* of the organization, illuminating your guiding *values,* and providing your *image* or picture of the future. These three ingredients—purpose, values, and image—are necessary for a vision to be strong, vital, and motivating.

Purpose

A *purpose statement* explains your company's reason for existence. It clearly defines what your company does and what it wants to accomplish. It tells others what business you are in—stated from the viewpoint of the customer and society. Companies usually find mission statements lying around that may be dusted off and used as a purpose statement. Often, this mission statement is *just* a purpose statement, not a vision, because the statement's writing style does not excite minds and hearts, and it lacks the necessary values and image ingredients.

All clear purpose statements link the organization to its customer's needs, from the viewpoint of the customer. While the organization's underlying purpose may be to grow and be profitable, those purposes are secondary to the organization's inherent customer and societal relationships. Although the profit motive may be energizing to internal people due to the implied payoff, the customer is not necessarily motivated by that purpose. However, a growth or profit purpose may not be intrinsically motivating to followers either. How many people want as a tombstone epitaph, "He/she was good at making a profit"? Thus, a growth or profit purpose does not answer the question, for what purpose? What purpose does the company serve *for the customer?*

Some Examples

Most successful businesses that enjoy high levels of commitment define themselves from the viewpoints of their customers and society. AT&T is now in the *communications* business, not the *telephone* business. Disney is in the *entertainment* business, not the *theme park* business. Cable News Network (CNN) is in the business of *providing hard-breaking news as it unfolds*, not in the *entertainment* business. Each of these companies defines its purpose in terms of the customer.

Serving Customers

Every organization serves someone, whether it's the American Nazi Party, the Klu Klux Klan, GTE, U.S. Defense Department, or Monsanto Chemicals. Linking organizational purpose with a needed service lets employees attach greater meaning to their work life. Employee pride derives from a meaningful organizational purpose, not from a narrow product or profit focus.

Mary Parker Follett, a pioneering business consultant, was asked to work with a financially troubled company that made window shades. The executives defined their purpose as being in the business of producing window shades. With Follett's help, they began to think in terms of the customer and found they were in the business of light control. When considering their business from the viewpoint of the customer, they realized that people bought window shades because they really wanted to control the amount of light coming through their windows. This realization opened new opportunities for product development and sales, because there were many ways to control light.

Stanley Magic Door decided they were not in the business of making automatic doors. Instead, they were in the business of facilitating and controlling the access of people and things through buildings. This redefined purpose produced greater employee appreciation and excitement for the company's products, and also created quite different implications for the company's future.

Defining purpose from the viewpoint of the customer asks the follower/stakeholder to examine his or her everyday actions in light of the organization's purpose to the customer. This connection can give greater meaning to follower efforts and create new business possibilities. The purpose becomes a driving force in daily organizational life.

Serving Society

However, there is not only a customer focus, but also a larger societal focus that needs consideration when defining organizational purpose. What service does the organization provide society? This question is important because most traditionalists, inbetweeners, and synthesizers want their organizations to embody a noble purpose or relevance to society. An organization's noble purpose generates power through employee commitment and excitement; an organization that is visibly disconnected from its society cannot, over the long term, survive.

Almost all work contains a higher social purpose, and it is the social implications with which people must become conscious if they are to bring deeper meaning to their work. Consider the example of the *Sesame Street* program. Joan Ganz Cooney is quoted as saying, "Everybody had this immense sense of purpose . . . it never occurred to us that we could not change the world."[4] *Sesame Street*'s mission of preparing inner-city children for school and engaging parents in the process never waned.

Not only employees are affected by the company's purpose to society. So too are its customers. Buyer preferences are influenced by the organization's image within society. For example, many consumers boycotted Dow Chemical products because it produced napalm, even after production was stopped. There are numerous other examples, from the boycott of companies investing in South Africa to the economic impact on Exxon after the 1989 Alaska oil spill. Organizations that espouse social service, but evidence other behaviors, run the risk of employee "whistle blowing," and legal or economic calamity.

Values

Purpose is one of three ingredients required for a compelling vision, but clear purpose alone is not enough to create strong commitment in those who need to accomplish that purpose. Clear purpose explains what you do, but the purpose can be accomplished in various ways, unless there are guidelines or values that shape the "hows" of the purpose.

Stating values and making them part of the vision evokes the passion necessary to remain focused in the face of obstacles, adversity, and change. Values evoke people's emotions and feelings. Values can nourish standards. A vision is motivating and forceful when it clearly resonates with the values of the individuals within the organization. When this happens, you don't need to sell the vision. People naturally enlist.

The vision's ends and means values must be clear and specify in broad, general ways *how* your organization's purpose will be served. For example, the values of CNN are to provide news information that is timely and accurate. It is not just producing news, but it is presenting it in an accurate and timely way.

Values inherent in the vision must, of course, be "chosen" by organizational members, if they are to positively guide actions. If chosen, then people will more likely manage themselves by those values. In other words, *management occurs by values, not by individual managers.* Too often, companies publish a set of values that are either disconnected from their members' daily work activities or espoused, but not exemplified, by managers. For example, managers may ask others to stop eating sugar but continue to do so themselves. Too often, organizations hold espoused or idealized values, yet act on a very different set of "real" values.

When people act in concert with their values, it is a source of social and personal esteem. When an organization's expressed and acted-on values are in accord, then they (1) provide employees with a source of emotional commitment and energy, and (2) allow integration and congruence of goals with action throughout the organization.[5]

Image

The third ingredient of a forceful vision is an image of the future. This image is a mental *picture* of a highly desirable future state. It is a "vision" of what happens when the purpose and values are fulfilled. It is a picture of the end result, not the process of getting there. However, images are not always expressed in pictures. Images can also be articulated in analogies, metaphors, and stories that convey both understanding and feeling, much like this book's onions, diamonds, sugar, and pig analogies.

Your image of the future illuminates the end result you intend to achieve. It is more than just a vague daydream or whimsical wish. It is something that stirs your blood, excites you, changes your body chemistry, and puts a spring in your step. It might be as personal as standing on the gold medal platform while the national anthem is playing and the flag is being raised. It might be an organizational image of children full of wonderment, joy, and excitement as they use a product that you designed for learning. It might be a room full of enthusiastic customers who want to thank you and your company for what your product or service provided them. The power of an image lies in conceiving the end state.

A clearly expressed image (1) lets you and others know what success will look and feel like, and (2) creates a symbol to guide the actions of self and others.

Gravity

Gravity is a very curious force of nature. It is a "process structure" that maintains its impact over time, yet is without tangible form. You can't see, touch, taste, or hear gravity. Gravity fields, like other process structures such as magnetic fields, are known only through their effects on physical forms.[6] All process structures are powerful, invisible forces that shape behavior.

Organizational vision is a process structure. A well conceived, widely expressed, and consistently modeled vision influences individuals working within the organizational setting. In the absence of a shared organizational vision, people rely on their personal means and ends value to guide their actions. There is no "pull" of a collective organizational vision to shape individual behavior. However, when the organization's vision is clear and faithfully communicated, the benefits are quite easily seen. A shared vision can (1) unleash employee energy, (2) provide a "field" of empowerment, (3) give perspective to individuals and teams as to how they "fit" in the organization, (4) promote cooperation, and (5) contribute to proactive action.

While you may be very clear about your organizational vision, you must also have a personal leadership vision that includes a personal purpose, personal values, and a personal image of what it "looks" like when you are leading the way you imagine it to be. So let's look at your personal leadership vision.

Starfish

A man was walking on a long, deserted stretch of beach just after a storm. Several hundred yards ahead, he could see a solitary figure that seemed to be running to the shoreline, then back to the beach to retrieve something, and then down again to the shoreline. As the man moved closer to the figure, he could see that it was a 12-year-old boy who was hurriedly picking up starfish that recently washed onto the beach, and then throwing them back into the ocean. When the man was close to the boy, he asked, "What are you doing?" The boy answered, "I'm trying to save these starfish, sir." The man saw it as an impossible task, given the many starfish still left on the beach. He announced, "Well, son, that's impossible. You can't make a difference." The boy didn't even break stride. As he threw another starfish back, he gently replied, "It makes a difference to *that* one!"[7]

There are several important points to be gained from this story: (1) the boy acknowledges a dream or vision, (2) he expresses that dream despite difficult odds or conventional wisdom, (3) he acts on a dream that he may not fully realize, and (4) he treats saving each starfish as a single incident within the bigger dream.

What's Your Personal Leadership Vision?

What is your dream? What future end-state allows you to live your leadership life deliberately? To be a leader, you must affirm a socially purposeful dream that enlists the hearts and minds of others. You must be willing to express and strive for your dream, despite competing forces that make the dream difficult to obtain. You must act locally, but think globally. You must treat daily activities as incidents within the larger context of your leadership dream.

You are reading this book with some expectations for self-growth, such as being a better leader. This book provides several models to help you gain self-understanding. It also helps you to be more aware of your responsibility to act across the one-to-one, group, and organizational context. If, as a result of reading this book, your vision extends beyond you (if it goes beyond your own welfare), then your vision may be worthy of followership. To be aware of a dream that lives in the hearts of others and is sensed in your own heart is only a *needed beginning*. You must also ask questions. What is the key social purpose of your organization? How can you express it through metaphors and analogies to others? What values are motivating to you and to others as your organization moves toward that dream or vision?

Power and Leadership Purpose

Without a vision or dream that is bigger than yourself, you are more likely to serve only yourself. Serving only yourself does not allow you to be *in role*. You become wrapped up in self, instead of living in the basic responsibility of context. You, as a leader, do have a responsibility to yourself. However, that responsibility is for self-growth and self-development *in the service of others*. To grow, you must see the leadership position as a role—a role of service toward a vision for others and self.

Being in the service of others lets you see reality as others see it. But seeing reality as others see it doesn't mean it *must* be that way. It only means that you maintain a basis for understanding others' dreams and how their reality resonates with yours. Additionally, you must see others as you see yourself. You must treat them as you would treat yourself. To lead others, you must understand yourself and look for the same dreams in others.

The covenant that is established between a follower and a leader, and/or between an employee and the organization, is determined by the leader's driving purpose and values. Is it to make money or to serve the customer/

society? Without an explicitly stated social purpose, the meaning of work becomes self-centered, and the covenant becomes everyone for him or herself. Without social purpose, power is driven by the unquestioned norms of hierarchy and economics.

A projected image of both profit and social service can be simultaneously present in the minds of organizational followers. However, effective leaders do not allow profit to take precedence over social service, either by word or action. In a free society, followers continue to lend their hearts and minds to an endeavor by judging the integrity of leadership in light of social purpose. Their confidence lies in the integrity of the process and the purpose that the leader represents. Without social purpose and the leader's faithfulness to such social purpose, the follower sees no clear moral business criteria on which to assess the actions of the leader. Therefore, both the leader and follower fall back on their personal value systems and dispositions. The result is disorder and a lack of common purpose.

Power, within most organizations, is exercised through hierarchical and economic control. This kind of control motivates people through their need for "things" such as compensation, job security, and desire for hierarchical position. This form of control establishes a transaction between the leader and the follower that is based on a return of money for effort and action. There is no heart, no personal excitement, and no moral imperative in this transaction.

Power of this type is the rule in many organizations of today. In fact, many leaders judge their success by the amount of transactional control they possess within their organizations. This type of control explains the "politics" and shadow side of many of today's organizations. It produces much of the cynicism, apathy, and fear in today's organizations. Without the purpose of service, power is a means looking for an end—much like a gun looking for a target. It is contingent on the emotional, moral, and spiritual well-being of the individual who wields it.

There is quite a difference when power is based on a common dream or vision of service. This type of vision rekindles the individual's spirit to be of service. A vision with social purpose links individuals to moral values, asks them to take responsibility for what they believe, and act for the benefit of others *and* themselves. A social vision calls on the courage, determination, and character of each organizational member to live this vision, and values those who are committed to the same vision. A vision balances traditional control with moral mandates. As a leader, you are connecting the inner life of every follower with the same vision. You are bringing meaning to the lives of those you seek to serve.

Personality in Action

An individual's personality is a combination of his or her point of view, disposition, and history of living with these values and preferences. An individual's personality identifies the traits, essential qualities, and attributes described through the D-I-S-C and T-I-C-S models. Personality implies patterned behavior *in* a context.

The combination of disposition and points of view shapes the way you go about influencing others. Research presented thus far confirms this point. Disposition seems to correlate with specific leader behaviors more strongly and frequently than does point of view. Disposition drives the *way* someone leads, while values shape *what* people feel they are being led toward. The follower notices *how* the leader influences, which is based on the leader's disposition. The follower also perceives the *ends* toward which the influence is aimed. The leader's valuing points of view exhibit a stronger effect on the covenant that is or is not formed between the leader and follower, than does the leader's disposition.

LEARNINGS

The "So What" of Personality on Leadership Behavior

The remainder of this book is dedicated to helping you understand the implications and whether you understand yourself and are willing to use

CHAPTER 7 ■ VISION AND LEARNING

those understandings to enhance the way you lead. You have learned about disposition, values, and leading in a one-to-one context. Now, let's look at how leaders with certain dispositions or values are "inclined" to lead in one-to-one contexts. If you can see the impact of certain personality variables on leadership behaviors, then you can become "free" from your own uninformed behavior. You can change the way you lead to better obtain the results you and your follower(s) desire.

Disposition and Leadership Behaviors

As you examine Chart 7.1 on page 222, you will see, on the vertical axis of the first two sections of the chart, a list of the directive and supportive behaviors in the situational leadership model. The third section of the chart contains certain aspects of follower motivation and morale. Across the top, in the horizontal axis, are listed the D, I, S, and C variables, divided into goal-driven (GD) and fear-driven (FD) sections.

The data was obtained from almost 250 upper middle level leaders in more than a dozen companies. Over 1,200 followers were asked to report which behaviors, in a one-to-one context, were most typical of their leaders, as well as how they felt about certain motivation and morale issues. The leaders responded to questionnaires that disclosed their disposition and value bases.[8] The leaders were categorized, based on disposition and point of view; correlations were produced of followers' perceptions of leaders' behaviors. An asterisk identifies any perception that is statistically significant.

As you can see from the data in Chart 7.1, self-perceptions of disposition are connected to specific leader behaviors, as perceived by followers. There are distinctive relationships between D, I, S, or C dispositions and how leaders use directive and supportive behaviors in a one-to-one context. "D" and "C" leaders are prone to use directive behaviors, while "S" and "I" leaders are prone to use supportive behaviors. This is not absolute, but the general patterns are credible. Everyone is capable of many of these leader behaviors. What is shown here are central tendencies.

THE LEADER WITHIN: LEARNING ENOUGH ABOUT YOURSELF TO LEAD OTHERS

CHART 7.1 *Disposition and One-to-One Leader Behaviors*

	D		I		S		C	
	GD	FD	GD	FD	GD	FD	GD	FD
Directive Behaviors								
goal set	*		*		*			*
planning						*	*	*
priorities						*	*	*
roles						*	*	*
timelines		*				*	*	*
method of evaluation		*					*	*
show how					*			

	D		I		S		C	
	GD	FD	GD	FD	GD	FD	GD	FD
Supportive Behaviors								
listen		*	*	*	*	*		
praise		*	*	*	*			
ask for input		*	*	*	*	*		*
share organizational info.		*	*	*		*	*	
share info. about self		*	*					
problem solve					*	*		*
rationale building				*	*	*		

	D		I		S		C	
	GD	FD	GD	FD	GD	FD	GD	FD
Follower Motivation and Morale								
work involvement								
coworker competence	high					low		
team atmosphere	high		high			low		
opportunity for growth							low	
tension level	low					high		
organizational climate				high				
morale								
commitment						low		

* followers see the leader as using these behaviors
GD = Goal Driven
FD = Fear Driven

"D-ness" and Leadership Behavior in a One-to-One Context

As shown in Chart 7.1, the leader with a "D" disposition really doesn't provide much directive and supportive behavior in goal-driven situations, except to "point the way" through goal setting. "D" leaders are results oriented; they tend to delegate (S4) a great deal of work, regardless of direct report competency. They tend to be trailblazers who want and expect others to be competent and committed to implementing their ideas. In fact, some employees may hate to come to work on Monday because the "D" used all weekend to think about additional results he or she wants to accomplish. However, the problem is that the employee has yet to implement all of last Monday's list.

Directive Behavior

"D" leaders tend to be direct. How things are done is not as important as what and how much gets done. Repetitive tasks will seem dull to the "D" leader. They might even tell a follower, "I don't care how you do it, just get it done." Because the "Ds" know what they want, people view them as decisive. The only significant statistic is that the "D" tends to set goals.

Under stressful fear-driven conditions, "D" leaders will tend to emphasize timelines; and to increase the chances of getting results, they will establish methods of evaluation. Even under stress, "D" leaders show little interest in discussing how or in what sequence things will get done. This lack of setting priorities creates headaches for both "Ds" and their followers. Because "D" leaders want to accomplish several innovative ideas or multifaceted results, projects may conflict. If followers do not understand the "Ds" priorities, then they will not know what to do first. Thus, followers may not know how to allocate their time and things may not get done properly or on time.

Supportive Behaviors

First notice there are no significant connections in the goal-driven (GD) column. This implies that, as a rule, the "D" does not tend to use supportive behaviors. Only under stressful conditions do "D" leaders begin to listen, praise, ask for input, share information about the organization's operations, and disclose personal information. They show some sensitivity by becoming more supportive under pressure. They start to listen to employee ideas and suggestions, while praising and acknowledging employee results. In tough circumstances, "D" leaders will praise their people and realize they cannot get along without them. "D" leaders possess the skills to be supportive, but it may take "an act of Congress" to get them to use those skills.

Because "D" leaders seldom discuss problems and alternative solutions with followers, procedures tend to be ignored. In fact, for "D" leaders, the status quo is there to be changed. Due to the "D's" lack of problem solving and rationale building, followers may never really learn *how* to do something. The follower may never develop certain technical skills, and the leader may never appreciate the effort or skill required to do a particular job. Under stressful circumstances, "D" leaders move to supportive behavior, not because they want to be kind to people or develop relationships, but because it will be instrumental in achieving the results they desire.

Growth Actions

Pure "D" leaders become more effective if they take time to listen to their followers as intently as they do with those outside the organization. In fact, the "D" knows how to listen but usually does so more frequently when things become stressful. The wise thing would be to listen *before* things are stressful.

"D" leaders tend to act first, without much concern for how they or anyone else will accomplish the outcomes the "D" wants. "D" leaders can benefit from understanding how the outcome can be accomplished, thereby setting more realistic outcomes. In fact, they sometimes know what they ask cannot be done; but by asking the impossible, they get more than mediocrity. This approach, over time, tends to wear down the follower and produce employee spectators—particularly without the coaching or assistance required to achieve the expected outcomes.

"I-ness" and Leadership Behavior in a One-to-One Context

As shown in Chart 7.1 on page 222, the "I" leadership character is typified by supportive behaviors. "I" leaders tend to be follower-oriented leaders who like people and want to be liked and respected in return. They prefer lots of interaction with all types of people with diverse backgrounds. They accept people at face value—believing that job performance and human frailties are interwoven. "I" leaders want people to feel good about themselves and expect performance to take care of itself.

"I" leaders meet people easily, tend to have a good sense of humor, and tend to be quite verbal. Because they are so verbal and want to be liked by others, they praise people a great deal. "I" leaders look for verbal and nonverbal cues to rate how well they are accepted by others. These cues enable them to adjust their behavior, demonstrate concern and interest, and gain acceptance. "I" leaders appreciate direct, open communication on both personal and business matters. Followers who control their thoughts and emotions and provide few nonverbal cues drain the "I" leader's energy.

Directive Behaviors

"I" leaders are not seen as frequently using directive behaviors in a one-to-one context. At minimum, the "I" leader may discuss goals to help the follower see the relationship between the job and the organization's plans. The technology of the work (hows, product specifications, or the tactical aspects of product manufacturing) may not be nearly as interesting to them as the political life of the organization.

Under either stressful or normal conditions, the "I" leader requires a great deal of unnatural energy to plan, define roles, set priorities, create timelines, or show someone how to do a specific task. Paperwork and document analysis are difficult because people stimulate the "I" leaders, not "things" and details. "I" leaders tend to spend much of their day with followers, both in and out of the office.

Supportive Behaviors

"I" leaders tend to shape follower performance in a one-to-one context by being supportive. They use personal power when seeking mutual trust and respect with the follower. "I" leaders naturally tend toward a high supporting, low directing Style 3. They can be good listeners, although they sometimes talk too much. They solicit the followers' ideas to get them to solve their own problems, such as better technical solutions.

It is easy for "I" leaders to share information about themselves and how the organization is functioning. They establish networks quickly, which lets them link followers with others who can help. This enhances their credibility with followers. The only supportive behavior that is not used frequently is problem solving. Analyzing alternatives, exploring pros and cons, and structuring detailed implementation plans are tedious tasks for "I" leaders. They tend to leave the details to those who prefer them. Under stress, not much changes for "I" leaders except that self-disclosure and rationale building become less frequent. They may exaggerate praise to reduce conflict, gain acceptance, and bolster their image. However, unwarranted praise without relevant performance may seem somewhat manipulative and self-serving to the follower.

"I" leaders are "natural" users of S3 behavior in a one-to-one context. However, they find that using directive behaviors drains their energy; when they do use directive behaviors, it will usually be "softened" with supportive behaviors or Style 2. They are more concerned with people than with things, ideas, or results. The "I" leader views work as especially hard when dealing with followers who do not have the needed skills and competencies to perform their jobs.

Growth Action

The single best growth action for "I" leaders is to realize that they will not be liked by everyone. Seeking others' approval may not result in pleasing all of the people all of the time. "I" leaders may benefit from taking a stand on issues that may be somewhat unpopular, but may ultimately benefit all concerned.

"I" leaders can benefit from helping their followers set priorities, define timelines and methods of evaluation, and show how to achieve certain outcomes. The "I" leader also should consider being more organized in daily routine and physical surroundings, thus eliminating some external stimuli.

Reserving private time to assess priorities and action items during a specific period of their business day will help "I" leaders be more organized, which will lead to quality time with their followers.

"S-ness" and Leadership Behavior in a One-to-One Context

As shown in Chart 7.1 on page 222, "S" leaders tend to use both supporting and directing behaviors. They are the only dispositional type seen as showing the follower how to do a task; therefore, they are natural teachers for followers who must learn a particular task. "S" leaders are seen as quiet, logical, and supportive. They are also seen as consistent in their approach to business issues and problems. "S" leaders want followers to approach assignments based on proven practices, because that is the way they would do it.

Directive Behaviors

"S" leaders prefer direct involvement when working on tasks, and want to see projects to completion; the more tangible and practical the project, the better. They need a stable work environment for timely accomplishment of work projects, and like to examine a situation and plan each step before acting.

Though their approach is people based, they are not easily sidetracked with interpersonal issues. "S" leaders are usually easygoing, pleasant, and relaxed. They are both supportive and logical with followers. In conflict situations, they tend to accommodate others and comply with required changes to reduce instability or conflict.

"S" leaders, when goal driven, tend to use only the directive behaviors of goals setting and showing how when working with followers. While these are core directive behaviors needed to help followers grow, it does not feel "heavy-handed" due to the absence of timeline and priority pressures. "S" leaders generally clarify *what* projects or goals they want accomplished and *how* to accomplish them. The "hows" are based on established, proven practices. "S" leaders want to serve people, not pressure them. Under normal circumstances, "S" leaders seek to create a stable work environment, not an overly demanding work environment in which followers cannot get things done fast enough.

Under stressful situations, "S" leaders switch from a *"what* and *how"* focus to a *"when, with whom,* and *in what order"* focus. This shift is usually caused by pressure emanating from one or two levels above the "S" leader. If a higher level boss wants something done faster or wants a change, "S" leaders will comply. Under stressful situations, "S" leaders behave more directively by planning work in advance, setting priorities, creating timelines for the follower, and defining roles. Fewer decision-making prerogatives are in the hands of the follower until things settle down.

Followers view this directive behavior shift as pressure from levels above the "S" leader, and learn the pros and cons of accommodation by watching the "S" leader. Followers will tolerate this shift because the "S" leader offers supportive behaviors to accompany the directive behavior. Followers still believe the "S" leader is concerned about them, as well as outcomes.

Supportive Behaviors

"S" leaders do not change much under stress when using supportive behaviors. Their natural energy is demonstrated when listening, praising, and asking for follower input. While they do not disclose much about themselves, "S" leaders take the time to attend to the followers' problems—both work related and nonwork related. When dealing with followers' problems, they respond rationally, indirectly, and slowly.

Under stress, "S" leaders share more information about the organization. They tend to give the follower more information about the politics and/or rationale involved in certain decisions and about factors that may be influencing problems under discussion. Sharing information, "S" leaders embrace both managing the conflict in a situation *and* continuing to support their followers. They tend to praise people less because they are less sure of themselves and more introspective.

The "S" leaders' outlook stems from moderation—between change and stability, emotion and rationality, and support and direction. Under stressful conditions, their need to reduce conflict and ambiguity results in conforming to expectations. "Ss" are natural S3 (high supporting/low directing) leaders, who can quickly use S2 (high direction/high support) when pressure arises. They may have trouble confronting employees who are assertive or are not performing, and they may overlook things to keep the peace.

Growth Action

The biggest single growth action for "S" leaders is to *go toward* any conflict that they may experience. The "S" leaders' tendency to withdraw or become immobilized when confronted with conflicts tends to lessen their effectiveness. Thus, their challenge is to initiate and change a situation or practice that is no longer effective. Problems don't usually go away by waiting for them to "take care of themselves." Decisive action and new routines must be established. "S" leaders must face change and conflict with the optimism and skills they already possess, which are usually considerable when drawn on.

"C-ness" and Leadership Behavior in a One-to-One Context

The "C" leaders' disposition tends to bias their leadership behaviors toward directive behaviors, as shown in Chart 7.1 on page 222. Their disposition may result in followers feeling less support. "C" leaders prefer a controlled, process-based, and orderly work approach in which rational decision making, planning, and unemotional interactions can minimize conflict and aggression. They avoid directly aggressive behaviors in self and others. They control their emotions and prefer others to do the same.

"C" leaders like involvement with technical issues and ideas, rather than follower problems. Aggression in others or strong assertions without factual presentation and backup seem out of place and may even be viewed as insulting. An emotional follower, one who rocks the boat procedurally or interpersonally, will be avoided. "C" leaders find it much easier to work with people who comply with established procedures and show clear conceptual thinking. They judge others on their ability to analyze and express themselves logically.

"C" leaders show a strong preference to do things correctly, according to rules, procedures, or policies. They emphasize accuracy and quality in all they do to reduce the probability of dissension, criticism, and ridicule. Their sense of self is tied up in the quality of work they and their followers produce. "C" leaders believe they can increase quality output through thoughtful analysis, planning and adhering to procedures, and paying close attention to key details.

Directive Behaviors

"C" leaders are prone to using most of the directive behaviors advocated in the Situational Leadership® II model. They are in agreement with the importance of planning, identifying priorities, clarifying roles for the follower, establishing timelines, and determining methods by which to judge the quality and quantity of work.

"C" leaders tend to focus on microissues, procedures, and systems that define boundaries, limitations, and expectations. They tend not to set goals (except under pressure) or provide the big-picture rationale needed for the follower to understand why something must be done just so. They do not spend much time showing or telling a follower how to do something. "C" leaders think that the follower can best learn how to do something by reading the manuals, following standard operating procedures, or studying the technology in classes. They prefer to spend their time evaluating output, then providing further direction to gain the desired result. They will structure training classes and write handbooks or manuals that followers can use.

Under stressful circumstances, "C" leaders will goal set with followers and provide more "big-picture" information by linking followers' efforts to the larger organizational goals. Followers may tend to view the rationale provided as justification for existing rules and procedures. Under stress, directive behaviors do not change much, although "C" leaders may become more cautious, fastidious, and worried. They tend to become more argumentative or even nit-picking, and they may overanalyze people and tasks.

Supportive Behaviors

Except for sharing information about the organization and its systems, "C" leaders' supportive behavior is seen as minimal. They prefer not to show much emotion—verbally or nonverbally—regardless of people's needs. They control their own emotional intensity and expect others to do the same. They believe that logic and analysis should govern the relationship between the leader and followers. It takes unusual energy for the natural "C" leader to appear authentically and visibly supportive.

Under stressful circumstances, they try to ask followers for input and suggestions more frequently. The request for input is typically about task-related matters, rather than interpersonal matters. They also tend to explore problems more fully under stress and spend more time examining the alternatives and consequences. This trend to problem solve with followers can contribute to their general pattern of overanalysis, nit-picking, and "worried" behavior. In the absence of praising, self-disclosure, or listening, their problem-solving efforts may seem like overly cautious, uptight leader interference, rather than genuinely supportive behavior.

Because "C" leaders prefer to be directive, they tend to be somewhat facilitative to followers who want to learn "from the ground up." These followers bring enthusiasm to the game, but few skills. "C" leaders tend to use S1 or S4 leadership styles, and their focus is well suited to managing quality processes and systems in more complex situations with longer timelines, such as research and development functions. Because of their controlled emotional responses, they may not be seen as very supportive to their followers.

Growth Action

The most concerted growth action "C" leaders can take is to recognize and address the feelings they experience. After their feelings and emotions are understood, "C" leaders must allow expression in appropriate situations.

The question "C" leaders must answer is how to put pleasure and emotion in their own workday, as well as in others' work experience. It is not that "C" leaders lack emotions, but it is the effective expression of such emotions that allows others to recognize and express their own.

Values and Leadership Behaviors

Values are a key, but neglected and underestimated, part of most leaders' understanding of how to lead. Most leaders fail to comprehend the potential impact and energy that comes from the stimulation of followers' personal and organizational values. Leaders must reflect, through their actions and words, the common values that live in their hearts *and* in the hearts of their followers. Followers must be convinced that the leader is a resource and ally for their dreams and can be counted on to remind them of those dreams when forgotten.

The research summarized in Chart 7.2 on page 233 demonstrates that the leader's values influence the way the follower sees the organization more frequently than the leader's disposition. As you examine Chart 7.2, several points can be made. First, the follower's perceptions of directive and supportive leader behaviors do not correlate with the leader's own points of view (values). Second, the leader persona is reflected through the leader's value base. Third, the traditionalist point of view seems to be dependent on the organization's approach to leadership. Finally, the follower's perception of self commitment and morale is strongly correlated with the leader's values or points of view.

Leader Values and Follower Perceptions of Leader Behaviors

As you examine others' perceptions (OP column), you can see there are very few correlations or connections between points of view and the use of directive and supportive behaviors, except for the synthesizer point of view.

The absence of correlations or connections means that, for the most part, disposition, not values, drives the way a leader acts in leadership situa-

CHART 7.2 *Values Points of View and One-to-One Leader Behaviors*

SP = Self perception of leader behaviors
OP = Others' perception of leader behaviors

Directive Behaviors

	Traditionalist		Inbetweener		Challenger		Synthesizer	
	SP	OP	SP	OP	SP	OP	SP	OP
goal set			*					
planning		++	*					++
priorities								++
roles								
timelines					*			++
method of evaluation					*			
show how			*	X	*			

Supportive Behaviors

	Traditionalist		Inbetweener		Challenger		Synthesizer	
	SP	OP	SP	OP	SP	OP	SP	OP
listen			*				*	X
praise			*		*			
ask for input								X
share organizational info.								
share info. about self			*		*			X
problem solve								
rationale building			*					X

Group Motivation and Morale

	Traditionalist		Inbetweener		Challenger		Synthesizer	
	SP	OP	SP	OP	SP	OP	SP	OP
work involvement			low		low			
coworker competency			low		low		high	high
team atmosphere			low		low		high	
opportunity for growth	high				low			
tension level								
organizational climate							high	high
morale			high		low			
commitment			high		high	low	high	

* denotes that leader sees self as using these behaviors
x denotes that followers see the leader as using these behaviors
++ denotes that followers see the leader as not using these behaviors

tions. As you examine Chart 7.1 (page 222) you can see that there are 49 significant correlations (Follower Perceptions) with DISC patterns and directive and supportive behaviors. As seen in Chart 7.2 (page 233), there are only nine significant correlations (Follower Perceptions) with points of view (values) and the directive and supportive behaviors. In other words, disposition exhibits more influence on the *way* leaders implement their leadership function. For example, disposition seems to determine if and how a leader sets goals or praises, but the leader's values or point of view does not.

Chart 7.2 shows that followers see traditionalists as not using planning behaviors, inbetweeners as showing how to do a task, and challengers as not using any particular leader behaviors.

The only point of view that seems to influence follower perception of leader behavior is the synthesizer point of view. The synthesizer value base results in followers perceiving the leader as *not* using directive behaviors such as planning, priority setting, or emphasizing timelines. However, the synthesizer is seen as a listener and one who asks for input, shares information about the self, and prompts rationale building. The synthesizer point of view appears to *drive* these leader behaviors, which results in the leader being values driven as well as disposition driven when working with followers. Given the importance of their own personal values of inner congruence and justice, synthesizers want to listen to others, ask for input, and build teams.

Persona and Values Point of View

As you examine self-perceptions (SP column) in light of the others' perceptions (OP column) you can see that various points of view appear to produce some self-delusions concerning how leaders believe they function versus what is actually experienced and reported by followers.

The persona of the inbetweener and challenger is quite interesting. The inbetweener point of view seems to result in the leader perceiving him or herself as using the directive behaviors of goal setting, planning, and showing the follower how to do a specific task. Followers' perceptions do not confirm these first two behaviors, but they do confirm the behavior of showing how. Notice the inbetweener point of view results in the leader *thinking* that he or she listens, praises, shares information about the self, and engages in rationale building; but none of these self-perceptions are confirmed by the followers' perceptions.

Remember that the inbetweener point of view holds personal ends and social means values. The leader with an inbetweener point of view can be easily deluded into thinking that his or her social means values of growth, equality, and helpfulness are seen as supportive, but this does not appear to be the case. The persona, the person that the leader presents to the outside world, puts social means first, but the follower may view this as insincere because the follower also sees the personal ends that drive the leader. These values can be so "in-between" that the follower has no sense that the leader will take a stand on anything of significance, let alone believe that the leader *values* sound management practices. Leaders who hold the inbetweener point of view may not be seen as connecting their values to the way they influence. Instead, the persona or "self" they want to present to the outside world is seen by their followers as being different from the leaders' "true" intent.

Leaders who hold a challenger point of view also tend to delude themselves. Challengers tend to see themselves as using directive behaviors, such as establishing timelines, defining methods of evaluation, and showing the follower how to do a particular task. This is not confirmed by follower perceptions. The challenger perceives that they use praising behaviors and sharing information about themselves. These behaviors are also not confirmed by follower perceptions. Challengers, like the inbetweeners, tend to think that their values are reflected in their leadership practices, but this is not supported by follower perceptions. As with the inbetweener point of view, the challenger value base is seen as being more disposition driven than values driven.

The persona of the synthesizer seems to be more values driven than the traditionalist, inbetweener, or challenger. (You might want to review the description of the synthesizer point of view, which starts on page 143 of

Chapter 4). It seems that the synthesizer's end value of integration, and means values of logic, justice, and inner congruence, are consistent with their leadership approach as reported by their followers. Interestingly enough, they don't see themselves as doing so, except in the case of listening behavior.

Traditionalists and the Organization

A logical, confirmed finding is that traditionalist leaders' perceptions show almost no self or others' correlations with leader behaviors. Except for the fact that followers see traditionalists as not using planning behaviors, there are no other connections between follower perceptions and leader value bases. There is also no relationship between self-perceptions of leader behavior and value base.

The lack of correlations between the self-value base to follower perceptions is explainable in that traditionalist leaders establish their values through the reference group to which they belong. Research proves that traditionalist leaders tend to advocate or support the management or leadership approach stated by the organization for which they work. When further analysis was done, there were correlations found by companies. While the correlations were different for the traditionalist across different companies, this was not the case with the other three valuing points of view. In other words, the variation in correlations between follower perceptions and traditionalist values was due to the differences of the organization to which they belonged.

Traditionalist leaders tend to use leader behaviors that are acceptable or expressed by the company in which they work. This implies that if a company has an inadequate set of management practices in place, the traditionalist may do little to openly counteract them. Conversely, if a company has vigorous employee-oriented leader practices in place, the traditionalist leader will do his or her best to openly support those practices.

CHAPTER 7 ■ VISION AND LEARNING

Morale and Leader Values

The most important finding from the research is that the *leaders' values or point of view has a greater impact on the followers' view of motivation and morale than does the leaders' disposition*. As you examine Chart 7.1, you can see that disposition does correlate, to some degree, with follower perceptions of team atmosphere, opportunities for growth in the company, tension level, and climate and commitment to the company. However, these correlations are few compared to the number of correlations found with values and leader behaviors (Chart 7.2, page 233). Remember that both Chart 7.1 and Chart 7.2 are basically comparing follower perceptions of leaders' use of direction and support, although in Chart 7.2 we included the leaders' self-perceptions. Use the OP column of Chart 7.2, when comparing to Chart 7.1.

There are a greater number of correlations between leader value systems and follower perceptions of company motivation and morale than between leader disposition and company morale. It seems that while leaders' personal values are not a predictor of leader behaviors, they may be a predictor of motivation and morale. A secondary point is that employee motivation and morale is not solely contingent on leader behavior as manifested through directive and supportive elements.

Challenger Point of View and Follower Morale

As shown in Chart 7.2, page 233, the leader who holds a challenger point of view tends to have demotivated followers. As you ponder this correlation, remember that challengers hold personal ends and personal means values. This point of view is concerned with self-rights and personal freedom.

As indicated by the low scores, followers who work with a challenger leader tend not to find the work involving, are not likely to see their coworkers as competent, do not sense a team atmosphere, and do not see opportunity for professional growth. They are not happy in the work environment, as indicated by the low morale scores, and do not feel much commitment to remain with the organization. Because those perceptions are not held by the followers who work with traditionalists or synthesizer leaders, it could be concluded that the leader who holds a challenger or inbetweener point of view may be creating, or is at least partly responsible for creating, a toxic work environment for followers.

If you are a leader who holds a challenger viewpoint, you should be concerned with the impact your values may have on your followers' motivation and morale. You tend to be seen as self-oriented and protective of your freedom, and this may cause followers to feel the same. The emotional state of your followers will range from open defiance, to passive resistance, to uncommitted compliance. You may even need to coerce them to perform. This, of course, is not effective leadership. You may want to consider changing your point of view, leading a group of challengers, or stepping out of the leadership position you hold.

Inbetweener Point of View and Follower Morale

As shown in Chart 7.2, if you hold an inbetweener point of view, your persona is not likely to be seen as you would expect it to be. You tend to delude yourself by thinking that your values of seeing many points of view will result in others feeling positive about you. The means values of self-growth, equality, and helpfulness, and the ends values of self-expression and happiness *do not* produce positively motivated followers.

Followers may soon get the sense that the leader uses them. They may think the leader views people as serving a purpose—for information or joint business purposes. Followers who work with a leader who holds inbetweener values tend not to see the work they do as self-involving, do not see their coworkers as competent, and do not feel there is a team atmosphere in the company.

Because inbetweeners tend to waffle on issues and tend to continue to collect more and more information before making a decision, they exhibit a tendency to delay or change decisions. Inbetweeners tend to lack the

CHAPTER 7 ■ VISION AND LEARNING

courage to make tough decisions. They can't confront reality and therefore can be seen as not being there on substantive issues.

Inbetweeners tend to want to leave their options open. They want harmony among all concerned; yet, they want to meet their own self-interests. Inbetweeners tend to try to shape things in their favor. They inwardly ask how can I optimize my opportunities, not "our" opportunities. This dilemma leads, ultimately, to loss of respect and confidence by followers. Protracted decisions or indecision may ultimately diminish follower implementation, cause waste, and promote unnecessary conflict and tension.

If you hold an inbetweener point of view, you may undoubtedly feel hurt and misunderstood because you expect to be appreciated for your concern for others. Followers may see you as supportive or fair, but that does not cause them to respect or admire you as a leader. When followers try to act within a framework of clear and consistent values to make a work/organizational decision and you model a tolerance to a range of different values without advocating anything specific, followers become immobilized. Leader credibility may be lowered because there are no effective leadership behaviors being demonstrated. There is no clarity of purpose within which followers need to act in unison and, because there is no clarity, there is no genuine empowerment of people. Direction is lacking and consistent, purposeful organizational action is limited.

Leaders who hold inbetweener values must learn to take a stand based on past learning and key ongoing commitments. Review the growth actions recommended on page 142 of Chapter 4. Inbetweeners should try to build an organizational vision, and then consistently model the purpose expectations and organizational values that they established. They should also try to make decisions more quickly and more consistently within their vision framework. Lastly, like challengers, they too can benefit from understanding and prizing the advice of qualified internal and external people who operate from a different personal value base.

Synthesizer Point of View and Follower Morale

As shown by comparing synthesizer self-perceptions and those of followers in Chart 7.2, synthesizers are seen as using, or not using, many more leader behaviors than they give themselves credit for. If you are a synthesizer, followers see you as someone who does not follow a plan, set priorities, or emphasize deadlines. You are seen as someone who listens, frequently asks followers for their input, shares information about yourself, and emphasizes rationale building. These behaviors create a positive effect on the followers' perceptions of the organization's climate and sense of coworker competence.

A secondary analysis shows the inbetweener as someone who also listens, shares information about him or herself, and emphasizes a rationale building; but the effects on the followers' perceptions of group motivation and morale are different. The synthesizer value base tends to produce more positive follower perceptions of the organization. As a synthesizer, you tend to underestimate how your values influence your leader behaviors, but you are somewhat correct in believing that your employees will see the organizational climate as positive. Your means values of logic, justice, and inner congruence, and ends values of integration of self with others, tend to produce positive motivation and morale in followers you lead.

The End of the Beginning

As you can see from the models and research presented, good leadership starts from the inside out. The disposition and point of view you hold shape your capacity to first understand the context in which you lead and then the way you act, which may be functional or dysfunctional, depending on the situation. Each disposition and point of view can tend toward dysfunctionality, although some dispositions and value points of view are more prone to be less effective than others.

The questions still remain: Are you willing and capable to be more adaptable? Are you willing to use unfamiliar behaviors that may be required by the context and the situation? Are you willing to appreciate other aspects of yourself? Are you willing to pick up the starfish and make a difference by becoming committed to changing yourself? Are you willing and capable to apply the leadership and management practices described in this book?

EPILOGUE

We intentionally did not develop the topic of character as opposed to personality, although we are fortunate to know and observe leaders with character. Instead, our treatment of personality demonstrates its connection with leader behaviors.

However, in this epilogue, we take a moment to explain some fundamental insights concerning the topic of Character. The demonstration of Character is observed less frequently among leaders, and is qualitatively different from the exhibition of preference, habit, goal, fear, values, or personality in general.

The Expression of Character

The word "ethics," in our culture, is derived from the Greek word "ethos," which means Character. One dimension of ethos or Character concerns the relationship of the individual to the community. The community's expectations, standards, or ethics place "conditions" on the preferences, values, and ultimately, the behavior of the individual. Because both Character and character are essentially social, it is the individual's relationship with the demands of the community that needs to be understood to act ethically. The individual's Character is expressed as the interactive result (behaviors) of what he or she does with the community's expectations and standards.

Definition of Character

While Character is the resultant behavior of both disposition and values, it is more a product of the individual's values and less a product of disposition. In fact, we believe Character is the consistently thoughtful demonstration of an individual's *values* in light of community expectations. *It is individual or collective action, over time, toward a humane vision, in a context where individuals are faced with significant obstacles, competition, or temptations.*

There are many aspects to this definition. The most important is the ingredient of a humane vision. By humane vision, we mean a vision that involves the intellectual and emotional commitment to equity in all human relationships. Equity involves not only equality of opportunity but also fairness and justice. It involves social ends and social means. Equity means that what we do to others, we do to ourselves.

For instance, think about the values that Mahatma Gandhi, Mother Teresa, Abraham Lincoln, Susan B. Anthony, Martin Luther King, Jr., or Albert Schweitzer championed. Think of their visions. Do not dwell on their disposition, but instead recall their advocated values. Contrast their values and visions to the visions and values of Adolf Hitler, Saddam Hussein, or Joseph Stalin. Where is the equity in the visions of the latter? Where is the connection to self and others that ensures compassion and justice for all concerned? Where are the consistently demonstrated leadership actions that are in the best interests of all?

As an executive or business leader, you might feel somewhat removed from these questions. You might even say there is little connection with your leadership circumstance. It is the essence of a humane vision that we want you to understand. What kind of humanism is contained in the vision of your organization? What kind of equity is espoused in your organization's strategies, goals, policies, and procedures? Who are the second- and third-class citizens in your organization? What is the meaning of the work your organization does? Are your organization's members forced to find a humane vision outside of the organization's boundaries? What thought have you given to the promotion of equity in human relationships in your organization?

In essence, Character is about doing good rather than harm to others, whether the harm is intentional or not. This widely recognized critical dimension of Character in fact supersedes community or social views over time. Leaders who demonstrate such Character are respected, trusted, and admired by people. This consistent core principle is not limited to specific situations, roles, decisions, or eras in the life of their organization. Instead, it is a large part of the leaders' core self—how they define and thereafter conduct themselves—in all contexts and with all people. For those who develop this strength, Character is the unifying ingredient for all layers of the self—a unification that results in compelling leadership from the inside out.

The concept of equity in business organizations is not dealt with easily. There are some who did a credible job.[9] Creating a just organization is like "pushing a rope." It is not easy; it requires thought. It takes leading by example. Equity requires "wearing the cloth" of second-class citizens until "classness" is changed. It requires clarifying the social purpose of the organization so the purpose and meaning of the work is foremost, not the making of money. It means equitably sharing the wealth, status, power, and opportunity to perform with all followers who are competent and committed to do so.

Character on a Personal Level

To this point, we define Character, on an organizational level, by stating that there is always a moral dimension to leadership actions. It could be as insignificant as the impact of title you hold in the organization or where you park. It could be as important as the salary you receive or the information you are willing to share. Character on a personal level is demonstrated by the commitment you make to the vision of equity in human relationships, in any context.

The commitment to equity requires leaders to be in the service of others. It requires the patient understanding and effective management of those whose moral consciousness resides in the service of themselves. Your service must present a contrast of morals, which allows others to choose equity and justice.

Endnotes

1. Nair 1994. Reprinted with permission of the publisher. All rights reserved.
2. See Langeler 1990; Ferris 1992; Nanus 1992; Boyd 1991; Tregoe et al. 1989; Kauppinen and Ogg 1994.
3. See Stoner-Zemel and Zigarmi 1993 for in-depth discussion and process for alignment.
4. Gerard 1990.
5. Blanchard and O'Connor 1997.
6. For an in-depth treatment of science and leadership, see Wheatley 1992.
7. Barker.
8. The classic dispositions are presented here but all 16 dispositions were computed. See Zigarmi, O'Connor, and Blanchard 1992.
9. See Liebig 1990.

Bibliography

Abrams, J. and Zweig, C. *Meeting the Shadow.* New York: G. P. Putnam Sons, 1991.

Adams, J. P. *Transforming Work.* Alexandria, VA: Mills River Press, 1984.

Adizes, I. *Corporate Life Cycles: How and Why Corporations Grow and Die and What to Do About It.* Englewood Cliffs, NJ: Prentice Hall, 1988.

Adler, N. J. and Izreli, D. N. *Women in Management, World-Wide.* New York: M. E. Sharpe, 1989.

Alessandra, T., O'Connor, M. J., and Alessandra, J. *People Smart.* La Jolla, CA: Keynote Publishing Company, 1990.

Asimov, I. *Isaac Asimov's Treasury of Humor.* Boston: Houghton Mifflin, 1971.

Atwater, L. E. and Yammarino, F. J. "Does Self-Other Agreement on Leadership Perceptions Moderate the Validity of Leadership and Performance Predictions?" *Personal Psychology.* 45, No. 1., pp. 141-163, 1992.

Barker, J. "Discovering The Future: The Business of Paradigms Video." Minneapolis, MN: Chart House Learning Corporation.

Bass, B. M. and Yammarino, F. "Congruence of Self and Others' Leadership Ratings of Naval Officers for Understanding Successful Performance." *Applied Psychology: An International Review.* 40, pp. 437-454, 1991.

Bass, B. M. *Bass and Stogdill's Handbook of Leadership*, 3rd edition. New York: Free Press, A Division of Macmillan, Inc., 1990.

Bass, B. M. *Leadership and Performance Beyond Expectations.* New York: Macmillan, 1985.

Bem, S. L. "Theory and Measurement of Androgyny: A Reply to the Pedhazur-Tetenbaum and Locksley-Colten Critiques." *Journal of Personality and Social Psychology.* 37, pp. 1047-1054, 1979.

Bem, S. L. and Lenney, E. "Sex Typing and the Avoidance of Cross Sex Behavior." *Journal of Personality and Social Psychology.* 33, pp. 48-54, 1976.

Bennis, W. and Nanus, B. *Leaders: Strategies for Taking Charge*. New York: Harper and Row Publishers, 1985.

Bennis, W. *On Becoming a Leader.* Reading, MA: Addison-Wesley Publishing Company, Inc., 1989.

Birden, L. *Leadership Behavior Styles of Administration and School Climate in Area Vocational Schools in Oklahoma as Perceived by Teachers.* Unpublished Doctoral Dissertation. Oklahoma State University, Norman, OK. 1992

Blake, R. R. and Mouton, J. S. *The Managerial Guide.* Houston, TX: Gulf Publishing, 1964.

Blanchard, K., Carew, D., and Parisi-Carew, E. *The One Minute Manager Builds High Performing Teams.* Escondido, CA: Blanchard Training and Development, Inc., 1990.

Blanchard, K., Zigarmi, P., and Zigarmi, D. *Situational Leadership II Facilitators Guide*. Escondido, CA: Ken Blanchard Companies, 1994.

Blanchard, K. and O'Connor, M. *Managing by Values*. San Francisco, CA: Berrett-Koehler Publishers, Inc., 1997.

Blanchard, K. and Sargent, A. "The One Minute Manager Is an Androgynous Manager." *Training and Development Journal.* pp. 83-85, May 1984.

Blanchard, K., Zigarmi, P., and Zigarmi, D. *Leadership and the One Minute Manager.* New York: Morrow Publishers, 1985.

BIBLIOGRAPHY

Blanchard, K. H., Zigarmi, D., and Nelson, R. "Situational Leadership After 25 Years: A Retrospective." *Journal of Leadership Studies.* 8, No. 1., pp. 21-36, 1993.

Block, P. *Stewardship: Choosing Service over Self-Interest.* San Francisco, CA: Berret-Koehler Publishers, Inc., 1993.

Bly, R. *A Little Book on the Human Shadow.* San Francisco, CA: HarperCollins Harper, 1988.

Boyd, T. *Visions: From Leaders of Today for Leaders of Tomorrow.* Alexa Press, 1991.

Braddock, C. *Body Voices: Using the Power of Breath, Sound and Movement to Heal and Create New Boundaries.* Berkeley, CA: Page Mill Press, 1995.

Bradford, D. L. and Cohen, A. *Managing for Excellence.* New York: John Wiley and Sons, 1984.

Buckingham, M. "Marcus Buckingham Thinks Your Boss Has an Attitude Problem." *Fast Company.* p. 88, August 2001.

Burns, J. M. *Leadership.* New York: Harper and Row Publishers, 1978.

Carew, D., Parisi-Carew, E., and Blanchard, K. "Group Development and Situational Leadership II: A Model for Managing Groups." *Monograph.* Escondido, CA: Blanchard Training and Development, Inc., 1990.

Claro, J. (Ed.). *Random House Large Print Book of Jokes and Anecdotes.* New York: Random House, 1994.

Conger, J. A. *The Charismatic Leader: Behind the Mystique of Exceptional Leadership.* San Francisco, CA: Jossey-Bass, 1989.

Deal, T. E. and Kennedy, A. A. *Corporate Cultures: The Rites and Rituals of Corporate Life.* Reading, MA: Addison-Wesley Publishers, Inc., 1982.

Deci, E. *Why We Do What We Do: The Dynamics of Personal Autonomy.* New York: Grossett/Putnam Books, 1995.

DePalma, D. J. and Foley, J. M. *Moral Development: Current Theory and Research.* Hillsdale, NJ: Lawrence Erlbaum Associates Publishers, 1975.

DePree, M. *Leadership Is an Art.* New York: Doubleday, 1987.

Doehrman, M. "Center for Creative Leadership in Colo. Springs Advises Managers About Employee Job Satisfaction." *Colorado Springs Business Journal. 21,* November 2003.

Eby, L. T., Freeman, D. M., Rush, M. C., and Lance, C. E. "Motivational Bases of Affective Organizational Commitment: A Partial Test of an Integrative Theoretical Model." *Journal of Occupational and Organizational Psychology.* 72, No. 4, pp. 463-483, 1999.

Egan, G. *Working the Shadow Side: A Guide to Positive Behind-the-Scenes Management.* San Francisco, CA: Jossey-Bass, 1994.

England, G. W. "Personal Value Systems of American Managers." *Academy of Management Journal.* 10, 53-68, 1967.

Erickson, E. H. *Gandhi's Truth.* New York: W. W. Norton, 1969.

Eysenck, H. J. and Eysenck, M. W. *Personality and Individual Differences: A Natural Science Approach.* New York: Plenum Press, 1985.

Fagan, M. M., Bromley, K., and Welch, J. "Using Biographies to Teach Leadership." *Journal of Leadership Studies. 1*, No. 4, 1994.

Farh, J. and Dobbins, G. "Effects of Self Esteem on Leniency Bias in Self-Reports of Performance: A Structural Equation Model Analysis." *Personnel Psychology.* 42, pp. 835-850, 1989.

Feather, N. T. "Educational Choice and Student Attitudes in Relation to Terminal and Instrumental Values." *Australian Journal of Psychology.* 22, pp. 127-143, 1970.

Feather, N. T. "Masculinity, Femininity, Psychological Androgyny and the Structure of Values." *Journal of Personality and Social Psychology. 50*, pp. 94-99, 1984.

Ferris, G. "Building a Vision Community." *Journal for Quality and Participation.* Oct./Nov. 1992.

Fiedler, F. E. *A Theory of Leadership Effectiveness.* New York: McGraw-Hill Book Company, 1967.

Fletcher, J. K. "Castrating the Female Advantage: Feminist Standpoint Research and Management Science." *Journal of Management Inquiry. 3*, pp. 74-84, 1994.

Flocco, R. "An Examination of the Leader Behavior of School Business Administration." *Dissertation Abstracts International. 30*, pp. 84-85, 1969.

Fritz, R. *The Path of Least Resistance: Learning to Become the Creative Force in Your Own Life.* New York: Fawcett Columbine, 1984.

Fromm. E. "Character and the Social Process." In G. Lindzey and C. S. Hall (Eds.), *Theories of Personality: Primary Sources and Research.* New York: John Wiley and Sons, pp. 117-124, 1965.

BIBLIOGRAPHY

Gardner, H. *Leading Minds: An Anatomy of Leadership.* New York: Basic Books, 1995.

Gerard, J. "Sesame Street is Talking About Race from A to Z." *New York Times.* November 21, 1990.

Goldsmith, H. H. "Genetic Influences on Personality from Infancy to Adulthood." *Child Development.* 54, pp. 331-355, 1983.

Greenleaf, R. K. *The Servant as Leader.* Indianapolis, IN: Robert K. Greenleaf Center, 1991.

Greiner, L. "Evolution and Revolution as Organizations Grow." *Harvard Business Review.* pp. 37-46, Jul./Aug. 1977.

Hall, G. E., George, A. A., and Rutherford, W. L. *Measuring Stages of Concern About Innovation: A Manual for Use of the SOL Questionnaire.* Research and Development Center for Teacher Education, University of Texas at Austin, 1977.

Hall, G. and Hord, S. *Change in Schools: Facilitating the Process.* New York: State University of New York Press, 1987.

Hampden-Turner, C. *Maps of the Mind.* New York: Collier Books-Macmillan Publishing Company, 1981.

Harris, M. and Schaubroeck, J. "A Meta-Analysis of Self-Supervisor, Self-Peer and Peer/Supervisor Ratings." *Personnel Psychology.* 41, pp. 43-61, 1988.

Hersey, P. and Blanchard, K. H. "Life Cycle Theory of Leadership." *Training and Development Journal.* May 1969.

Hickman, C. R. *Mind of a Manager; Soul of a Leader.* New York: John Wiley and Sons, Inc., 1990.

Hofstede, G. *Culture Consequences: International Differences in Work-Related Values.* Beverly Hills, CA: Sage Publications, 1980.

Hough, L., Keyes, M., and Dunnette, M. "An Evaluation of Three 'Alternative' Selection Procedures." *Personnel Psychology.* 36, pp. 261-275, 1983.

Hudson Institute and Walker Information. "The 1999 National Business Ethics Study." *www. walkerinfo.com,* 1999.

Husted, B. "Bell South Exec Got $4.3 Million to Retire." *Atlanta Journal.* p. F1, March 24, 1995.

Jacobi, J. *The Psychology of C.G. Jung.* New Haven, CT: Yale University Press, 1973.

Jaworski, J. *Synchroncity: The Inner Path of Leadership.* San Francisco, CA: Berrett-Koehler Publishing, 1996.

Jensen, T. D., White, D. D., and Singh, R. "Impact of Gender, Hierarchial Position and Leadership Styles on Work-Related Issues." *Journal of Business Research. 20,* pp. 145-152, 1990.

Johnson, J. W. "Linking Employee Perceptions of Service Climate to Customer Satisfaction." *Personnel Psychology: Journal of Applied Research. 49,* No. 4, Winter 1996.

Johnson, R. A. *Owning Your Own Shadow: Understanding the Dark Side of the Psyche.* New York: HarperCollins, 1991.

Jung, C. G. *Man and His Symbols.* Garden City, NY: Doubleday and Company, 1964.

Jung, C. G. *Memories, Dreams and Reflections.* A. Jaffe (Ed.). New York: Vintage Books, 1961.

Jung, C. G. *Psychological Types.* New York: Harcourt and Brace, 1923.

Kagen, R. *In Over Our Heads: The Mental Demands of Modern Life.* Cambridge, MA: Harvard University Press, 1994.

Kahn, R. L., Wolfe, D. M., Quinn, R. P., and Snock, J. D. *Organizational Stress: Studies in Role Conflict and Ambiguity.* New York: John Wiley and Sons, Inc., 1964.

Kanter, R. M. *Men and Women of the Corporation.* New York: Basic Books, 1977.

Kauppinen, T. J. and Ogg, A. J. *Vision Into Action: The Leader's Guide to Driving Change in Turbulent Times.* San Diego, CA: Leadership Studies International, Inc., 1994.

Keirsey, D. and Bates, M. *Please Understand Me: Character and Temperament Types.* Del Mar, CA: Prometheus Nemesis Books, 1978.

Keleman, S. *Emotional Anatomy: The Structure of Experience.* Berkeley, CA: Center Press, 1985.

Keller, L. M., Bouchard, T. J., Arvey, R. D., Segal, N. L., and Dawis, R. V. "Work Values: Genetic and Environmental Influences." *Journal of Applied Psychology.* 77, No. 1, pp. 79-88, 1992.

Ket de Vries, M. F. R. *Prisoners of Leadership.* New York: John Wiley and Sons, 1989.

BIBLIOGRAPHY

Kim, S. "Participative Management and Job Satisfaction: Lessons for Management Leadership." *Public Administration Review.* 62, No. 2, 2002.

Kohlberg, L. "Continuities in Childhood and Adult Moral Development Revisited. In *Life-Span Developmental Psychology: Personality and Socialization.* Balters, P. B. and Schaie, K. W. (Eds.). New York: Academic Press, 1973.

Kohlberg, L. "Development of Moral Character and Moral Ideology." In *Review of Child Development Research.* Vol. 1. Hoffman, M. L. and Hoffman, L. W. (Eds.). New York: Russell Sage Foundation, 1964.

Kohlberg, L. "From Is to Ought, How to Commit, the Naturalistic Fallacy and Get Away With It in the Study of Moral Development." In *Cognitive Development and Epistemology.* Mischel, T. (Ed.). New York: Academic Press, 1971.

Kohlberg. L. *Stages in the Development of Moral Thought and Action.* New York: Holt, Rinehart & Winston, 1965.

Komaki, J. L. "Toward Effective Supervision: An Operant Analysis and Comparison of Managers at Work." *Journal for Applied Psychology.* 71, No. 2, pp. 270-279, 1986.

Komaki, J. L., Zlotnick, S., and Jensen, M. "Development of an Operant-Based Taxonomy and Observational Index of Supervisory Behavior." *Journal of Applied Psychology.* 71, No. 2, pp. 260-269, 1986.

Korabik, K. and Ayman, R. "Should Women Managers Have to Act Like Men?" *Journal of Management and Development.* 8, pp. 23-32, 1989.

Korman, A. K. "Consideration: Initiating Structure and Organizational Criteria—A Review." *Personnel Psychology: A Journal of Applied Research.* 19, No. 4, Winter 1966.

Kotter, J. P. *A Force for Change: How Leadership Differs from Management.* New York: Free Press, 1990.

Kouzes, J. M. and Posner, B. Z. *The Leadership Challenge: How to Get Extraordinary Things Done in Organizations.* San Francisco, CA: Jossey-Bass Publications, 1987.

Kroeger, O. and Thuesen, T. M. *Type Talk: Or How to Determine Your Personality Type and Change Your Life.* New York: Bantam Doubleday Dell Publishing Group, Inc., 1988.

Kurtines, W. and Greif, E. B. "The Development of Moral Thought: A Review and Evaluation of Kohlberg's Approach." *Psychological Bulletin.* 81, No. 8, August 1974.

Labich, K. "Kissing Off Coporate America." *Fortune.* pp. 44-50, Feb. 20, 1995.

Lacoursiere, R. B. *The Life Cycle of Group: Group Development Stage Theory.* New York: Human Service Press, 1980.

Langeler, G. H. "The Vision Trap." *Harvard Business Review.* March-April 1990.

Lee, C. "Beyond Teamwork." *Training Magazine.* 1993.

Levinson, D. J., with Darrow, C. N., Klein, E. B., Levinson, M. H., and McKee, B. *The Seasons of a Man's Life.* New York: Alfred A. Knopf, 1978.

Liebig, J. E. *Business Ethics: Profiles in Civic Virtue.* Golden, CO: Fulcrum Publishing, 1990.

Lobben, S. *An Analysis of the Relationships between Clinical Supervision and Situational Leadership: The Development Process to Increase Clinical Supervision Effectiveness.* Unpublished Doctoral Dissertation. University of Massachusetts, Amherst, MA, 1988.

Lombardo, M. M. "Value in Action: The Meaning of Executive Vignettes Technical Report #28." Greensboro, NC: Center for Creative Leadership, 1986.

Lorenz, K. *On Aggression.* New York: Harcourt Brace, 1966.

Loucks, S. F., Newlove, B. W., and Hall, G. E. *Measuring Levels of Use of the Innovation: A Manual for Trainers, Interviewers and Raters.* Research and Development Center for Teacher Education, University of Texas at Austin, 1975.

Luria, A. R. *The Nature of Human Conflicts.* New York: Washington Square Press, 1967.

Manchester, W. *The Last Lion: Winston Spencer Chruchill—Visions of Glory: 1874-1932.* New York: Laurel Trade Paperback, 1983.

Marston, W. M. *Emotions of Normal People.* Minneapolis, MN: Persona Press Inc., 1979.

Maslow, A. H. *Toward a Psychology of Being.* Princeton, NJ: Van Nostrand Press, 1968.

Massey, M. *The People Puzzle.* Reston, VA: Reston Publishing Co., 1979.

Massey, M. and O'Connor, M., *The Values Analysis Profile.* Minneapolis, MN: Performax Systems International, 1981.

Mintzberg, H. *The Nature of Managerial Work.* New York: Harper and Row, 1973.

Montagu, A. M. F. *Man and Aggression.* New York: Oxford University Press, 1968.

BIBLIOGRAPHY

Murphy, E. F., Eckstat, A., and Parker, T. "Sex and Gender Differences in Leadership." *Journal of Leadership Studies.* 2, No. 1, 1995.

Nair, K. *A Higher Standard of Leadership: Lessons from the Life of Gandhi.* San Francisco, CA: Berrett-Koehler Publishers, 1994.

Nanus, B. *Visionary Leadership: Creating a Compelling Sense of Direction for Your Organization.* San Francisco, CA: Jossey Bass, 1992.

Newlove, B. W. and Hall, G. E. *A Manual for Assessing Open-Ended Statements of Concern About an Innovation.* Research and Development Center for Teacher Education, University of Texas at Austin, 1976.

Nicholson, N. "How Hardwired Is Human Behavior?" *Harvard Business Review.* pp. 134-147, July-August 1998.

O'Connor, M. J. *The Professional Trainer and Consultant's Reference Encyclopedia to the TICS Model.* Naples, FL: Life Associates, Inc., 1986.

Ornstein, R. *The Roots of Self: Unraveling the Mystery of Who We Are.* San Francisco, CA: Harper, 1993.

Patterson, J. and Kim, P. *The Day America Told the Truth.* New York: Prentice Hall, 1991.

Person, C. S. *The Hero Within: Six Archetypes We Live By.* New York: HarperCollins Publishers, 1986.

Peters, T. J. and Waterman, R. H. *In Search of Excellence: Lessons from America's Best Run Companies.* New York: Harper and Row Publishers, 1982.

Petty, M. M., McGee, G. W., and Lavander, J. W. "A Meta-Analysis of the Relationships Between Individual Performance." *Accademy of Management Review.* 9, No. 4, pp. 712-721, 1984.

Podsakoff, P. and Organ, D. "Self-Reports on Organizational Research: Problems and Prospects." *Journal of Management.* 12, pp. 531-544, 1986.

Powell, G. N. "One More Time: Do Male and Female Managers Differ?" *Academy of Management Executive.* 4, pp. 68-91, 1990.

Powell, G. N. and Butterfield, A. "Investigating the 'Glass Ceiling' Phenomenon: An Empirical Study of Actual Promotions to Top Management." *Academy of Management Journal.* 37, pp. 68-86, 1994.

Prather, H. *Notes to Myself.* Moab, UT: Real People Press, 1970.

Prochaska, J. O., Clemente, C. L., and Norcross, J. C. "In Search of How People Change; Applications to Addictive Behaviors." *American Psychologist.* 47, No. 9, pp. 1102–1114, 1992.

Rainey, H. G. *Understanding and Managing Public Organizations.* San Francisco, CA: Jossey-Bass, 1997.

Raths, L. E., Harmin, M., and Simon, S. B. *Values and Teaching: Working with Values in the Classroom.* Columbus, OH: Charles E. Merrill Publishing Co., 1966.

Reddin, W. J. *Managerial Effectiveness.* New York: McGraw-Hill Book Company, 1970.

Reich, R. "Entrepreneurship Reconsidered: The Team as Hero." *Harvard Business Review.* 1978.

Riley, P. *The Winner Within.* New York: Berkley Books, 1993.

Robbins, A. *Awaking the Giant Within.* New York: Fireside Books, Simon and Schuster, 1991.

Rokeach, M. *Beliefs, Attitudes and Values: A Theory of Organization and Change.* San Francisco, CA: Jossey-Bass, Inc. Publishers, 1972.

Rokeach, M. *The Nature of Human Values.* New York: The Free Press, A Division of Macmillan Publishing Co., Inc., 1973.

Rokeach, M. and Ball-Rokeach, S. J. "Stability and Change in American Value Priorities." *American Psychologist.* 44, pp. 775–784, 1989.

Rokeach, M. *Understanding Human Values: Individual and Societal.* New York: Free Press, 1979.

Rokeach, M. *Beliefs, Attitudes and Values: A Theory of Organization and Change.* San Francisco, CA: Jossey-Bass, 1986.

Rosenblith, J. F. and Allinsmith, W. *The Causes of Behavior: Readings in Child Development and Educational Psychology.* Boston: Allyn and Bacon, Inc., 1966.

Sargent, A. G. *The Androgynous Manager: Blending Male and Female Managerial Styles for Today's Organization.* New York: American Management Association, 1983.

Sashkin, M. "The Visionary Leader." *Training and Development Journal.* May 1986.

Scharf, P. *Readings in Moral Education.* Minneapolis, MN: Winston Press Inc., 1978.

BIBLIOGRAPHY

Schein, V. E. and Mueller, R. "Sex Role Stereotyping and Requisite Management Characterisitics: A Cross-Cultural Look." *Journal of Organizational Behavior. 13*, pp. 439–447, 1992.

Schmit, M. J. and Allscheid, S. P. "Employee Attitudes and Customer Satisfaction: Making Theoretical and Empirical Connections." *Personnel Psychology: Journal of Applied Research. 48*, No. 3, Autumn 1995.

Seligman, M. E. *Learned Optimism: How to Change Your Mind and Your Life.* New York: Pocket Books, 1990.

Sheehy, G. *New Passages: Mapping Your Life Across Time.* New York: Random House, 1995.

Sheehy, G. *Passages: Predictable Crises of Adult Life.* New York: E. P. Dutton & Co., Inc., 1974.

Sonkin, S. *Study of the Relationship Between Power Bases and Situational Leadership Styles.* Unpublished Master's Thesis, University of Texas at Arlington, TX, 1991.

Stoner-Zemel, J. and Zigarmi, D. *Creating Your Organization's Future: Building a Shared Vision.* Escondido, CA: Blanchard Training and Development, Inc., 1993.

Stoner-Zemel, J. and Zigarmi, D. "From Vision to Reality." *Monograph.* Escondido, CA: Blanchard Training and Development Inc., 1993.

Stoner-Zemel, M. J. *Visionary Leadership, Management and High Performing Workunits: An Analysis of Workers' Perceptions.* Unpublished Doctoral Dissertation, University of Massachusetts, Amherst, MA, 1988.

Strauss, W. and Howe, N. *Generations: History of American Future 1584 to 2069.* New York: William Morrow, 1991.

Tellegen, A., Hykken, D. T., Bouchard, T. J. Jr., Wilcox, K. J., Segal, N. L., and Rich, S. "Personality Similarity in Twins Reared Apart and Together." *Journal of Personality and Social Psychology. 54*, pp. 1031–1039, 1988.

Tett, R. P., Jackson D. N., and Rothstein, M. "Personality Measures as Predictors of Job Performance: A Meta-Analytical Review. *Personnel Psychology. 44*, No. 4, 1991.

Tett, R. P. and Meyer, J. P. "Job Satisfaction, Organizational Commitment, Turnover Intention, and Turnover: Path Analysis Based on Meta-Analytic Findings." *Academy of Management Review. 46*, No. 2, pp. 259–293, 1993.

Tichy, N. M. and Deranna, M. A. "The Transformational Leader." *Training and Development Journal.* pp. 27–32, July 1986.

Tregoe, B. B., Zimmerman, J. W., Smith, R. A., and Tobin, P. M. *Vision in Action: Putting a Winning Strategy to Work.* New York: Fireside—Simon and Schuster, Inc., 1989.

USA Today, Editorial "CEO Greed Targeted." Sept. 17, 2002.

Vitullo-Martin, J., and Moskin, J. R. *The Executive's Book of Quotations.* New York: Oxford University Press, 1994.

Walker Information. "Loyalty in the Workplace: 2001 National Employee Benchmark Study." *www. walkerinfo.com*, 2001.

Weber, J. "Managerial Value Orientations: A Typology and Assessment." *International Journal of Value Based Management.* 3, No. 2, pp. 37–54, 1990.

Weber, J. "Manager's Moral Reasoning: Assessing Their Responses to Three Moral Dilemmas." *Human Relations.* 43, No. 7, pp. 293–318, 1990.

Wheatley, M. J. *Leadership and the New Science: Learning About Organizations from an Orderly Universe.* San Francisco, CA: Berrett-Koehler Publishers, 1992.

Wilkinson, A. *Perceived Supervisory Leadership Style, Flexibility and Effectiveness, Counselor Focus of Control and Dimensions of Job Satisfaction for State Rehabilitations Counselors.* Unpublished Doctoral Dissertation. Southern Illinois University, Edwardsville, IL, 1990.

Williamson, J. N. (Ed.). *The Leader-Manager.* New York: John Wiley and Sons, Inc., 1984.

Woodring, S. and Zigarmi, D. *The Team Leader's Idea-A-Day Guide.* Chicago: Dartnell, 1997.

Yoshikawa, E. *Musashi.* Tokyo: Kodansha International Ltd., 1981.

Yukl, G. A. *Leadership in Organizations.* Englewood Cliffs, NJ: Prentice-Hall, Inc., 1981.

Zalesnik, A. "Managers and Leaders: Are They Different?" *Harvard Business Review.* May–June 1977.

Zigarmi, D., Edeburn, C., and Blanchard, K. *The Reliability and Validity of the LBAII, 4th Edition.* Escondido, CA: Blanchard Training and Development, 1997.

Zigarmi, D., O'Connor, M., and Blanchard, K. H. *The Leadership Bridge: Situational Leadership II and DISC.* Escondido, CA: Blanchard Training and Development, Inc., 1992.

Index

A

Aaron, Hank, 122
Accepted realities, clinging to, 23
Accept versus control response mode, 71-72
Acquired disposition, 68, 102
Acquired preferences, 16
Actions and fear, 27-28
Adaptability and dispositions, 103-08
Allen, Woody, 21
Alternative realties and behaviors, 30-31
Alternatives, choosing from, 117-18
Annie Hall (film), 21
Assumed constraints, 23
Auerbach, Red, 41
Awareness of effect on people, lack of, 8

B

Behaviors, 41-42
   alternative realties and, 30-31
   change, major patterns of, 28-30
   directive element, 176-79
   influence behaviors, 175-76
   of managers and leaders compared, 172-73
   patterns of frequent, 31-32
   supportive element, 176-79

Beliefs:
   as basis for acceptance or rejection of others, 114
   importance of, 114
   overview, 113, 115-16
   reality, as basis of, 22
   self-change and, 114-15
   values and, 116-25
Belief window, 22
Bennis, Warren, 55
Berra, Yogi, 122
Blanchard, Ken, 180

C

Challenger point of view:
   follower morale and, 237-38
   general perspective of, 137
   generational viewpoint and, 158-59
   growth actions, 138
   life issues and, 137-38
   overview, 135, 138-39
   personal ends, 135
   personal means, 135-36
   self-esteem conflict, 136-37
   work style, 138
Change:
   behavior and patterns of, 28-30
   failure and, 33
   growth and, 20-21
   how people view you, changing, 8

Change-oriented versus continuity-oriented response mode, 78
Character:
  defined, 241-43
  expression of, 241
  on personal level, 243
Clinton, Hillary, 27
Coaching (style 2) behavior, 195-96, 201-03
Comfort zones, 47
Commitment:
  to organization, lack of, 9-10
  Situational Leadership II model, 182-84
Competence, 182-84
Confidence, 184
Confinement due to conforming to accepted realities, 23-24
Consequences and values, 118-19
Context:
  defined, 52-53
  group context, 59
  leader behaviors, 57
  one-to-one context, 58-59
  organizational context, 59-61
  response to, 61-62
  role behaviors, 53-55
  role concept and, 55-56
  roles, 53
  situation and, 57-58
Cooney, Joan Ganz, 214
Core unconscious self, 15-16
Corporate culture, 11
Covenant between each employee and the organization, 13-15

D

Decision making:
  direct accepters, 86
  direct controller, 82
  indirect accepters, 89
  indirect controllers, 92
  values, 124
Delegating (style 4) behavior, 196-97, 205
Developed values, 16, 49
Development cycle, 206
Development levels, 182-87
Direct accepters ("I" disposition):
  comments by, 87
  decision making, 86
  disposition and leadership behavior in a one-to-one context, 224-27
  evaluation of others, 86
  fears, 87
  goals, 86
  overview, 84-85
  public figures, 87
  strengths, 85
  tendencies of, 87
  use of time, 86
  weaknesses, 85
Direct controllers ("D" disposition):
  comments by, 84
  decision making and, 82
  disposition and leadership behavior in a one-to-one context, 222-24
  evaluation of others, 83
  fears, 83
  goals, 83
  overview, 81-82
  public figures, 83
  strengths of, 82
  tendencies of, 84
  use of time, 83
  weaknesses of, 82
Directing (style 1) behavior:
  delivery and perception of, 191-92
  example of, 191
  in a one-to-one context, when to use, 198-201
  overview, 189-91
  styles, 189-92
Directive element of behavior, 176-79

Direct versus indirect response mode, 74-75
Discomfort, 17-18
DISC principles:
  mixed-type dispositions, most people have, 100-02
  needs (goals and fears), all people are motivated by their, 97-100
  no best preference or DISC position, there is, 95-97
  overview, 69, 95
  people can become more versatile; other preferences can be developed, 107-08
  strengths or limitations of each personal preference and still undeveloped potentials, 104-07
  two preferences cannot, at any one time, be equally strong under pressure, 103-04
Disposition:
  accept versus control response mode, 71-72
  acquired disposition, 68, 102
  adaptability and, 103-08
  change-oriented versus continuity-oriented response mode, 78
  defined, 67
  direct accepters, 84-87
  direct controller, 81-84
  direct versus indirect response mode, 74-75
  DISC principles, 69, 95-110
  extroversion versus introversion response mode, 72-74
  flight versus fight response mode, 71
  indirect accepters, 87-91
  indirect controllers, 91-94
  judgment of, 68-69
  leadership behaviors. *See* disposition and leadership behaviors
  modes of responding, 70, 79-80
  optimistic versus pessimistic response mode, 77-78
  perceive versus judge response mode, 75-76
  personality, 46
  risk-taking versus risk-assessing response mode, 76-77
  values and, 153-54
  wired disposition, 67-68, 102
Dispositional layer, 15-17
Disposition and leadership behaviors:
  direct accepters ("I" disposition) and leadership behavior in a one-to-one context, 224-27
  direct controllers ("D" disposition) and leadership behavior in a one-to-one context, 222-24
  indirect accepters ("S" disposition) and leadership behavior in a one-to-one context, 227-29
  indirect controllers ("C" disposition) and leadership behavior in a one-to-one context, 229-32
  overview, 221-22
Disposition-values-persona connection, 49-50
Diversity within pattern and personality, 45
Driving force of executives, 12
Dynamic nature of personality, 43

E

Ego defense and values, 123
End values, 120-21
Energy and personality, 47-48
Ethics, 11, 241
Evaluation of others:
  direct accepters, 86
  direct controller, 83
  indirect accepters, 89
  indirect controllers, 93

Examples of typical leaders, 2–8
Expression of character, 241
Extroversion versus introversion response mode, 72–74

F

Failure and change, 33
Fear:
  actions and, 27–28
  persona and fear mode, 162–63
  response, 40
  self-esteem and, 163
  shadow self and, 24–25
  triggers, 98
Feminine behaviors, 26–27
Flight versus fight response mode, 71
Follett, Mary Parker, 213
Follower morale:
  challenger point of view, 237–38
  inbetweener point of view, 238–39
  synthesizer point of view, 240

G

Gandhi, Mahatma, 117
Generational points of view, 158–59
Generations (Howe & Strauss), 45
Goal response, 40
Group context, 59
Growth, capability for, 20

H

Happiness with job and relationship with boss, 1
Hersey, Paul, 180

I

Image and vision, 215–16
Impact on others, lack of understanding of, 8
Importance of leadership, 1

Inbetweener point of view:
  follower morale and, 238–39
  general perspective of, 141
  growth activities, 142–43
  life issues and, 141–42
  overview, 139, 143
  personal ends, 139–40
  relaters and, 159
  self-esteem conflict, 141
  social means, 140–41
  work style, 142
Indirect accepters ("S" disposition):
  comments by, 90
  decision making, 89
  disposition and leadership behavior in a one-to-one context, 227–29
  evaluation of others, 89
  fears, 90
  goals, 90
  overview, 87–88
  public figures, 90
  strengths, 88
  tendencies of, 90–91
  use of time, 89
  weaknesses, 89
Indirect controllers ("C" disposition):
  comments by, 94
  decision making, 92
  disposition and leadership behavior in a one-to-one context, 229–32
  evaluation of others, 93
  fears, 93–94
  goals, 93
  overview, 91
  public figures, 94
  strengths, 92
  tendencies of, 94
  use of time, 93
  weaknesses, 92
Influence behaviors, 175–76
Introverts and traditionalist point of view, 159–60

J
Jung, Carl, 66

K
Kierkegaard, Soren, 17, 153

L
Language and reality, 22-23
Layers of self, 15-17
Leader behaviors, 57
Leaders and managers compared, 172-73
Leadership:
  behaviors and values, 232
  best leadership style, lack of, 180-81
  defined, 174-75
  development cycle, 206
  lack of effective, 2
  one-to-one context and, 181-82
  regressive cycle, 206-07
  style. *See* styles of leadership
Life experiences influencing personality, 44-45
Loving tolerance of self, 17
Loyalty of employees, 9

M
Managers and leaders compared, 172-73
Masculine behaviors, 26-27
McDonough, William, 19
Means values, 120-21
Mental filters, 114
Michelangelo, 20
Mixed-type dispositions, 100-02
Morale and leader values, 237
Motivation, 124-25, 184

N
Needs (goals and fears), all people are motivated by their, 97-100
Negative response mode, 39-41
New York Federal Reserve Bank, 19

O
The Odd Couple (play), 80
One-to-one context:
  leadership and, 181-82
  overview, 58-59
  situational leadership and, 182
Onion analogy, 15-19, 50-51
Optimistic versus pessimistic response mode, 77-78
Organizational context, 59-61
Organizational cultures, 53
Organization and traditionalists, 236
Outward behavior, changing, 17-18

P
Patterns of frequent behaviors, 31-32
People skills, 5
Perceive versus judge response mode, 75-76
Perception:
  disposition and values, relationship between, 153-54
  lateness example, 152
  others' perception, 4-7, 156-57
  self-perception, 154-55
  support example, 152
Perpetuation of poor leadership, 9
Persona, 15-16
  defined, 164-65
  fear mode and, 162-63
  implications of, 165-66
  personality and, 49-50
  point of view and, 234-36
  role-dependent persona, 166-67
  self-esteem and, 161-64
  self-indulgent persona, 167-68
Personal fulfillment, sacrificing, 12
Personality:
  defined, 42-43

Personality *(cont.)*:
  disposition, 46
  disposition–values–persona connection, 49–50
  diversity within pattern and, 45
  dynamic nature of, 43
  energy and, 47–48
  life experiences influencing, 44–45
  model for experience, 38–39
  negative response mode, 39–41
  onion analogy and, 50–51
  overview, 37
  persona and, 49–50
  positive response mode, 39–41
  values and, 48–50
  vision and, 220
Personal leadership vision, 217–18
Personal values, 120–21
Perspective of leadership, 20
Place in organization for leadership, 18–19
Platinum Rule, 108–10
Points of view:
  challenger point of view, 135–39
  generational points of view, 158
  inbetweener point of view, 139–43
  overview, 125–26
  persona and, 234–36
  rights/responsibility focus, 127–29
  self/other focus, 126–27
  summary of, 149
  synthesizer point of view, 143–48
  traditionalist point of view, 130–34
Positive response mode, 39–41
Power and leadership purpose, 218–20
Preference:
  defined, 66–67
  origins of, 66
  unconscious preference, 65
Presentation of self and values, 123–24
Programmed values, 16, 49, 118
Projection, 25–26
Public figures:
  direct accepters, 87
  direct controller, 83
  indirect accepters, 90
  indirect controllers, 94
Public ownership of values, 119
Public reprimands, 29
Purpose statement, 212–14

R

Reality:
  accepted realities, clinging to, 23
  beliefs as basis of, 22
  confinement due to conforming to accepted realities, 23–24
  creating, 21–22
  language and, 22–23
Regressive cycle, 206–07
Rejection of others as basis for beliefs, 114
Relationship with boss and job happiness, 1
Resentment of employees, 8
Response modes, 79–80
  accept versus control response mode, 71–72
  change-oriented versus continuity-oriented response mode, 78
  direct versus indirect response mode, 74–75
  extroversion versus introversion response mode, 72–74
  flight versus fight response mode, 71
  negative response mode, 39–41
  optimistic versus pessimistic response mode, 77–78
  overview, 70
  perceive versus judge response mode, 75–76
  positive response mode, 39–41

risk-taking versus risk-assessing
 response mode, 76-77
Response to context, 61-62
Rights/responsibility focus, 127-29
Risk-taking versus risk-assessing
 response mode, 76-77
Role behavior:
 as basis for leadership, 54-55
 defined, 53
Role concept and context, 55-56
Role-dependent persona, 166-67
Role requirements, 53
Roles, 53
 concept of, 55-56
 leader behaviors as subsets of role
  behaviors, 57
Role set, 53

S

Salaries, executive, 19
Seeking position of leadership, what
 drives people to, 32-33
Self-change and beliefs, 114-15
Self-conflict resolution and values, 124
Self-esteem:
 fear and, 163
 persona and, 161-64
Self-indulgent persona, 167-68
Self-knowledge, lack of, 8, 10-13
Self/other focus, 126-27
Self-perception, 3-6, 154-55
Shadow self, 24-27
Simon, Neil, 80
Situational leadership, 205
 one-to-one context and, 182
 using, 208
Situational Leadership II model:
 commitment and, 182-84
 competence and, 182-84
 development levels, 182-87
 overview, 180

Situations:
 coaching (style 2) behavior in a one-
  to-one context, when to use,
  201-03
 and context, 57-58
 delegating (style 4) behavior in a
  one-to-one context, when to use,
  205
 directing (style 1) behavior in a one-
  to-one context, when to use,
  198-201
 overview, 198
 supporting (style 3) behavior in a
  one-to-one context, when to use,
  203-04
Socialization, 26-27
Social values, 120-21
Societal focus of organization, 214
Socrates, 13
Styles of leadership:
 best leadership style, lack of, 180-81
 coaching (style 2) behavior, 195-96
 delegating (style 4) behavior, 196-97
 directing (style 1) behavior, 189-92
 leadership, 175
 overview, 187-88
 supporting (style 3) behavior, 192-
  95
Supporting (style 3) behavior:
 example of, 193-95
 in a one-to-one context, when to
  use, 203-04
 overview, 192-93
Supportive element of behavior, 176-79
Synthesizer point of view:
 controllers and, 160
 follower morale and, 240
 general perspective of, 145-46
 growth activities, 147
 life issues and, 146
 overview, 143, 147-48
 personal means, 144-45

Synthesizer point of view *(cont.)*:
   self-esteem conflict, 145
   social ends, 144
   work style, 146-47

T

Task knowledge, 183
Team meetings:
   others' perception of typical leader at, 4-5
   self-perception of typical leader at, 4
Time and values, 119
Traditionalist point of view:
   general perspective of, 132
   growth actions, 133-34
   introverts and, 159-60
   life issues and, 132-33
   organization and, 236
   overview, 130, 134
   self-esteem conflict, 131
   social ends, 130
   social means, 130-31
   work style, 133
Transferable skills, 183
Treatment of employees, 13
Typical leaders:
   examples of, 2-8
   others' perceptions of, 4-7
   self-perceptions of, 3-6

U

Unconscious preference, 65

V

Values:
   alternatives, choosing from, 117-18
   beliefs and, 116-25
   choosing, 117-19
   consequences, choosing while anticipating, 118-19
   criteria for, 117-19
   decision making and, 124
   disposition and, 153-54
   ego defense and, 123
   end values, 120-21
   functions served by, 122-25
   leadership behaviors and, 232
   leader values and follower perceptions of leader behaviors, 232-34
   means values, 120-21
   morale and leader values, 237
   motivation and, 124-25
   overview, 116-17
   personality and, 48-50
   personal values, 120-21
   points of view. *See* points of view
   presentation of self and, 123-24
   process, 120
   programmed values, 118
   public ownership of, 119
   self-conflict resolution and, 124
   social values, 120-21
   time, acting on over, 119
   types of, 120-21
   value system, 121-22
   vision and, 214-15
Values layer, 15-17
Value system, 121-22
Vision:
   image and, 215-16
   overview, 211-12
   personality and, 220
   personal leadership vision, 217-18
   power and leadership purpose, 218-20
   purpose statement, 212-14
   societal focus of organization, 214
   values and, 214-15

W

Wired disposition, 67-68, 102
Wired preferences, 16

Reference critical business skills in an instant online.

Try it FREE! Sign up for a 30-day Enterprise Trial at www.safaribooksonline.com/bizdemo.asp

SEARCH electronic versions of hundreds of books simultaneously.

BROWSE books by category. Peruse the latest titles from today's most authoritative business authors.

FIND answers in an instant!

Search Safari! Zero in on exactly the information you need to complete the task at hand - from creating killer presentations, to understanding how supply chains work, to honing your interview skills. Search across all books in the library simultaneously to pinpoint exactly the chapter, sentence and example you need. Read books from cover to cover. Or, flip right to the page you need.

Preview Safari as our guest at bus.safaribooksonline.com or sign up for a free enterprise trial at www.safaribooksonline.com/bizdemo.asp. Also check out Safari's premier library for programmers and IT professionals at safari.informit.com.